Forty Years
with
London Transport

Companion Volumes

Liverpool Buses	Shearings
Glasgow Buses	Bus Story Early '70s — Proof of the Pudding
SHMD	Bus Story '60s — Turbulent Times

Other books from TPC

The Manchester Bus	The Manchester Tramways
Liverpool Transport	NBC Commemorative Volume
Eastern Coach Works Vol. 1	The Leyland Bus

Forthcoming Titles

Eastern Coach Works Vol. 2 — 1946-closure	Liverpool Transport Vol. 5
Bus Story — Late '70s	Metrolink
Tilling & Harrowing	

Illustrated list of all titles available on receipt of SAE

Designed, typeset and produced for the Publishers by
Mopok Graphics, 128 Pikes Lane, Glossop, Derbyshire
Printed and bound in Great Britain

Forty Years
with
London Transport

Colin Curtis OBE

B.Sc(Eng), C. Eng., M.I.Mech.E., M.I.R.T.E.

Edited by

Alan Townsin
and
John A. Senior

Transport Publishing Co Ltd : Glossop : Derbyshire : England

Preface

Having spent a lifetime connected with the bus industry it always struck me that much of the work done in helping to provide a reliable and efficient service went unsung. In this autobiography I have tried to recount some of the more interesting things that took place in the hope that the passenger and enthusiast would perhaps be able to appreciate more of what went on in order to give better value for his or her journey. I hope I have been able to convey the friendship that existed in the industry generally and that is meant in its widest sense even though there was a degree of competition. It always gave me great satisfaction to work for London Transport and to have made so many friends over some forty years. The wind of change is now upon us and I shall watch the fortunes of London Buses with great interest.

Finally, I should like to thank my former secretary, Mary Watson, who in retirement has typed my manuscript and given me her usual helpful advice.

The author at the wheel of a Daimler Fleetline.

Contents

When the author first joined London Transport, all but six of the first 49 production AEC Renown six-wheelers dating from early 1930 were still in service, together with the prototype, LT1, of August 1929. Here the last of the batch, LT50, is seen at the tree-lined Camden Town terminus of the 53A route a few months before withdrawal in September 1948. The open-staircase body was built at Chiswick Works by the London General Omnibus Co Ltd, for whose fleet the vehicle was destined.

Introduction

Colin Curtis belongs to that special group of people who can rightly be described as professional enthusiasts. From an early age, he knew exactly what he wanted to do to earn his living—working with buses.

Good results at school, and a perceptive Headmaster, took the youthful Curtis to a wartime engineering degree course at Brighton Technical College, coupled with a period as vacation student with the local Brighton Hove & District Omnibus Co Ltd. Graduating with Honours he expected to be directed to the Services, but was allowed to go to the AEC concern, 'Builders of London's Buses', to gain practical experience at its Southall, Middlesex works in 1947.

Advised to seek his fortune in the operating world, he applied to join London Transport, was accepted and then, in September 1947, began his steadily rising career of over 40 years with that organisation. Latterly he became Vehicle Engineering Manager (Buses) but he was already a figure widely known and respected on both the operating and manufacturing sides of the bus industry. Most of that time was spent at the famous Chiswick Works, working during the earlier years under the legendary A. A. M. Durrant, who had guided bus design policy from the formation of London Transport in 1933 until his retirement in 1965.

Being in such a position, able to observe all that was going on and, as the years went by, participate to a growing extent in the engineering development of Britain's largest bus fleet, would enable the author to tell a fascinating story under any circumstances. What makes it especially valuable is the way in which the ground rules of the whole enterprise completely changed during the period covered.

When Colin Curtis arrived at Chiswick, London Transport's influence over the design of its vehicles, already strong, was increasing. In the 1950s this produced what, in retrospect, seems likely to be regarded as the jewel in the crown of London bus designs, the Routemaster. Then, beginning in the 1960s, the wind of change blew steadily chillier.

The era of 'off the peg' bus purchase arrived, largely as part of national policy favouring the creation of large manufacturing groups. However, the sheer size of the London fleet meant that Chiswick could still exert useful leverage on the decisions being taken by the manufacturers, feeding in its immense experience of day-in day-out operation in all weathers in London traffic, still able to show up design weaknesses which had gone undetected elsewhere. Both sides found they had much to learn, especially as buses were becoming more complex and some of the reliability associated with rugged simplicity was being lost.

The concept of a large central works which not only overhauled the buses but acted as a centre for research and development went back long before the formation of London Transport in 1933. Chiswick Works had been established by the London General Omnibus Co Ltd in 1920-21. Moreover, the close liaison with the AEC concern, originally set up in 1912 primarily to supply LGOC's needs in bus chassis manufacture, had continued virtually unaltered even though AEC became a completely separate business from 1933. Mergers within the manufacturing industry gradually diminished AEC's role and the lines of London Transport's contact with manufacture extended further afield, first to Daimler at Coventry and then Leyland in Lancashire or, latterly, Cumbria.

This process was not without pain. Colin Curtis's description of Daimler's George Fabel sitting in a Fleetline with his head in his hands after it had been demonstrated how a London bus was liable to be driven is perhaps one of the most revealing passages in the book. Yet good liaison was established with Daimler, only to be disrupted in the mid-1970s as British Leyland increasingly centralised its activities, producing a relationship less responsive even to as pre-eminent an operator as that of London Transport.

More fundamentally still, the whole concept of a large unified bus and underground rail system, having its own engineering facilities, began to be questioned in the early 1980s. Colin Curtis found himself fighting a rearguard action, firstly to show how the Experimental Department produced direct financial savings to counterbalance its costs and then by taking in work from other organisations. Despite this, it was decided above his head to close the department in 1986 and it makes poignant reading to learn how what was considered the bare essential equipment from the birthplace of the Routemaster—truly a centre of excellence—was stored in a succession of lock-up garages and railway arches.

This book, as well as telling a fascinating story of triumph and, for the time being at least, decline, contains a mine of information on practical problems met and overcome that will be of special interest to engineers, as well as providing insight for enthusiasts. One cannot help wondering how long it will be before the value of something like London Transport's characteristic blend of willingness to pursue engineering advances with an insistence on stern practicality will be realised and again regarded as an essential to a thriving modern city.

Alan Townsin
Series Editor

Although AEC buses were the usual choice for London Transport until 1970, there had been plenty of exceptions. Here D269, one of the batch of 100 Daimler CWA6 added to the fleet in the later months of 1946, all allocated to Sutton garage, is seen at Epsom in company with RTL270, one of the Leyland buses built to RT specification, in this case dating from June 1949. Both had bodywork built by Park Royal, the Daimler being to a design derived from wartime practice while that on the RTL was to the closely-standardised design produced for RT-class buses on either AEC or Leyland chassis.

In later years, London Transport accepted 'off-the-shelf' bus designs. One of the more successful was the MCW Metrobus, of which deliveries began in 1978. The example shown, M537, entered service in July 1981 and is seen in 1983 on the Airbus service introduced to provide a direct link between Heathrow Airport and central London.

1. Brighton and Southall

My first contact with the bus industry was as a small boy when I was involved in head-on collision with a Thomas Tilling bus on Route 8 in Brighton. Having got over this, my interest was taken up wondering which actual bus I had hit and it was then I found that the buses ran in numerical order, each route having its own stud of buses. This particular route was run by 1932 AEC Regent open-staircase double-deckers GW 6279-6282 and the Company numbers were the same as the registration numbers — in those days Thomas Tilling was running buses under its own name in both London, where they were registered, and Brighton.

This stimulated my interest in buses, particularly the Brighton and Hove section of Thomas Tilling, which carried on to the years when it became Brighton Hove & District Omnibus Company Limited from 1935. In 1939 a joint organisation was set up with Brighton Corporation Transport Department under the new name of Brighton Hove & District Transport, both operators using the same red and cream livery. Another interesting fact emerged in that each driver had his own bus, working alternate 'early and late', the conductor dropping back a bus each fortnight.

My studies then took me to Varndean Grammar School and although the war years did not favour a career in the bus industry I managed to maintain my interest in Brighton Hove & District, by spending evenings at Conway Street learning about schedules and other facets of the business. This was achieved through my Headmaster, Mr Eric Hutchins, who knew the Traffic Manager of Brighton Hove & District, Mr H. G. Baker. In my eyes 'H.G.' was a man I looked up to and

could imagine that in his later role as a Magistrate he would dispense justice in a very fair way. He was in every way a perfect gentleman and the industry was the loser when he tragically died.

As a result of my Higher School Certificate examination I was awarded a State Bursary in Engineering at the Brighton Technical College. Again through the good offices of my Headmaster I was able to fix up to spend a period as a student at the Conway Street workshops of the bus company so that I could get the feel of things as by now I realised that buses were my bent.

I spent two months at Conway Street, and the variety of vehicles operated by Brighton Hove & District made the work doubly interesting. At that time the fleet was still largely AEC Regent buses of the early 'thirties, originally petrol-engined although many had received Gardner 5LW five-cylinder oil engines and others AEC 7.7-litre units; in addition a rebodying programme was in hand. Bristol chassis, also with 5LW engines, had been chosen from 1936 for double-deck fleet renewals, but there were also eight AEC trolleybuses dating from 1939 which did not go into service until 1944-6 and a small number of Dennis buses — Lance double-deckers and small Ace and Dart single-deckers.

This was good experience, if only of how not to do things. My first experience in getting a bus finished in time for the evening service occurred on a Dennis Ace 28-seat vehicle used on Route 2a and Route 9. Single-deckers were very sparse in the fleet and spares were just as limited. Somehow or other a con rod bolt had not been tightened properly, and the result

My first contact with a bus — literally — was in Brighton with a Thomas Tilling AEC Regent dating from 1932 and belonging to the same batch as GW 6278, shown here in the early war period, by which date the fleet had become Brighton Hove & District. Like many others in the BH&D fleet, it had been fitted with a Gardner 5LW oil engine in place of the original petrol engine in 1937, though retaining the original Tilling open-staircase body. This particular bus is seen as running in 1939-40, converted again to run on producer gas, with plant built under the outside staircase and auxiliary petrol tank on the front bulkhead, as mentioned in Chapter Seven.

Brighton Hove & District ran a handful of small Dennis single-deckers on routes where double-deckers were unsuitable, that shown, No. 6306, being one of a pair of Ace models with 20-seat bodywork by Eastern Counties dating from 1934. It was such a bus that suffered a conn-rod through the side of the crankcase as the result of an insufficiently tightened bolt.

was that the bus did not complete the evening journey on Route 9 to Mile Oak, returning instead with a gaping hole in the crankcase.

I started at the 'Tech' in September 1944 on what was to be a crash course with no summer break. During my stay in my capacity as the Secretary of the Engineering Society I kept up my interest in transport by arranging visits to many transport and transport-related organisations. It was amazing how keen organisations were to receive visits from such societies.

Towards the end of our course we were all subjected to interview by the War Office Selection Board. Some went to the interview feeling that whatever was said it was to be the Services anyway. I had now set my sights on getting into Engineering and four of us on the course had been granted permission to take an Electrical/Mechanical degree course as opposed to the more or less mandatory Electrical/Civil/Mechanical course. It was obvious that originally this was done to allow a greater degree of freedom in allocation.

At the end of my studies, and to my surprise, instead of being sent to the Services as were most of my colleagues, I was allocated to Aircraft Production. I duly attended for interview in Coventry but the size of the Drawing Office frightened me. After discussion with the Selection Board it was agreed that I could go to AEC at Southall as a Student Apprentice to gain practical experience in building vehicles, which included army lorries at that time of course.

I duly reported to AEC whereas many of my colleagues joined HM Forces in various arms. Looking back at my time at Southall I was lucky in that I was able to choose the areas to which I was to be attached and naturally chose those in connection with vehicle building plus, of course, the Experimental Department. Having spent my period at the Technical College on what could only be described as a crash course, I found the demand on brain usage replaced by more manual work.

Starting at 7.30am at AEC was no hardship as I had always been an early riser, but working until 5.30pm seemed to make a long day. We worked on Saturdays, although that was only

a half day, which continued for some years when I moved to London Transport. Wages totalled some £3. 7s. 6d. (£3.37½p) per week and considering I was in lodgings this meant I was not all that flush. Often the cycle was pressed into service rather than spend 4d. (1.7p approximately) each way on the 92 bus, especially as I managed to go back to my digs for lunch.

Incidentally, I often wondered why LT — in full, it was still the London Passenger Transport Board at that time, often called simply 'the Board' — ran Bristol K6A models on the 92 route rather than AEC buses. Perhaps it was a gentle reminder to AEC that there were other makes of bus. These vehicles came from the batch of 20 with Duple relaxed utility bodies (numbered B10-29) that had been delivered early in 1946 as the wartime arrangements for bus supply were just coming to an end. At least they had AEC 7.7-litre engines, basically as found in most of what was still LT's largest bus class at the time, the STL type on AEC Regent chassis.

A large version of the AEC triangle was displayed over the Southall works, facing what was then the Great Western Railway main line. It, and the proud slogan below, were outlined by neon lights at night.

My bus service to work when I started with AEC was London Transport's 92, and it seemed ironical that, at the time, it was operated by Bristol buses, even though they were of the K6A type with AEC engine. Here B18, of the batch of 20 such buses with Duple 'relaxed utility' bodywork placed in service early in 1946, is seen heading for what was then called Hanwell garage (later renamed Southall), its home base, which was within a few hundred yards of the main entrance to the AEC works.

How glad I was that the nine wartime Bristol K5G buses B1-9, were held to the nearby 97 service which I didn't use, as at that time these still had the Gardner 5LW engines with which they had been built, efficient but the passengers got the full benefit of their five-cylinder roughness thanks to the simple bolted-in engine mounting. In those days Hanwell garage, as it was then (later called Southall though the old HW code remained) also operated Leyland PD1 buses of the 1946 batch (STD 112-176), on the 55 route whereas Turnham Green (garage code V), a garage with which I was later to become deeply involved, was still struggling with ST-type petrol-engined AEC Regent buses dating back to 1930-31 as their contribution to the same route. Another interesting duty was the provision of a daily bus — in those days an LT-type AEC Renown six-wheeler from Leyton garage — to bring workers who still lived in Walthamstow, on the opposite side of London, from the days of AEC's works in Ferry Lane there before the Southall factory opened in 1926-27.

At the time, 1947, the first batches of the post-war RTs were in build and I had a good insight into the construction of all the components. Models in production at AEC in 1947 included the Mark III passenger range — Regent (both London RT and

AEC buses were to be seen on other routes serving the AEC Southall works, however. Here an AEC Regent on the 83 is seen leaving the Lyndhurst Avenue stop in Uxbridge Road, from which a tunnel under the GWR railway embankment led into the works. Trolleybuses on the 607 route to Uxbridge also used this stop and the special works bus, by then provided by LT, still giving transport to those long-service AEC workers who lived in Walthamstow (from which district the works had moved in 1926-27) awaited its passengers on the opposite side of the road. The vehicle shown, STL282, dated from January 1934 and was one of a batch with Daimler preselective gearboxes which had originally entered service with petrol engines removed from AEC Renown LT-class six-wheelers then being converted to oil. They had themselves been converted to oil with AEC 7.7-litre direct-injection engines, in this case in November 1939. They had flexible engine mountings as converted and thus gave a quieter ride to passengers than most STL buses, despite the more 'basic' style of the Chiswick-built body than the more familiar style adopted later in 1934. It is seen, still in old-style livery, shortly before withdrawal in 1952.

The post-war version of the AEC 9.6-litre engine had not long been in production when I joined the firm in 1947 — the example shown is an early A207 goods version with exhauster for vacuum brakes and small dynamo. The Experimental Department arrived at a cure for a water circulation and consequent overheating problem while I was there, later examples having a water pipe running above the exhaust manifold to draw water from the rear end of the engine.

provincial) and Regal, the latter including left-hand drive export models. The Regent II was still in production, though the 20 built for London Transport and added to its STL class were already in service, and the Regal I was also still in build. On the goods side the main volumn of output was split between the Monarch four-wheel and the Mammoth Major six- and eight-wheeler models.

Perhaps the hardest part of the job was the road test of the chassis which involved taking a weighted chassis as far as the outskirts of Oxford where adjustments had to be made in the light of what was shown up on the test. I shall never forget the breakfast stop which was always made on the outskirts of High Wycombe and was much needed as we were in the throes of a fuel crisis in a very cold winter.

During my stay at Southall we came across a problem with the 9.6-litre engine where sand from the casting process had been left behind and caused failure of the main bearings. The order was given to drop all sumps on these engines and with the 3RT (the standard post-war version of the RT chassis) it was not possible to do this without dropping the front axle by releasing the rear spring shackles. If my memory serves me rightly we were expected to do one-and-a-half engines per day. If the bearing was scored the engine had to come out! The use of a protective shellac coating soon obviated the problem.

Later in my period in AEC's Experimental Department I was involved in a further problem with seizure of the engine which was traced to an inadequate water supply to the cylinders. By fitting transparent side cover plates we soon saw that the water flow around the cylinders reduced almost to nothing as one proceeded from No. 1 to No. 6 cylinder. The problem really arose because the water flow entered and left the cylinder heads at the front of the engine. Modifications to

create a flow in-at-the-front and out-of-the-back soon cured the problem. Engines built with this modification generally received new unit numbers — A218 in place of A208 for the provincial Regent III for example — but the A204 engines in the RT were all modified so the unit number did not change. This helped me in my belief that in solving problems one first finds the cause and then eliminates it. This is so different from the current tendency to change the system and start on another learning curve.

With the end of my time at AEC approaching it became necessary to look to the future. Clearly in the manufacturing area it was a much more sheltered atmosphere, protected from the cruel world. My stay in the Service Department had shown me another side of the business, often dealing with jobs that the operator had started but failed to finish. I sought advice from the Experimental Engineer, Mr Jock Trench, who advised me to try the outside world and gain operating experience even though AEC had offered me a post. I heeded his advice and in spite of the offer I duly applied to London Transport in the Development Section at Chiswick where I was interviewed by Mr J. W. Wicks. After an agonising wait I was offered a post as a General Technical Assistant in what was known as the Technical Office.

London Transport's bus fleet had survived the war years outwardly in surprisingly good shape, but inevitably it had taken its toll. All the buses in this London Bridge scene of October 1946 would either have been scrapped or have been nearing the end of their days had there not been a war, quite apart from suffering from reduced overhaul facilities. Approaching the camera is STL22, one of the early ex-LGOC petrol-engined 60-seat examples of this class of AEC Regent buses dating from just before London Transport was formed in 1933 — it was to soldier on until May 1948. Following is STD47, one of the 100 Leyland Titan TD4 buses of 1937, all of which were to run for seven more years. One of the STL buses of the mid-1930s on the left was among those receiving an extensive body rebuild to extend their lives.

The entrance to Chiswick Works, a familiar sight to me almost daily for over 40 years. In addition to its function as Road Services Engineering Department and Supplies and Services Department, the premises included the Central Laboratory, a Medical Centre, the Recruitment Centre for all departments and the Training School for Bus Staff. The photograph was taken in November 1958 and the single-decker visible is T719, the first of the post-war batch of 14T12 AEC Regal buses dating from 1946, withdrawn from service with the rest of the batch that month and probably making its last visit to Chiswick.

2. Early days with LT

I shall always remember my first day working for London Transport, in September 1947. I travelled from Brighton where I was living, using the Southern and District Line trains and reported for duty at Chiswick. The day began at 8.30am and at that time everyone in the office worked a five-and-a-half day week. There were some 13 people in the Technical Office which was situated within the Chiswick Works. Our chief was Albert Higgins and he was directly responsible to J. W. Wicks.

London Transport was a vast organisation, of course, and at that time employed some 93,000 people in various occupations to do with the provision of transport in the Capital and its environs. Although LT operated electric trains, tramcars, trolleybuses and motor buses my work was concerned solely with the last-mentioned. Others in the Technical Office were involved in such diverse areas as recovery of vehicles, writing maintenance manuals etc as well as acting as technical secretaries.

There were many legendary figures in the hierarchy of course, and I soon came into contact with Albert Miller, Chief Engineer of Self-Changing Gears, Stanley Markland of Leyland and John Rackham of AEC as well as, later, Gordon Parnell of Lockheed, people whose names were well-known to me through my wider transport interests.

During the period between 1947 and 1950 I was employed as a General Technical Assistant working mainly on chassis, and in a department of some 70 people whose efforts were directed towards bus design, development and maintenance. As trams then trolleybuses were scrapped so we took over the former depots as bus garages.

We were self-contained, and thus working in parallel with the works and garage people. It was our responsibility to locate faults, devise solutions and eliminate problems, in addition to looking to the future in matters of Research and Development, of which I shall say more in a later chapter.

As a new and junior member of the Department I was not aware of the reasons for many of our actions, of course, but my day-to-day work brought me into contact with the steadily increasing fleet of RTs which were gradually replacing the pre-war double-deckers, as well as bringing about a major change in operating practice as the hitherto unfamiliar air-pressure brakes and gear operating system gradually became the norm.

Having associated myself more with engines than vehicle components whilst at Southall, I was a little disappointed to find that I was to work on the chassis side of the Technical Office under the Assistant Engineer (Development — Buses). Looking back over those days I would not have had it any different now.

Although I had spent a short time in helping to build RT type chassis whilst with AEC I soon learned how little I knew.

The licensing shop in Chiswick Works on 26th November 1947. Three new RT-type buses are to be seen together with newly-overhauled vehicles, all of AEC make. In the foreground RT450, with Weymann-built body, is alongside STL541, a 1934 Regent converted to diesel in 1939. In the row behind, RT229 and 227, both with Park Royal bodies, are to be seen with, between them, T411, one of the 1936 batch of Regal single-deckers of the 9T9 type and STL1845, one of the so-called 'tunnel STL' buses of 1937, with body of special profile to allow operation through the Blackwall and Rotherhithe tunnels under the Thames.

BRAKING SYSTEMS

CODE	No. OF SERVOS	WHETHER LOCKHEED	MAIN SERVO BORE	AUX SERVO BORE	LOCKHEED MASTR. CYL BORE	FR. WHEEL CYL. BORE	R. WHEEL CYL. BORE	LOCK CYL. & TANK COMBINED	COMP SERVO & LOCK	RESERVR. CAPAC.
6 & 8LT	1	YES	150	–	$1\frac{3}{4}$"	$1\frac{1}{4}$"	$1\frac{1}{4}$"	YES	NO	$1\frac{1}{2}$ PNT.
1,2,1/4,6,8STL.	1	"	"	–	"	"	$1\frac{1}{2}$"	"	"	"
5,9,1/9,2/9,3/9,4/9 10,1/10,11,14STL,9T.	1	"	175	–	2"	"	"	"	"	"
1,2,3,4,5,6Q	1	"	"	–	"	"	$1\frac{1}{4}$"	"	"	"
18STL,14T	3	NO	"	150	–	–	–	–	–	–
1STD	1	YES	"	–	2"	$1\frac{1}{4}$"	$1\frac{1}{4}$"	YES	NO	$1\frac{1}{2}$
3STD	3	NO	150	150	–	–	–	–	–	–
4STD,1TD	3	"	"	150	–	–	–	–	–	–
15,16,1/16,2/16 STL.	1	YES	175	–	$1\frac{3}{4}$"	$1\frac{1}{4}$"	$1\frac{1}{2}$"	NO	YES	CANNISTER 1
10,1/10T	1	"	200	–	2"	"	"	NO	"	CANNISTER 1
1,2B	3	NO	150	150	–	–	–	–	–	
1,1/D	1	YES	175	–	2"	$1\frac{1}{4}$"	$1\frac{3}{4}$"	NO	YES	CANNISTER 1
2,1/2,3,1/3,G	1	"	"	–	"	"	$1\frac{1}{2}$"	NO	"	CANNISTER 1
1ST ※	1	NO	150	–	–	–	–	–	–	
1/2LT	2	"	"	TANDEM 150	–	–	–	–	–	
2ST,4,7,10,11,12LT 3,11T,LTL	3	"	"	150	–	–	–	–	–	
GS	1	YES HYDR.$_C$	198	–	1·5"	1·0"	$1\frac{5}{16}$"	NO	NO	1 PINT

DIVERTER VALVE

This chart relates to the vacuum servo brake systems used on the majority of London Transport buses in service in the early post-war period, though the small GS single-deckers of a later era had been added subsequently. It also shows how the chassis code system could be used to indicate variations. It would be impractical to give details of all the codes mentioned, some of which cover very minor distinctions but it can be seen that most of the STL-type AEC Regent buses and several other types had vacuum-hydraulic brakes, the latter part of the system being of Lockheed make. Some of the sub-variants were very numerous — the 4/9STL code applied to the 902 buses numbered STL614-2515 being the largest single group. The triple servo brake mechanism used on some types of the early 1930s came back into favour on such models as the 3STD (Leyland TD7), 4STD and 1TD (Leyland PD1 and PS1), B (Bristol K-types) and the post-war 18STL and 14T (AEC Regent and Regal).

NOTE:- TF & RT FITTED WITH AIR PRESSURE BRAKES.

※ CERTAIN 1ST HAVE BEEN CONVERTED TO TRIPLE SERVO.

At this time the RT family was very small in numbers and the existing fleet consisted of a multitude of types; this is illustrated in a table showing the braking systems of the fleet at the time. With only RT and TF types with air pressure brakes (though there had been some experimental installation in a few STL-class buses), I had a lot to learn! By today's standards it was a formidable task so those who today think they have problems don't know how lucky they are.

The RTs were based on an AEC chassis (the Regent III) built largely to suit LT's needs, and most were to carry bodywork either by Park Royal or Weymann to identical standard laid down in detail by London Transport engineers.

Huge orders had been placed—trams would also need to be replaced by buses before abandonment of the tramway system in 1952—and although delivery was slow at first it reached about ten per week before the end of 1947. In 1949-50, with the additional input of Leyland chassis and further bodybuilders RT-family buses were entering the fleet at a peak rate of over 30 per week. It slowed somewhat later but over the whole period from 1947 up to the end of production in 1954 average output was about eighteen per week. Eventually there would be some 4,825 RT buses including the 151 dating from 1939-42, plus 1,631 Leyland RTL and 500 Leyland RTW.

Although the enthusiast may think that when you've seen one RT you've seen them all he will soon realise from reading this chapter that a policy of continuously monitoring performance and improving the specification meant that there were in fact several variants. To the untutored eye they appeared virtually identical but to those who drove and maintained them these differences were very important.

Perhaps it might be as well to explain the nomenclature of identification of the vehicle. The bonnet code, such as STL, RT etc governs the basic type but the whole vehicle is identified by a code using numbers in front and behind the RT

The first of the post-war RT-type buses to enter service was RT402 which began the initial batch of examples with Weymann-built bodywork allocated fleet numbers running up to RT651. It entered service on 10th May 1947 from Leyton garage and is seen at Victoria in company with G66, a Guy Arab of the early wartime type with Park Royal utility body dating from 1943. The first RT with Park Royal body, RT152, went into service a fortnight later but delivery was slow from both bodybuilders at first, only 26 having been put on the road up to the beginning of September 1947.

letters. Those in front refer to the chassis whereas those behind refer to the body, thus we have 1/3RT3/1. In other words the basic chassis is 3RT the 1/3 indicating a minor change which doesn't affect the general interchangeability of the chassis. In a similar way RT3 represents the basic body with the 3/1 indicating minor changes. The numbers need not be the same for body and chassis, for instance 8RM10 which covered the RCL coach version of the Routemaster. Usually with a big change in the body, such as from bus to coach in the case of the RCL, the number changes.

Although the post-war 3RT3 did not look unlike the 'pre-war' 2RT2 (strictly speaking, they had entered service during the early war years, beginning in 1940), the body construction was different in that much had been learned from aircraft production during the war years. Nearly everything was jig-built, involving a lengthy process of the precise design of body components, and bodies had to be completely interchangeable between chassis to assist with the vehicle overhaul. Usually the body took longer to overhaul than the chassis, by about one week, so that a body rarely if ever met its original chassis again. London Transport was allowed to change chassis numbers. Thus the bus going in for overhaul would give its number to an outgoing vehicle. So throughout its life the body and chassis

These detail views of a later RT dating from 1951 indicate the location of the various numbers and codes which were used to identify London Transport vehicles. The fleet number RT2565 appeared on the bonnet (hence sometimes being described as bonnet number) as well as the cab side and inside the rear platform. At that stage registration numbers rarely matched though LYF 1-500 were all used on various batches of RT, RTL or RF buses of that period. The chassis type code, 3RT, appeared on the small brass plate on the offside dumb iron (1), whilst the body code RT8 was on a similar plate (2) attached to the body just above the bonnet top — the complete vehicle being described as 3RT8. The AEC chassis number, in this case 09615884, was on another brass plate on the nearside dumb iron (3), while the London Transport body number, 5832, was shown inside the front canopy. The removable plates by the cab door show the garage to which the bus was allocated, J being the code for Holloway, and the running number of the working on the route it was on.

would have a host of bonnet numbers. The body could also change its colour from red to green!

It had been found in the days of the London General Omnibus Company (LGOC), the main operator of London buses in the days before the formation of London Transport in 1933, that a ratio of building 103 bodies to every 100 chassis worked out about right in allowing time for the slower process of body overhaul. In those days it was normal for bodies to be removed for an annual overhaul — the combination of solid-

The removal of bodywork from chassis for overhaul was standard practice at Chiswick. In this scene, dating from soon after the 1939-45 war, the chassis of one of the LT-type AEC Renown six-wheel buses dating from 1931 is being towed out from under the body after it has been raised. Like almost all of the type, the chassis had an 8.8-litre oil engine, probably being converted at some time during 1933-39 though a few had always been oil-engined.

This scene within Chiswick Works on 22nd October 1947 was one I might well have witnessed as I had begun work there only a few weeks previously. The chassis of STL1860, a standard example of 1937, though belonging to one of the 'Tunnel' buses, is given a brief road test after overhaul, using the gradient in 'The Dip' specially constructed for the purpose (there was a similar facility within the AEC works at Southall). The Experimental Department was at the far end of the Dip and the main workshops to the left — the lorries (the nearest being an AEC Regal converted from a Green Line coach) were probably loading up with reconditioned units for delivery to garages.

tyred chassis, wooden-framed bodywork and many streets still paved with stone setts makes this frequency, originally laid down by the Metropolitan Police, understandable.

In later years, the interval gradually extended, and during the 1939-45 war the practice of body removal for overhaul largely stopped. It was resumed subsequently but when Aldenham overhaul works got into its stride in 1955, as described in a later chapter, it was decided not only to build a small batch of 'float' bodies again (this had not been done since 1939) but also to permanently delicense 158 buses of various types. The various bonnet, registration and chassis numbers of these effectively disappeared, in some cases for many years, to cover the vehicle under overhaul. Thus newly overhauled buses took on the identities of vehicles arriving for attention, often on the same day. This saved quite a lot of money, quite apart from the paperwork involved in surrendering and renewing licences for periods which would rarely have matched the period for which refunds could be obtained.

Chassis for London Transport did not have the chassis number stamped on the frame, but the number was given on a brass plate usually on the dumb iron where it could easily be changed. For internal records, a similar brass plate was affixed to the top face of nearside frame members, visible when the bonnet was opened, so a complete history was maintained. Similarly there was a body number, usually painted under the canopy. The Routemaster was a special case, as it did not have a true chassis, only what were called the A and B frames which had their own series of numbers (though AEC did issue chassis numbers conforming to its usual system), but the system was carried on, as before. This procedure was reviewed when the Greater London Council took over responsibility for LT matters in 1970, but it continued until the lifting of bodies ceased.

At the start of post-war production the RTs came with Park Royal or Weymann bodies but the body builders were not keeping pace with the AEC chassis output. There was an interesting development following this situation arising — AEC were severely stretched in trying to meet national demands and Liverpool were pressing the Ministry to assist them in finding new buses after a disastrous fire in one of their tram depots in November 1947. The Ministry realised that LT could afford to allow AEC to divert some of its output to Liverpool but people in LT had other ideas! Only the veiled threat of 'intervention' and 'allocation' resolved the situation and AEC were allowed to build a batch of chassis for Liverpool to help them out — in practice, the effect seemed to be slight.

The Park Royal vehicles started at RT152 and the Weymann at RT402. Much of the preliminary work for the post-war RT had been carried out on some of the pre-war RTs. For instance the chassis modifications had been carried out on RT52. The history of the various changes makes interesting reading and is reproduced in this Chapter. The body of RT19 was fitted to RT52 and the chassis of RT19 was converted to what was to become the 3RT prototype with the body of RT1, which was closer in its form of construction to the proposed post-war standard. It may be of interest to note that the apparent RT1, as now preserved, is really the original RT1 body of 1939 mounted on the post-war chassis from RT1420.

Apart from these variants, the evolution of the 3RT fleet makes interesting reading. The genuine 2RT had a shaft-

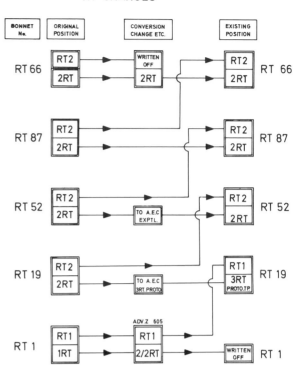

RT CHANGES

The interconnected way in which five of the early RT buses were involved in the development work which led to the post-war 3RT standard is shown in this chart. Chassis type codes are 1RT and 2RT while the body types are RT1 and RT2.

The modified chassis of RT19 was fitted with the 1939 body from the original prototype, RT1, re-entering service in this form in November 1945. It is seen as running a few years later from Putney Bridge (F) garage. In later years this body was transferred to a post-war chassis, RT1420, and used as a mobile instruction unit numbered in the service fleet as 1037J. Subsequently this vehicle was restored as 'RT1', though the original chassis of RT1 was used for such spares as were common to the 2RT version and the remains broken up in September 1946 — some items were non-standard and replacements no longer obtainable.

By the time this view of RT123 was taken it had acquired the 'all-red' livery adopted in 1950. New in September 1941, it displays the curved shape of the cab side window and windscreen which readily identified the RT2 body from the front — compare with RT1239, new in September 1949, alongside. The latter happens to have been one of the Saunders-bodied buses but their bodywork, coded RT3/3, was to the standard early post-war outline. The photograph was taken outside Peckham garage, but RT123 was from Chelverton Road, Putney, as indicated by its AF garage plate, whilst RT1239 was from Nunhead (AH).

driven rotary compressor and dynamo. The dynamo speed was inadequate (a measure to correct this is described later) and a change was made to keep the shaft-driven dynamo, but belt driving a more powerful reciprocating compressor. The rotary compressor had given rise to oil carry-over problems and needed an oil separator. This second group of RTs was coded 1/2RT but the unbalanced belt load on the gearbox gave rise to bearing failure. Finally a further change was made in belt driving the compressor on the opposing side of the gearbox to the dynamo. These were coded 3/2RT. The code 2/2RT is understood to have been issued for a plan to update RT1's chassis, which proved uneconomic as many of its components were of a 'one-off' character.

This group of vehicles ran, in the main, from Chelverton Road and Putney Bridge garages and much of their success was due to the efforts of the Day Foreman, at Chelverton Road, Johnny Johnson. He knew every bus individually. Unusual things happened to 'his' buses — for instance fitters were allowed to strip the top speed clutch in the gearbox whereas it was usually the custom to return gearboxes to Chiswick for overhaul. Because of the shortcomings of the 2RT gearbox whereby the end thrust was taken through to the rear bearing of the box, changes were made in the future to contain the

This picture of the chassis of RT2, taken at AEC when it was new in late 1939 shows the arrangement of the dynamo and the small rotary compressor originally fitted to the 2RT-type buses, both being mounted centrally in the chassis and driven by a shaft, just visible alongside the fluid flywheel in this view, from the front of the engine.

thrust within the top speed itself. Unfortunately it was not possible to fit two equal thrust bearings and the smaller of the two bearings gave rise to a shorter-than-designed life. It was by no means uncommon when riding in a standard post-war RT to find that quite a pronounced whine would begin when the driver engaged top gear, because of this.

Returning now to the shaft-driven dynamo, of which there were approximately forty-eight when I came on the scene, battery failures were all too common and with the help of Mr Albert Miller, who was the Chief Engineer of Self Changing Gears at Coventry, a geared-up drive was designed. This consisted of a miniature gearbox fitted on the front end of the dynamo which had an overspeed and free wheel clutch mechanism. This worked quite well except that the gearbox needed to be filled with oil. One doesn't need much imagination to find that on occasions it was forgotten and seizure of the overdrive occurred. As an alternative the automatic chassis lubrication system was plumbed in to it, but this gave inadequate supply. However the device proved that with a little more capacity for oil, the charging problem could be solved.

Because the 2RTs worked from two distinct garages the drivers also were very familiar with them. Once other garages started to receive the 3RT we had problems because they had been used to driving buses with vacuum servo brakes and pedal pressures which were much heavier than with 3RT buses. It so

The dynamo and compressor drive arrangement adopted for the post-war 3RT chassis is seen in this drawing.

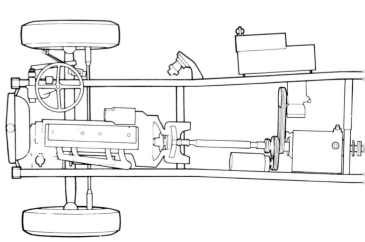

happened that Chelverton Road ran the 28 route jointly with Middle Row who had 3RTs. The brake linings in use on the vehicles at this time were the woven type—asbestos weave impregnated with resins—and because of the overbraking by the Middle Row 3RT drivers, brake fade (deterioration in braking efficiency) resulted. Drivers had formed the habit of racing to a stop and yanking on the handbrake to stop the bus just at the stop—and they were pretty expert at it. Nevertheless this was a situation that could not be tolerated and the largest exercise of brake testing was carried out including the use of the new moulded type lining which was then making itself known. These contained asbestos in powder form with other products made either in a dry or wet mix which was then cured in a fixture made like baking a cake.

In essence the test method used was a soak test where the brakes are gradually heated up by a drag test and at stated intervals stopping tests are taken using a Tapley meter to measure the rate of deceleration from a full brake application. From this can be obtained a graph of efficiency against temperature. Further checks have to be taken during the life span of a brake lining as the friction tends to drop off with age, sometimes due to glazing, so reheat tests are taken at stipulated mileages. Finally wear rates are recorded of linings and drums, as some linings have given very good wear rates themselves but wore away the cast iron drum! I can recall one Duron lining of years ago that didn't wear at all but the drum certainly did. It all depends on the materials in the lining—a trade secret—and it is London Transport policy to stipulate the friction requirement for the lining at certain temperatures and not materials from which the lining is made.

The desperation experienced over the Middle Row situation was such that every possible combination of lining was tried, and out of all the tests came a combination fitment of a moulded shoe liner (Capasco HF 6A5) for the leading shoe and a woven one (Chekko XL 3) for the trailing. This gave excellent resistance to fade and in principle has continued to this day.

The theory behind it, or one that appears to fit the facts, is that the woven lining has a higher cold friction level which fades very quickly with temperature whilst the moulded starts at a lower friction level but does not fade so easily, thus the general fall-off is much less. A typical brake performance curve is illustrated showing that friction also falls with age. These curves were obtained in a deliberate heat-up test when values of retardation were recorded at rising temperatures followed by a recovery test. Since this procedure gave a good indication of the performance of the brake lining under service conditions it was decreed by the Chief Mechanical Engineer, Mr Bill Durrant, that every choice of brake lining must firstly satisfy this 'Middle Row' test before adoption. This policy is still being followed, by and large, today.

Having successfully overcome the fade problem the task was then tackled of finding alternative manufacturers so that supplies were guaranteed, and this was achieved with a modicum of success in the case of the moulded lining, but an alternative to the woven one was difficult to find. Eventually it was agreed to use just the one woven type. Chekko XL 3, and hope that supplies would be guaranteed. But as everyone knows this never happens and in later years Chekko were bought out by Mintex (British Belting and Asbestos).

Brake fade curves reveal the variation in performance in relation to temperature, in this case carried out on a Leyland National using Beral 1537 linings. The footbrake retardation is shown in the graph and handbrake figures are tabulated above. Repeated use, as liable to be needed in London conditions, makes rises in temperature inevitable.

However, this is part of a later story when it was a case of 'all hands to the pump'.

The success of the work carried out on braking systems and lining materials may be judged by the life obtained—up to 20,000 miles on an RT. In later years the 'off the peg' buses frequently achieved as little as 8,000 miles brake shoe life.

It was realised at the time of the introduction of the air-pressure brake that there would be a tendency for over-braking since the pedal effort required on the STL could go up to a maximum of 100lbs whereas the RT peaked at 80-85lbs. To this end a 'dead' spring was fitted in the brake valve so that when the driver reached what was considered to be the average required pressure he felt a resistance. Further braking, if needed, could be achieved by increasing the pedal pressure. Unfortunately it served to tell the driver that he was fading the brakes because he had to go into a heavier range. Once the older type vehicles were withdrawn it was decided to remove this spring inside the brake valve and the driver was given straight lining braking up to 80-85lbs./sq.ins.

London Transport had always been a pioneer in bus design, partly through its connection with AEC at Southall, although always open to fresh ideas from other sources, and had been a great believer in automatic brake adjusters. A design known as the RP system, which came from its inventors, T. Rowland and W. Parker who were successive Chief Engineers with Birmingham Corporation, often referred to as the 'ratchet and pawl', was quite an innovation. A mechanism was mounted on one of the brake shoes which measured the movement of the shoe and on the release of the brake caused a ratchet mechanism to wind out the nose piece in the shoes thus taking up the clearance. The calculations for the mechanism were complex since they had to take into account drum expansion due to force, drum expansion due to temperature as well as to allow for brake liner wear. Above all, when the brake drum cooled down the brakes did not have to bind. As has already been stated the RT brakes tended to get hot due to abuse in the early days and it was found that the adjuster mechanism tended to over-compensate and cause binding brakes. The ingenious idea was put forward to open the hole in the positioning link in the ratchet motor by about .015ins which just did the trick.

This led to another problem, however, which came my way with the wartime Guy Arab buses, of which there were 435. These had vacuum brakes and needed a fairly hefty pedal effort so the brakes did not get that hot. In consequence brake shoe clearances were not maintained and once over .060ins clearance delayed-brake-calls were received. For this reason Clayton Dewandre, who manufactured the mechanism, produced a four pawl adjuster for these servo brakes.

Gearbox developments

Returning now to our RT story. The question of top speed failure has been discussed and the next question to arise was the fierce gearchange; this often resulted when the driver quickly released the 'clutch' pedal. A simple explanation of the workings of the Wilson type gearbox is that it consists of an epicyclic gear system which rotates within a drum and each ratio is obtained by gripping the outside of the drum by means of what is termed a brake band. This brake band is activated by a linkage incorporating a toggle mechanism which has the effect of increasing the grip as it tightens. For convenience the 1st, 2nd and 3rd gear bands were set to a pre-determined position when applied. Theoretically as the gears are engaged in turn during each restart from rest each change-up requires a decreased loading, as the torque loading required lessens as the vehicle accelerates away, and an ingenious automatic adjuster device 'felt' the amount of toggle action, resetting the grip to compensate for lining wear.

Unfortunately some drivers got into the habit of changing down from top gear to 3rd with excessive sharpness when approaching a stop which put a severe reverse loading action on the brake band and eventually it broke. This meant a gearbox removal from the bus and a complete strip down. It was decided the only way to overcome this was to reduce the 3rd speed setting so that the reverse loading in this situation was less and therefore not so critical. In order to ensure that the automatic adjuster worked it was necessary to make a further modification to the tail of the automatic adjuster ring. This

modification also reduced the kick-back when making a quick upchange from 2nd to 3rd. This simple modification almost entirely eliminated brake band failures and was soon adopted across the fleet. The modifications to the gearbox would fill a book on their own but this example will suffice to show that service operation can throw up some irritating and expensive problems which could sometimes be cured quite simply.

I think it's time I returned to Chiswick, and turned to some of the more important things that occupied my time, although the day was punctuated by events of the type described earlier. Our Chief Mechanical Engineer, Bill Durrant, always believed that buses should be made more than just fool-proof so that however they were driven it was very difficult to break them. He also believed that the driver should be able to concentrate on the driving and not have to worry too much about the complications of gear changing. It was for this reason that fluid transmissions, ie fluid flywheels and preselector gearboxes, were almost standard in the fleet.

My boss at the time, Mr Albert Higgins, had been working on a design with Self Changing Gears to produce a gearbox that did not need a clutch pedal, or, more correctly, gearchange pedal since on a preselector this pedal is linked to the gearbox and effects the change which has been selected in advance by the hand lever. Some work had been done pre-war in this direction with STL760 at Merton which had been fitted with an automatic gearbox control developed by Mr Albert Miller who, at the time he began work on the idea, owned a garage at Stornaway on the remote Isle of Lewis. He was later, as already mentioned, to become Chief Engineer of Self Changing Gears and then Director and it was he with whom I came in contact on this project. Basically the gearbox was an epicyclic one with oil control cylinders to engage the gears, thus giving the possibility of full throttle changes without a jerk. The box was referred to as the RV7 but once in service they were always referred to as the 'one leggers' because there was no 'clutch' pedal, one leg being used for the brake and throttle. First of all the gearbox was fitted to a 3RT chassis loaded with weights and driven behind a service vehicle on Route 17 which at this time ran between Shepherds Bush and London Bridge. Acting as the Assessor, it was my job to record oil pressures and temperatures in the gearbox throughout the journey, sitting in the open on the chassis. Often I deserted the chassis to ride on the platform of the bus we were following as protection from the rain, returning periodically to the chassis to take the readings. For some reason this sort of job always came my way in the winter months.

The gearbox having survived these tests, the chassis was sent away for bodying at Park Royal and returned as RT778. Turnham Green garage, being near to Chiswick, was an ideal operating garage for experimental vehicles when it was desired to gain experience of new ideas under service conditions, and was in the process of receiving RTs for the 91 route. Thus RT778 was later followed by its sisters RT2207, 2208 and 2273 and it was arranged that they ran on distinct running numbers so that each driver would have a week on the bus, Turnham Green garage having a weekly rota as opposed to a daily rota as in some others. With these vehicles I almost became part of the garage staff, and the connection was strengthened with the addition of another batch of experimental vehicles. From these four vehicles much was

London Transport was often at the forefront of bus design; STL757, originally dating from 1935, had been one of ten STL-type AEC Regent buses fitted with air-pressure brakes in the period around 1937 when features to be adopted on the RT were being evaluated. There had been earlier experiments in the late 1920s and air brakes had become usual on trolleybuses but the RT was the vehicle which eventually led the way for general adoption of air brakes on British buses. By the time it was seen in this post-war view at Kensal Rise, STL757 had reverted to standard, the body being one of those rebuilt by Mann Egerton, in this case in October 1947. Another similar bus, STL760, had been used to experiment with air operation of the Wilson preselective gearbox in June 1937 and then, in November of that year, with a prototype of the Miller automatic version of the Wilson unit which ran for about 18,000 miles in the period up to November 1939.

The first 'one-legger' — RT778, fitted with Self-Changing Gears RV7 gearbox, soon after arrival at Turnham Green in September 1948, after bodying.

learned about the behaviour of gearboxes which changed gear under full torque conditions and it gave me an excellent insight into the requirements of gearboxes for London bus work.

Needless to say all did not always go to plan and it so happened that new vehicles were in short supply. Things were not helped by an incident at Leatherhead by the Senior PSV Ministry Examiner who found an old ST bus on Route 65, also operated by Turnham Green buses, on which he had earlier given an immediate Prohibition Notice when it had been operating from Holloway. Apparently it had been transferred, in ignorance, and Turnham Green felt his anger when he proceeded to give the ST vehicles PSV 71 Stop Notices as they arrived at Leatherhead but allowing them to work back to Kew Bridge. STL vehicles were drafted in after it was realised what was happening but then it was found that the drivers had only been passed by LT examiners to drive on clash

boxes! Incidentally this latter phrase was the usual one within LT for what was apt to be called a crash gearbox elsewhere — ie a conventional gearbox without benefit of synchromesh. Basically they had sliding-mesh engagement but AEC's clash boxes had constant-mesh third gear since 1931-32, giving a slightly easier change, with a shorter lever movement into that gear.

Such situations as this reacted on development projects and one day full service was not met, there being one bus short of requirement. I was summoned to Dollis Hill which was the Divisional Office of 'C' Division, before Tom Stammers, the Divisional Engineer, and asked to explain. After listening to me he asked if an additional spare STL would assist during our development days. The offer was gladly accepted and a very happy atmosphere existed between us, and still does, even though Tommy has been retired this many a year. This is

Turnham Green (V) garage, positioned only a short distance from Chiswick works, was often used when experimental vehicles were put into service, and route 91 was thus a likely location for such buses. Here the Leyland RT-series prototype, numbered RTL501 because it had been planned that 500 Leyland-bodied vehicles would be given the earlier numbers in the series, is seen soon after entering service in June 1948. The design was intended to give complete interchangeability of bodies with AEC RT-type chassis, and in fact this vehicle was fitted with a Park Royal-built body diverted from RT657.

typical of the way we worked, appreciating there was a need for each other, all working together with a common purpose of producing a better bus for London.

It was nothing during the bus shortage years of 1948 onwards, when the fleet was ageing after several years of operation with difficulties of spares, to operate the experimental vehicle during the day and report to Turnham Green after the bus came off service to change a gearbox before going home, ensuring the service would be met in the morning.

Being close to Chiswick, it was natural that Turnham Green became almost an experimental garage and it was then decided to introduce some RTs with power hydraulic brakes. This system was the joint brain child of my boss Albert Higgins and Automative Products Limited, better known by the name of Lockheed, who had considerable experience with hydraulic systems on aircraft where reliability was the name of the game. One RT was converted from air brake operation to power hydraulics. For the power source a seven-cylinder radial pump was used which pumped oil into three hydraulic accumulators which contained air within a rubber bladder. As the fluid was pumped into the accumulator it compressed the air within the bladder. This rise in pressure of the air reacted against the oil which was thus automatically and continually under pressure. When the system reached a pre-determined pressure a valve on the end of one accumulator, called the cut-out valve, snapped open to allow the pump to circulate through the brake valve and back to the header tank. Two accumulators served the brakes and the third supplied pressure to the preselective gearbox, also included in the hydraulic system.

It soon became obvious from the tests with the chassis that the quicker build-up times of the system allowed the brake pressure to be kept well above the maximum brake line pressure that the driver required and therefore throughout the day the driver could rely on full brake pressure, and the low-pressure warning device, which arranged for a warning 'flag' to drop into the driver's line of sight at the top of the windscreen could be set to operate at a higher pressure. With the air system it was not possible to do this and there was always a worry in that in the case of an accident the driver could claim that his air pressure was not up to the maximum he could expect. The chassis was bodied and numbered RT902 and joined the experimental-gearbox vehicles at Turnham Green. Whilst the drivers were not told of the nature of the brakes they soon twigged that something was different. In releasing air brakes there is usually a hissing noise but the hydraulic bus is silent. The application was much smoother and almost gave the impression of a weak brake yet the stopping distance was very good. There was no option but to come clean and let on.

Number RT902 did however develop a curious quirk in that if the 'clutch' pedal was violently operated it was possible to miss a gear. This arose, as we later discovered, because the supply pipe did not release the fluid quickly enough so that the operating strut in the gearbox of the outgoing gear moved out of the 'bus bar' groove and the ingoing gear did not drop in. Thus the gearbox piston would come right to the top of the cylinder and a false neutral was obtained. Whilst trying to iron out the fault I can recall an occasion in Hounslow High Street where I met up with a fire engine on the wrong side of the road racing to a fire when I lost my gears. It was an agonising time, nose to nose with the fire engine, trying to regain gears which, after what seemed an age, came back again. The simple remedy was to fit a larger supply pipe and the trouble disappeared.

It was then decided to equip six more vehicles with this brake system and arrangements were made to use numbers ending in 1-6 as RT3381, 2782, 3483, 3504, 3535 and 3646. Whilst this was convenient for recognition there was a slight snag in that there was a change in the build programme and RT3504 was green, having been built for the Country Bus department. This caused a problem for a little while until it was decided that Reigate would be the base for this vehicle. Reigate was the seat of the Divisional Engineer (South) and living on the borders of that area, I had already developed a rapport with the staff. So Turnham Green ended up with six Lockheed vehicles and Reigate with one. At that time Reigate operated three Chiswick staff buses which were a hangover from the East Surrey days when there was a works there which had closed on the formation of LPTB. It was handy to put RT3504 on this duty when attention was required with the vehicle, otherwise an afternoon visit was made to Reigate, afterwards travelling on the bus as running number RG2 on Route 405 to Three Bridges where it changed to a 405B and dropped me off at my door on its return home to Reigate.

In the early days a visit to a Country garage was usually a day's visit out but this time it had been reduced to half a day. In later life it reduced either to an early morning visit before 7.30am or an evening visit on the way home, about 6.00pm. It was always a pleasure to see one's friends in the

The Country Area had a different way of life. Some surprisingly quiet scenes could be found within the London Transport operating area. This 20-seat Leyland Cub, C69 of the 1935 batch with Short Bros bodywork, is seen soon after entering service, on route 450, linking Dartford and Gravesend via the villages of Bean and Betsham.

Country — a different way of life, being much more separated from the hub of the organisation and left to run on its own much more. Service was the motto and the service had to run even if it meant that a peculiar type, such as a GS, had to cover for a double-deck. Nevertheless there was a friendly spirit in Central but somehow a much more hectic life.

It was always a great sadness to me when the Country area was 'given away' by the GLC (for which I have never forgiven them) because it wasn't realised that Country buses ran through central London. In those early days it was nothing for red double-deckers to be drafted to Country to strengthen Green Line, especially during the days of the New Towns. In fact one of my tasks on a Friday was to take a Control car to Reigate from Turnham Green for week-end operations.

The success of the hydraulic-brake buses soon made Clayton Dewandre consider the implications. For many years Clayton, and also Westinghouse, had been the suppliers of air pressure equipment to the commercial vehicle industry and they could see a loss of business if power hydraulics took over.

It may perhaps be worth dwelling on the advantages of hydraulics over air. Firstly on the conversion of the RT to hydraulics well over 112lbs was saved in equipment weight. Secondly the working agent being a fluid there was no pressure drop in the line as the fluid acted like a solid rod, and once pressurised at one end the effect was immediately felt at the other; hence the brakes were more progressive.

Using mineral oil as a working agent there was no fear of corrosion — or freezing for that matter — and in all my 40 years I never experienced freezing of the brake system on a hydraulically braked vehicle. I understand that this was found to be an important advantage of the Routemaster buses operated in the more severe climate of County Durham by the Northern General Transport Co Ltd. The level of stored energy was much higher at any time compared with air. Because build up times were much superior, with the setting of the warning flag to indicate low pressure at a higher value, it

was no longer possible (or necessary!) to accept a driver's story that his flag dropped and he therefore had insufficient brake. With the advent of the Routemaster, drivers soon learned that this was no excuse and ceased to put this forward as a reason for an accident. The only disadvantage was the occasional loss of working fluid, which could not so readily be replaced as air, but later, with the advent of warning devices in the head tank to indicate low level, this ceased to be a problem.

Therefore Clayton produced a power hydraulic brake system which, after an initial trial on RT 2532, and not without difficulties, led to 20 more vehicles being converted. This was too great a number to allocate to Turnham Green in its entirety, so they were split between Hounslow and the Green with one that happened to be in Country-area livery being sent to join its sister at Reigate. The experience of these vehicles was such that it was decided by my chief, Albert Higgins, to utilise this system for the new Routemaster vehicle, but more of that later.

Many other tasks were undertaken during those quieter years — further attempts were made to improve the preselective gearbox on the RT by employing a revised bus bar linkage which altered the application torque build-up while closing the brake band on the speed drum. Whilst this was successful it meant changing another vital part, namely the bus bar bracket which was bolted to the bus bar and could only be reached by stripping the gearbox. Instead the old bracket and bus bar with its knife edge, which was apt to break off, rendering the bus immobile, remained standard. Careful inspection was maintained on the production of this bus bar bracket to see that sharp corners were avoided during the machining operation at AEC.

Another problem that arose was the material from which this bracket was made, normally being what was known as EN36, a steel high in resistance to impact failure. On the AEC lists alternative materials were quoted as a general guide and for EN36 the suggested one was EN352. Suddenly a spate of

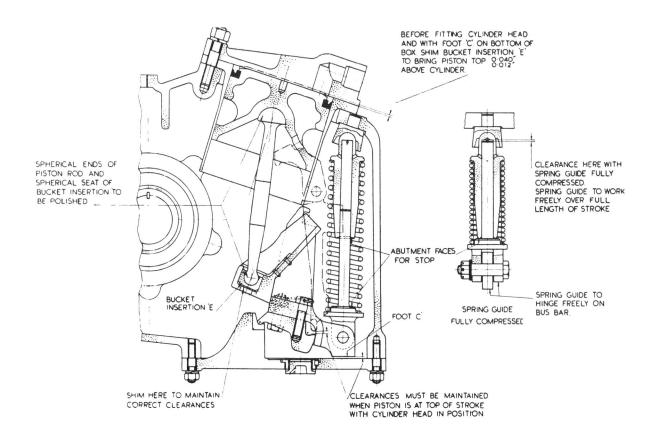

BEFORE FITTING CYLINDER HEAD
AND WITH FOOT 'C' ON BOTTOM OF
BOX, SHIM BUCKET INSERTION 'E'
TO BRING PISTON TOP $^{0.040"}_{0.012"}$
ABOVE CYLINDER.

SPHERICAL ENDS OF
PISTON ROD AND
SPHERICAL SEAT OF
BUCKET INSERTION TO
BE POLISHED

CLEARANCE HERE WITH
SPRING GUIDE FULLY
COMPRESSED.
SPRING GUIDE TO WORK
FREELY OVER FULL
LENGTH OF STROKE

ABUTMENT FACES
FOR STOP

BUCKET
INSERTION 'E'

SPRING GUIDE TO
HINGE FREELY ON
BUS BAR.

FOOT 'C'

SPRING GUIDE
FULLY COMPRESSED

SHIM HERE TO MAINTAIN
CORRECT CLEARANCES

CLEARANCES MUST BE MAINTAINED
WHEN PISTON IS AT TOP OF STROKE
WITH CYLINDER HEAD IN POSITION

This drawing of the air cylinder and part of the internal operating mechanism of an RT gearbox shows potential sources of trouble and the action taken to eliminate them. Careful study often allowed simple solutions, greatly improving reliability and extending life between overhauls.

failures developed and in those days AEC practice was to stamp the article with the material number from which it was made; these bore the legend EN36. Just as a check, an examination was made and it was found to be EN352. The explanation was that the person making the bracket saw the drawing was stamped EN36 so he just stamped it accordingly. In any case EN352 was not really a satisfactory alternative, so it was rejected for this part.

Part of the somewhat complex operating mechanism in the gearbox is illustrated.

Also indicated is a modification which gave a few traumatic days until it was solved. As is customary, troubles of this nature seem to occur over Bank Holiday periods and in this case complaints arose of being unable to obtain gears. The garage where the trouble arose was Middle Row, now closed, and thinking it was an air pressure problem, in conjunction with the Garage Engineer, Dick Turtle, we ran a vehicle with the aid of an air bottle. Whilst this didn't prove anything, it was a little hazardous as the foot brake of the bus ceased to be operative. For those who knew Middle Row with its collection of isolated areas, some of the walls were nearly demolished. In the end it was found that the bus bar return spring took up a curvature and the end of its guide dug into the spring. Tapering the end of the guide solved the problem and a fleet modification was put in hand.

Not all my work centred on brakes and gearboxes, however. It had been traditional to fit all London buses with a worm type

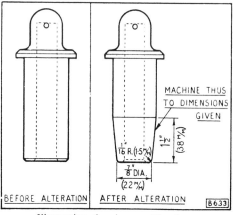

MACHINE THUS
TO DIMENSIONS
GIVEN

$\frac{1}{16}$ R.(1.5 ⁿ/ₘ)

$1\frac{1}{2}$
(38 ⁿ/ₘ)

$\frac{7}{8}$ DIA.
(22 ⁿ/ₘ)

BEFORE ALTERATION

AFTER ALTERATION

B633

Illustration showing modification
to upper return spring guide.

rear axle mainly because of long life and ease of assembly during overhaul, as well as the low-level propellor-shaft line it facilitated. It is possible on the AEC differential to view the wormwheel teeth through the filler opening in the top of the casing and someone must have looked in there on a fairly new axle on a bus and it seemed as if great lumps had been plucked from the phosphor bronze of the wheel. Therefore an experiment was set up to examine some crown wheels during their early service life and it was apparent that in the first few months pieces do get plucked off, but it does not get any worse. Furthermore it would seem that these small craters, for want of a better word, act as little reservoirs for the oil and give a lubrication film between the wormwheel and worm.

Another problem that caused irritation was heavy steering. The AEC design of front axle used a taper roller race to support

These three views, taken when the last preselective Wilson-type RT gearbox to be overhauled in Chiswick Works was going through in 1979, shows how the main assemblies were fitted together. In the view above, the fitter is completing the assembly of the baseplate with the brake bands for first, second and reverse gears, holding the bus bar bracket mentioned in the text. In the top-right view, the gearbox casing is lowered on to the baseplate assembly. In the third view, the method of up-ending the running gear, with its series of sun-and-planet gears within the various brake drums, so as to ensure it all stays together while the assembled casing is lowered on to it, is shown. What becomes the front of the unit, with the pulley for the compressor and dynamo drive, is at the bottom and the output shaft is yet to be fitted on what is to be the rear face of the unit, to take the drive from within the gear sets. The later types of gearbox using the same basic principles but with automatic control have similar internal parts.

the king pin in the axles and under certain operations an indentation appeared on the tracks, leading to a localised heaviness in the steering effort. Remember there was no power assistance on models up to and including the RT family. This indentation became particularly evident on the 10T10 Green Line coaches because there was a lot less turning of the steering due to there being fewer stops per mile. Tests were done at a later stage to measure the frequency of turns and their actual angular turn and it was surprising how many manoeuvres there were just either side of the straight-ahead position, with rapidly decreasing frequency as the angle of turn became greater. Because of this the front axle life became limited to two years, but it was essential to ensure that the maximum life was present when the axle was built.

On the other hand Leyland chose to use thrust buttons to support the load and these could easily be changed in the axle. However, a lot of work had to be done to determine the surface shape of the button and the heat treatment. The working surfaces needed a plentiful supply of oil from the automatic lubrication system which for various reasons was not always present. It did mean that, once the treated surface wore, steering became very heavy and resulted in driver complaints. Naturally comparisons would be made between different makes and classes!

Since we are considering lubrication, perhaps it is appropriate to look into it further. For many years it had been the practice to lubricate the wearing parts of a bus manually. To make the job easier a greaser was connected to a battery of grease nipples situated at a convenient point on the chassis. The theory was that by applying a hand-operated pump, which became known as a 'blue pig', grease was pumped along the pipe lines to the appropriate point. A second man watched to see that grease reached the point concerned, when the operator would change the greaser to the next point on the battery plate. Thus to do the job properly it was a two-man job and very expensive in labour.

Thought turned to making the system more automatic and it is true to say that London Transport gave a lead in this direction with the help, initially, of Clayton Dewandre of Lincoln.

It was considered that with an air pressure braking system it might be a good idea to operate a power lubricator so that every time the brakes were applied one of a collection of lubricating lines would receive a shot of oil. It was later found that braking was a good measure of the work a bus did as far as Central London was concerned but not quite so applicable to the Country area of London Transport. Indeed on a Green Line vehicle working with about two stops per mile it was totally inadequate. Large scale trials were carried out on the 15STL class with power-operated automatic lubrication referred to as the RP system, being another invention of the Rowland and Parker partnership. Such a system became universal on the pre-war RT and the post-war RT. It was even carried through on the Fleetlines where some were fitted from scrapped RTs when Clayton Dewandre could not supply new units.

During the RT days there was another firm, Tecalamit, who were marketing a belt-driven lubricator, some of which London Transport fitted experimentally. This was quite a robust unit and the advent of power hydraulics enabled a redesign to be done which produced a much smaller unit and it first saw the light of day on six Fleetlines that were converted to Clayton Dewandre hydraulic braking. Then, for some reason best known to Clayton, they pulled out of the lubrication market and it left the way clear for Tecalamit at Plymouth. With the design of the much smaller and efficient hydraulic unit developed specifically for London Transport, they then produced an air-operated version of lubricator which started to come in on the later Fleetlines — but still using the brake line method of operation. This method continued with the B15 Titans but the law was suddenly altered on the grounds of safety such that the brakes must not be liable to be affected by the operation or failure of a satellite system operated from them. The mileage-operated lubrication system had then to be employed but other alternatives such as using timers are on the market. All current big buses are fitted with these systems, which are now known under the Interlube name, still from Plymouth.

There have been some criticisms of power systems, such as a chafed pipe causing seizure of a vital part. However, if all points are inspected for receipt of lubricant instead of relying on adding lubricant to the tank, much of this can be avoided. Since the running of buses has a high usage of labour (about 70%) anything to reduce the manual effort must be a step in the right direction. To be able to keep the lubricant in contact with the working surfaces must be right, rather than pumping grease on a rota. In addition, rota periods were being increased, the wisdom of which is open to some question, and there is a greater chance of more wear. Indeed the STL tests did show that the shackle pin wear was considerably reduced with automatic lubrication.

Another point of controversy had been whether grease or oil should be used. Experience has shown that if the space between the two moving parts is filled with a product it will keep out the muck and dirt but of course it must be viscous to enable it to flow. There has been a great move on goods vehicles to fit automatic lubrication as vehicles are away from base for long periods — including trailers where maintenance has been generally poor. Perhaps the accountants in the bus business will look more favourably at this essential extra.

The reader will realise that my life was occupied with a wide variety of matters affecting the operation, safety and economy of our buses, and as my career progressed I would be able to make more impact with my findings and proposals.

My colleagues and I were contributing to the improved safety and better availability of 7,000 buses and coaches which were, between them, covering over 278 million miles per annum. Miles lost through failure were very low and the cost-effectiveness of our department was obviously related at least partially to this figure.

This photograph of a Clayton Dewandre automatic lubricator installation on the offside of an RT chassis was dated July 1945 and this strongly suggests that the chassis would be that of RT19, then being modified to act as a prototype for the post-war RT. The modified compressor position and drive is visible at the top left of the picture. The angle-iron assembly built on top of the frame was probably a temporary seat for use by observers when out on road test in chassis form.

Standing at the canal end of Park Royal's works ready for delivery just before I joined London Transport is RT168 — it entered service in September 1947. Note that at that date the full title of the undertaking was still the London Passenger Transport Board. The round white patch on the rear panel was a legacy of wartime practice when it had been provided to improve visibility for following vehicles in the black-out. After the austerity of the war years these buses made an impressive sight.

Although the production of the closely jig-built standard RT bodywork had taken longer than usual to get underway, by the time I arrived in the autumn of 1947, deliveries were rapidly building up. This picture of the 1000th Park Royal-bodied RT was taken at the main entrance to that concern's offices — the vehicle (RT1543) entered service in August 1949.

Hammersmith Broadway, July 1947. Nearest the camera is RT131, one of the 2RT buses dating from 1940, followed by ST and LT buses dating from 1931 and 1932 respectively. The car traffic includes four Hillman Minx, two Standard and examples of Morris and Wolseley.

3. The existing fleet 1947-50

When I joined London Transport in 1947, the huge vehicle replacement programme based on the RT had only just began to get under way. The original prototype, RT1, had already been withdrawn as its chassis had many non-standard parts of which spares were not available. The batch of 150 production buses of the 2RT2 type that had entered service between January 1940 and February 1942 had played a useful role in revealing items of the design that needed improvement, but were already well-worn buses with arduous wartime service behind them.

The first post-war RT chassis was delivered from AEC to Chiswick in March 1946 and deliveries continued steadily for the rest of that year but had actually been halted temporarily by Christmas of that year, not resuming until May 1947. The

problem was delay in body construction and consequent lack of space to store the chassis. It had been decided that bodybuilding at Chiswick, where most of London's buses had been bodied since the LGOC central works opened there in 1921, would cease, there being an enormous backlog of overhaul to the existing fleet due to war conditions which meant that no capacity could be spared for new construction.

However, although it was agreed before the end of the war that Park Royal and Weymann would each build large numbers of bodies for the RT chassis, it was decided that these were not merely to conform to London Transport ideas on appearance and finish, as had been the case with 'outside' bodybuilders in the 'thirties but would be jig-built to identical design throughout so that parts would be completely

Typical of an unrebuilt later-type standard STL-class bus as running in the early post-war years is STL2383, still in the version of pre-war red and white livery as modified with red-oxide roof and other details during the war period. It was placed in service in November 1937 and was representative of the STL with 'lighthouse' route number box built into the front of the roof panels, though this was not used as a result of wartime reduction of destination display still in force. The chassis of these buses were reliable and gave quite nimble performance with their preselective gearboxes, but wartime neglect had often taken its toll of the Chiswick-built bodywork. The heavy vertical external metal straps added to the pillars were an attempt to prolong life short of rebuilding but this vehicle was not untypical in having to be withdrawn relatively early, in this case in July 1950.

interchangeable for subsequent overhaul and repair. This policy was derived from wartime experience with the London Aircraft Production consortium which produced Handley Page Halifax four-engined bombers and included both Chiswick works and the Park Royal concern as well as three other companies. It had been co-ordinated by London Transport and the experience of much more precise manufacture than had been used in bus bodybuilding was seen as one worth copying. Extra staff were recruited for the Chiswick drawing office in August 1945 but it was a massive task and it was not until 28th April 1947 that the first bodied

vehicle arrived from Weymann, this being RT402, followed a fortnight later by RT152 from Park Royal.

It took several more months before production built up, and only 26 post-war RT buses were in service by the end of August 1947. Though this had grown to 171 by the end of the year, the bulk of London Transport bus services were to continue to be run by other types of vehicle for several years. It was not until 1950 that the RT family gained an overall majority and various older types remained in service for several years after that.

(continued overleaf)

London Transport licensed fleet at end of May 1947

Double-deckers (total 5,769)

Type	Make and model	Quantity
LT	AEC Renown six-wheel	1,184
ST	AEC Regent (25ft.)	932
STL	AEC Regent (26ft.)	2,584
STD	Leyland Titan	176
RT	AEC Regent RT	149
B	Bristol K-type	29
G	Guy Arab	435
D	Daimler CWA6 and CWD6	280

Single-deckers (total 1,082)

Type	Make and model	Quantity
T	AEC Regal	461
LT	AEC Renown six-wheel	189
Q	AEC Q-type	218
LTC	AEC Renown six-wheel	24
TF	Leyland ('flat' engine)	49
TD	Leyland Tiger PS1	29
C	Leyland Cub	73
CR	Leyland Cub (rear engine)	39

Grand total 6,851

Note that the above does not include vehicles owned but not licensed at that date, some classes being well below their potential strength, an obvious example being the TF, of which 76 were still around. On the other hand, some classes were remarkably close to their full original strength. For example, the LT-class double-deckers licensed at that date represented 96.9% of the total number of vehicles built, despite all dating from 1929-32 and hence all fifteen to eighteen years old.

Similarly the STL class was still deployed at 96.4% of its original numbers despite having been the 'front-line troops', in regular service throughout the period of wartime bombing. The ST-class was at a slightly lower proportion, 81.8%, quite a number of the ex-Tilling vehicles with open-staircase bodies having been withdrawn by then. Classes with 100% licensed included the STD Leyland Titans of 1937-46 and the wartime G-type and B-type Guy and Bristol buses.

The original STL type, as introduced by the LGOC at the beginning of 1933 and 100 examples built, was an attempt to provide maximum capacity on a two-axle chassis. The combination of the then recently-introduced 16ft. 3in.-wheelbase AEC Regent chassis with light bodywork allowed 60 seats to be provided, as many as in the final LT-class six-wheelers. However, weight and dimensional restrictions made it impractical at that date to fit oil engines. Seen here shortly before withdrawal in November 1948 is STL45.

The original plan for the post-war fleet renewal programme was to withdraw open-staircase buses first, but wide variations of body condition made that impossible. Of the 150 open-staircase buses that had been the first batches of the LT class of six-wheel AEC Renown buses to enter service with LGOC, dating from 1929 (LT1) or 1930 (the rest), only eighteen had been withdrawn by the time I arrived at Chiswick in September 1947. Seen here leaving Victoria towards the end of its days is LT67, which survived until May 1949 — like all but one of the type, it remained petrol-engined to the end. The last four lasted until February 1950.

At the end of 1947, the STL class of AEC Regent was still the largest class, with 2,529 licensed for service out of the total of 2,679 of this type that had entered service between 1932 and 1946. At that stage, apart from wartime bombing casualties, few of this type had been scrapped. About 2,000, dating from 1934-39, had the 7.7-litre AEC oil engine and preselective gearbox and these still formed the core of the London bus fleet, though some of the earlier examples were petrol-engined. The standard STL could be quite nimble in

traffic and was generally reliable, having the benefit of both Southall and Chiswick's knowledge and experience.

At that stage there were still many older buses in service, going right back to open-staircase six-wheel AEC Renown LT-class double-deckers of 1929-30. These were petrol-engined, as were over 600 of the early short-wheelbase ST-type AEC Regent buses of 1930-31 still scheduled for service in October 1947; the ST class originally numbered 1,139. A diminishing

The largest bus fleet to be added to that of the LGOC after the formation of London Transport was that of Thomas Tilling, acquired in October 1933. Among the vehicles transferred were 191 petrol-engined AEC Regent double-deckers of the early short-wheelbase type, duly given ST-class fleet numbers ST837-1027, following on from those of buses on similar chassis from LGOC. The open-staircase bodywork was as had been familiar to me from my boyhood, as Tilling had run other buses of the same type in Brighton. Seen here early in 1949 is ST945 which had been new in December 1930, running from Potters Bar garage on route 29 — such buses were used as garage 'spares' and carried only limited destination display. The sagging of the body was very typical of these buses in their final years — this one was withdrawn and scrapped in September 1949.

Possibly the last photograph to be taken of ST1 is this view taken outside Holloway garage in December 1949 — it was withdrawn that month. Built in October 1929, this had been the LGOC's prototype for the type, though its chassis was by no means the first AEC Regent, its chassis number being 661074. It had received a later standard ST-type body dating from 1931, becoming virtually a standard member of the class. Apart from seven exceptions, the vehicles numbered up to ST836 were similar.

The LT class of AEC Renown six-wheelers was still a mainstay of the fleet in 1947, some 1,184 licensed double-deckers of this type forming the second largest class. Most had AEC 8.8-litre oil engines, the majority of these being conversions in which the original petrol engines were replaced and although the vehicles dated from 1931-32, their engines had either been built or converted to the smooth-running pot-cavity direct injection system subsequently adopted for the early RT buses. The vehicle shown, LT156, was one of the first built with 56-seat enclosed-staircase bodywork (as standardised for all but one of LT151-950), dating from January 1931, receiving its oil engine in November 1938. It had been fitted with a body of the slightly modified type originally fitted to the LT501-850 batch, with revised destination display, during overhaul, and was one of the buses whose bodywork was renovated by Mann Egerton. It was withdrawn in June 1949.

minority of the latter (from the former Thomas Tilling Ltd fleet operated in London until the formation of London Transport in 1933) were also open-staircase though the majority, from LGOC, had closed-stair bodywork.

The bulk of the 1,061 LT-class double-deckers with closed-staircase bodywork placed in service by LGOC in 1931-32 had been converted to oil, using the 8.8-litre AEC engine that was in many ways the predecessor of the 9.6-litre (though some had always been so powered), and apart from some wartime casualties and a few withdrawn due to body defects, most were still in service in 1947.

Body condition was indeed the key problem so far as the pre-war fleet was concerned and although it had been hoped to withdraw the petrol-engined buses first, and particularly those with open staircases, vehicles of other types were having to be scrapped as being beyond economic repair and even the oil-engined STL-type buses were by no means immune from severe decay. The standard Chiswick-built bodies had not been expected to remain in service more than ten years or so when designed and neglect of repair in wartime had allowed damp and consequent rotting of their mainly ash frames to take hold.

The body shops at Chiswick, even though relieved of new body construction, could not cope with the huge volume of work and many vehicles of ST, LT and STL types had been sent to outside contractors for both repair and more extensive body overhaul from 1945, and in particular the Norwich firm of Mann Egerton carried out body overhauls on some 511 STL-type buses between February 1947 and March 1949. Had the war not intervened, almost the whole pre-war fleet would either have gone or be nearing the end of its days by 1949 and such overhauls were intended to keep enough STL-type buses in sound condition to enable the class to continue in service until phased out by about 1954, as was indeed achieved.

The style of body used for 262 LT-type buses built in 1932 (LT951-999, 1204-1416) was nicknamed 'Bluebird' because of the colour of upholstery although the design was more fundamentally different than implied by this detail, with 60-seat capacity and a more square-cut outline. The LT class was the subject of much pioneer work on mechanical design and LT1380 was one of those which were built from new with oil engines, its 8.8-litre engine originally being of the Ricardo indirect-injection type. It entered service in June 1932 and was scrapped in May 1949.

The only pre-war London Transport double-deck motor buses on other than AEC chassis still in use were 100 Leyland Titans built in 1937. Both the TD4 chassis and the Leyland metal-framed bodies incorporated features to London Transport requirements and outwardly they bore a general resemblance to the contemporary STL which accounts for the class letters, STD, which they bore — an earlier batch of Titans from independent operators had been TD. The entire class was allocated to Hendon (AE) garage, which seemed to take a pride in their appearance. Although they had clash gearboxes which might have been expected to accelerate their demise, none were withdrawn until 1953, a tribute to the quality of the bodywork in particular, though the direct-injection 8.6-litre engines had impressed LT and influenced subsequent engine design policy.

The STD class was relatively small, by London standards, the largest batch being 100 buses built in 1937. These were Leyland Titan TD4 buses with body also built by Leyland to London Transport's requirements. They were durable and refined buses and all 100 survived until 1953, the last being withdrawn in 1954 — seen here on the 113 route, one of those on which they worked from Hendon garage for most of that time, is STD34.

London Transport received an allocation of 34 AEC Regents with clash gearboxes from the limited number of bus chassis released to operators under wartime control in 1941 and sometimes known as 'unfrozen' vehicles. To get them into service without delay they were fitted with spare bodies from the float and thus STL2679 entered service in February 1942 with a 60-seat body originally fitted to STL170 and which dated from early 1933. It is seen in the Licensing Shop at Aldenham in February 1952, shortly after withdrawal from public service, though it continued in use as a staff bus until 1954.

Wartime

Construction of new bus chassis had dried up early in the war but in 1941 permission was given for manufacturers to complete batches of chassis from stocks of parts in hand. A total of about 352 double-decker chassis were made available in this way, of which London Transport was allocated 54, consisting of 34 AEC Regent, 11 Leyland Titan TD7 and 9 Bristol K5G. The Regent models were added to the STL class but differed from the 1939 LPTB standard in having clash gearboxes and because of this were allocated to the country area. Authority was given for 34 bodies (including 20 lowbridge versions, a layout not previously built at Chiswick) to be built by London Transport but the chassis arrived before these could even be put in hand — materials were becoming scarce — and eighteen received existing bodies from the overhaul float, mostly of types found on oil-engined STL chassis but including two of the original square-fronted 60-seat type used on the first STL buses of 1932-33. The remainder received new bodies, though none of the 20 lowbridge type included in the batch intended for these chassis, which later found their way on to various standard STL chassis drawn from the overhaul process.

The eleven Leyland TD7 chassis, classified STD to follow on from the 1937 batch, and the nine Bristol K5G models mentioned in Chapter One, which revived a famous classification by being simply designated 'B' (though STB had been contemplated), all received bodies built to the Ministry of Supply utility specification.

Subsequently, production of new chassis by Guy and Daimler for utility bodywork was authorised and, between 1942 and 1946, London Transport was allocated 435 Guy and 181 Daimler buses of this character, respectively the G and D classes.

Guy Motors Ltd, based in Wolverhampton, had become one of the mainstays of the bus industry during the war, building the famous Arab model which saw service in many parts of the country, including the 435 in London. After the first 71 of these, which were Arab I models, they had the extended Arab II bonnet which would have accommodated the long Gardner six-cylinder engine. Supplies of this were very limited, being intended for areas with hilly terrain.

The first utility bus body of all was that on STD101, the first of eleven Leyland Titan TD7 chassis supplied to London Transport as part of its 'unfrozen' allocation. The body, by Park Royal, was built to a specification designed to economise on labour and scarce materials and further similar Park Royal bodies were built on the nine Bristol K5G, also part of the same allocation in 1942, and then on 200 of the Guy Arab buses built between 1942 and 1946. The batch of TD7 buses were allocated to Victoria (GM) garage and were never as popular there as the pre-war STD class buses were at Hendon — the TD7 had a slow gear-change — and the Victoria drivers refused to continue driving them in 1951, so they were transferred to non-public duties.

Of the 435 wartime Guy Arab buses allocated to London Transport, most were of the Arab II type with forward-mounted radiator, but all had the Gardner 5LW engine and hence limited performance with their increased weight due to the non-availability of aluminium and rather ponderous gear-change. The most angular were the 49 with bodywork by Massey Bros supplied in 1945 — the only buses in the fleet by that Wigan-based concern — among which was G263, one of Enfield (E) garage's large fleet of Guy Arab models, seen here at Golders Green on the 102.

The wartime Daimler CWA6 used the AEC 7.7-litre engine and so was nearer to London Transport standard policy than its radiator shape suggested. Merton and Sutton garages were their main stronghold, and this view shows D71, one of a batch with Brush utility bodywork dating from 1945, in Kingsway on route 77A, one of the routes with which they were associated until 1952.

London was not regarded as qualifying so all 435 had the less powerful five-cylinder Gardner unit.

The transmission, as introduced in 1942, comprised a double-plate clutch, and a true clash gearbox of the original type with sliding-mesh engagement for all indirect gears was not one of its strong points, having been inherited from much earlier Guy models. It also had a gate reversed left to right from the usual layout, apt to cause confusion when a driver changed from one model to another although in itself no real problem when duties all involved the same type of bus.

At the end of the war, Guy took the opportunity to begin the process of updating the Arab chassis and the first major change was the adoption of a new gearbox, with constant-mesh for all forward gears, a single-plate clutch being adopted at the same time. The gear lever movements became the conventional layout, Guy fitting a red gear lever knob to indicate vehicles to the new design. The change came in before the completion of the wartime contracts though the vehicles didn't reach operators after bodying until about the beginning of 1946. London Transport received 34 such buses, placed in service between January and April 1946, being fleet numbers G301-311, G340-357, and G431-435. They were actually the last chassis for London from the wartime Guy allocations though the fleet numbers related to the bodybuilders' batches.

Unfortunately at the garages they became intermingled with the much larger numbers of Guys with the earlier type

The final addition to the STD class consisted of 65 buses on Leyland Titan PD1 chassis supplied in 1946. The Leyland bodywork was finished to London Transport standards in some respects, although the modifications from standard were much less extensive than on the original STD buses of 1937. Here STD158 from Victoria garage operates one of that garage's workings on the 77A.

gearbox. Clearly this was an intolerable situation and I believe some changes of units were made to create uniformity.

The Daimler was closer to LPTB standards, especially as most of the wartime chassis were CWA6 models with AEC 7.7-litre engines, while the preselector gearbox was very similar to that of the standard STL — in fact early STL preselectors (and the minority of LT-type buses so fitted) had Daimler-built gearboxes. When Bristol resumed chassis production towards the end of the war, it was also allocated AEC engines and a further 20 K-type buses supplied to the LPTB fleet in the winter of 1945-46 were so powered, these being the B10-29 batch I used to travel in on my journeys to AEC as mentioned in Chapter One. This prompted the conversion of the nine vehicles supplied in 1942 from Gardner to AEC, in 1948-49 — by that date, Chiswick had numbers of sound 7.7-litre engines from scrapped STLs.

It was foreseen that there would be a gap before RT deliveries came on stream and interim orders were placed for double-deckers approaching peacetime standards but not to accepted London specifications. A final 20 STL buses entered service in January-February 1946 as STL2682-2701 — before the last of the wartime Guys arrived — these having chassis officially designated Regent II by AEC but in reality very like the unfrozen ones of 1941-42, with clash gearbox, although the brakes were of a new triple-servo type. The Weymann metal-framed body was to that firm's standard style as supplied to other operators, and the complete vehicles designated 18STL20.

Another 100 Daimler CWA6 were delivered later in the year, with Park Royal bodywork derived from a utility design but with improved finish which became D182-281. There were also 65 Leyland Titans (STD 112-176) of the new PD1 model complete with that manufacturer's standard metal-framed body and altered only in detail respects from what one might call the 'standard provincial municipal bus'.

Leyland additions to the RT fleet.

Although the initial post-war order for 1,000 AEC RT chassis was in hand by the summer of 1946, it was realised that AEC would not be able to produce chassis fast enough to meet the combined demands of fleet renewal and the replacement of the remaining trams, itself calling for 1,148 buses, it was reckoned at the time. An approach was made to Leyland, initially on the basis of a possible order for 1,000 chassis — by November 1946 this had been increased by the addition of a further 500 with Leyland-built bodywork.

The basic principle was that these would conform to the RT concept not only in looking very similar but also in offering similar performance and commonality for drivers, with air-operated preselective gearbox and brake system as well as the same strict conformity with all body mounting dimensions. The Leyland O.600 9.8-litre engine with its flexible-link mounting was accepted as an equivalent to the AEC 9.6-litre unit, as were major units such as axles. However, much redesign was necessary, from the frame profile to such features as steering column angle, and the end result was very different to the standard Leyland PD2 using the same engine. Even the wheelbase was increased, if only by 1 inch.

After long discussions with Leyland, firm orders were placed and ultimately the total supplied rose to 2,131, including the 500 complete with Leyland-built bodywork, which it was agreed would be of the 8ft. width by then permissible on approved routes and accordingly designated RTW, these vehicles being coded 6RT6. The 7ft. 6in. version was to be RTL, these chassis being 7RT and originally it was planned that Metro-Cammell would build 1,000 bodies for them, to the same RT3 specification as Park Royal and Weymann. Later it was agreed that Metro-Cammell could use its own form of framing, but with RT appearance but the number of these was eventually reduced to 450. The Metro-Cammell version of the RT body was given the designation RT7 and the vehicles so fitted were RTL 551-1000. As it turned out, different type of body mounting confined these bodies to this batch of chassis despite the conformity to RT dimensional standards.

Earlier it had been suggested that even the 8ft. buses should have been given the fleet numbers RTL 1-500, with the 7ft. 6in. version following on as RTL 501 upwards. However, it was realised that there would be problems if the two different widths had the same bonnet letters and hence the wide vehicles became RTW.

The prototype RTL was given the fleet number RTL 501 when it was completed in 1948, production vehicles taking the numbers RTL 1 up, continuing to RTL 1631, the last vehicle, in 1954.

The direct inter-changeability of bodies was confirmed by the mounting of a Park Royal body, which had been intended to be on RT 657, on RTL 501, this being of the type with 'light-house' route number box in the roof then still current. In the event Park Royal was to build most of the production bodies on RTL chassis. It entered service in June 1948 and like all good prototypes was allocated to Turnham Green, with all

The first eleven production RTL buses were allocated to Sidcup garage in December 1948 and this view shows RTL11 when new. By that time Park Royal had switched production to the RT3/1 type of body, with no 'lighthouse' for the route number — the roof-level display was considered vulnerable to damage by tree branches. The RTL chassis was based on the Leyland PD2, having similar mechanical units apart from the preselective transmission and air-pressure brakes, but strict dimensional interchangeability with the AEC-built RT produced an appearance which could be described as RT with a Leyland 'face'.

The first 8ft.-wide example of the Leyland RT-family buses, RTW1, was allocated to Tottenham (AR) garage in March 1949 where it is seen, although it did not enter service on route 41 until May. Leyland built the bodywork on the 500 buses of this type to London Transport specification in regard to appearance, fittings and finish, but they were based on Leyland's standard body constructional design. The extra 6in. of width altered the proportions of the bus quite noticeably.

the other experimentals, and gave a good deal of trouble with cylinder head gaskets as described later.

Because of their extra width, when the first RTWs arrived in April 1949 it was decided that they should be allocated to the suburbs. In order to test whether the extra width would cause problems in London, arrangements were made to transfer them to routes serving Kensington High Street and, later, Piccadilly Circus. As now seems obvious, but had to be confirmed for the benefit of the ever-cautious authorities, no problems arose from their operation and they were permitted by the Police to operate anywhere in Central London.

Partly because of difficulty in getting the idling of the engine correct, another subject touched upon later, the Leyland vehicles were prone to uneven tick-over, causing vibration of the steering column. Some of this was due to the steering column mounting, and RTL 1337 was taken as new and used for development purposes in respect of the steering column mounting, resulting in the installation of a revised front cross member. This was successful and the final batch of vehicles 1469-1631, having been built as standard, were converted to the new arrangement with a fair degree of success. Eventually RTL 1337, which would normally have received an MXX registration, was put into service and given an out of sequence council plate number—OLD 813, taken from the batch issued to the last RTLs.

From a mechanical point of view the RTW differed little from the RTL—mainly in that it had a wider front axle; a standard rear axle was used, apart from the extended hubs. The production of this front axle was interesting in that it was made in two pieces joined off-centre whereas the RTL had a single-piece forged beam. There was a scare, involving taking vehicles off the road for checking for a few days, when one of the wider front axles cracked, but, as far as memory allows, I think this was an isolated incident.

Not very much large scale development was done on the Leyland vehicles, other than RTW 489, which had a Pneumo-Cyclic gearbox fitted. This was the Leyland version of the basic RV16 direct air selection gearbox, similar to that fitted to RT 3684 at Turnham Green. In both versions the air to operate the gears was brought to the selector head in the driver's cab and the driver moved the lever when he required the gear instead of the hitherto usual pre-selection method. In essence it could be described as the air version of the 'one legger' RV7, also at Turnham Green. Bringing the pipes up the side of the steering column made it rather untidy on RT 3684 but Leyland used a small turret head to the left of the driver, mounted on a small pedestal, rather reminiscent of the very early design used for AEC buses with Daimler preselective gearboxes in 1931-32. The RTW was allocated to Riverside and ran on Route 11. It was popular with the drivers and the box remained fitted until the bus was sold out of service.

The Leyland RTs operated in London from 1948-1967, subsequently seeing service throughout the world from South Africa to Niagara Falls and Yugoslavia to Ceylon. Their demise was hastened by the drastic reduction in services which followed the eight week strike in 1958. Literally hundreds of buses became surplus as former passengers found new ways of getting to work, and although some were simply delicensed and found useful employment again when trolleybus replacement began, they were sold off earlier than the bulk of RTs.

Hired Bristol buses

Another, short-term, solution to the post-war shortage had included a large-scale hiring of buses from the Tilling Group, beginning in December 1948, when post-war RT deliveries had only reached about 700 and the shortage of serviceable vehicles was still severe. London had hired vehicles during the war and also from local coach operators in 1947-49 but this, however, was a hiring of a different type and there were some understandable howls of protest from operators who found that their much-needed brand new vehicles were to be delivered direct to the capital. One hundred and eighty double-deckers were diverted in this way, all Bristol K-type with either AEC or Gardner 5LW engines, bodied by Eastern Coach Works of Lowestoft, and diverted from companies in the Tilling group, by then under the control of the British Transport Commission as was London Transport itself.

London Transport's shortage of serviceable buses led to the temporary hiring of new Bristol K-type buses from Tilling companies which had become part of the British Transport Commission empire, as was LTE itself. Most were of the lowbridge type, but they were to be found on routes distributed over most of the London area. Here a United Automobile Services Bristol K5G with standard Eastern Coach Works lowbridge body is seen at Victoria on the 16 in July 1949. Numbered BDO109 in that fleet, it had been delivered the previous month. It remained in service with United until 1965.

The vehicles performed satisfactorily, as one would expect of new machines which were standard in fleets throughout England, Wales and in the case of one company, southern Scotland. Out of the total, 135 had lowbridge bodywork not hitherto seen on routes running into central London and inevitably unpopular with passengers and conductors. They were to be kept for one year and, in fact, the first ten were replaced by new buses before the scheme was ended in 1950.

They were very different indeed from our own RTs, being very similar in chassis specification to the B-class Bristol K-type buses of 1942 and 1946 that had been allocated to LT under the wartime scheme. In 1950, after they had all been returned, an internal report was produced for the LT Executive comparing their specification and performance with LT vehicles. It makes interesting reading and one wonders whether its purpose was to reinforce the London thinking on transmission and engines, for instance, by pointing out the deficiencies of the Bristols in London's traffic, or whether someone had genuinely wondered if off-the-peg buses were the way forward for the future. I have included the text which I feel may interest the reader.

MEMORANDUM FOR THE EXECUTIVE

SUBMITTED BY: CHIEF MECHANICAL ENGINEER (ROAD SERVICES), OPERATING MANAGER (CENTRAL ROAD SERVICES), AND OPERATING MANAGER (COUNTRY BUSES AND COACHES).

SUBJECT: THE PERFORMANCE OF THE BRISTOL BUSES HIRED FROM THE TILLING COMPANIES.

DATE: 10TH AUGUST, 1950

The Tilling Companies loaned to London Transport a total of 190 Bristol double-deck buses, most of which completed a year's service, or approximately 40,000 miles, in London during 1949 and 1950. The maximum number of buses in service at any one time was 180, three quarters of which were of the awkward 'low bridge' type which many provincial operators are obliged to operate on account of over-bridges of restricted clearance.

The majority of the buses came to London straight from the Lowestoft factory of Eastern Coach Works Ltd., who built the bodies. There was good opportunity, therefore, to ascertain how the provincial type of bus would perform under the arduous conditions of London's services and, in particular, make some check upon the very high reputation for mechanical efficiency which these vehicles have acquired amongst the provincial operators.

Of the total number of loaned buses, 170 were allocated on a fairly even basis to 26 'parent' garages in the Central Area and 10 to 2 Country Garages; for reasons of economy in training drivers, and in the provision of destination blinds, etc., they were restricted to about thirty routes, more than half of which, however, traversed the inner area. The Bristol buses ran in direct competition with all types of London Transport buses and on 14 routes they ran with the latest type of RT series of buses.

The performance of the buses during the first 12 months of their lives in terms of trouble-free and efficient running certainly upheld their high reputation in provincial service. It is doubtful whether any other 'foreign' make of vehicle could have given our garage staffs so little trouble and fitted so well into our maintenance procedure. The reliability of the buses, particularly insofar as failures and delays in service were concerned, was the more notable in view of the several features regarded as sub-standard by the operating crews who have become used to the more refined modern London bus especially designed to suit the particular conditions of the metropolis. The knowledge that the visiting buses were on loan for a limited period, however, tended to cause the crews to overlook features which they would resist on permanent vehicles.

Examination of the Bristol chassis and its Eastern Coach Works body gives the clue to their reliable running. Both units verge on austerity and are devoid of refinements for passengers or crew; they are products of intensive operating/engineering development of a basic type of vehicle over many years. Rugged simplicity, with wearing surfaces more generous and more lightly stressed than other designs are essential features of the chassis, which is therefore capable of operation for extended periods without attention other than minor adjustment, and this has been made simple and almost fool-proof. The absence of change for the sake of fashion or sales requirements is very marked and every chassis item bears the stamp of painstaking development towards the goal of utmost longevity.

Unfortunately, however, the Bristol vehicle, apart from its reliability and ease of maintenance, is somewhat lacking in terms of road performance in relation to the requirements of London traffic. This is traceable to the policy of perpetuating a sound basic design dating from the middle-thirties, at which point in time London Transport had found it necessary to embark upon a more advanced type of vehicle in which, firstly, refinement of running would appeal to passengers and ease the work of the crews, and, secondly, increased rates of acceleration and braking would reduce traffic congestion due to liveliness in relation to other traffic, and give more scope for making up time lost due to the ever-increasing traffic delays with its effect on scheduled speeds.

Thus the Bristol vehicle, in terms of London requirements, is deficient in acceleration to the extent of requiring between 24 and 50% more time (according to engine fitted) to accelerate from rest to 20 miles per hour — the most frequently used and important speed range. Whereas the London driver has only to depress his accelerator to start smoothly, and then effortlessly to operate the semi-automatic transmission to produce rapid acceleration, the Bristol driver has to exercise greater skill and effort in the various movements involved in clutch, throttle and gear shifting operations. Similarly, in braking, the Bristol demands more of the driver, culminating in a 200lb. emergency effort as compared with 125lb. of the RT. In the latter vehicle an almost unlimited braking power is obtained by a graduated travel and proportionately increasing weight of pedal depression, whereas in the Bristol, the brakes, which are mechanically operated with servo assistance, tend to suffer by comparison from lack of progressive action and variability according to adjustment.

The relatively inferior acceleration of the Bristol is due partly to the slower clash gear change and partly to the smaller engine used. Many buses loaned to London had as little as 85 maximum brake horse power available from their 5 cylinder Gardner engines: others had 95 b.h.p. available from the 7.7 litre A.E.C.engines as standardised by London Transport from 1934 but abandoned in 1938 in favour of the present 125 b.h.p. of the 9,6 litre engine. In terms of 'torque', or pulling characteristics at the engine speed most influential on liveliness, the RT London bus has an advantage of more than 30% over the Bristol.

The use of relatively low-powered engines on the Bristol buses results in more gear changing, slower hill climbing and the production of more noise and vibration than the larger engine working easily within its limits. By our latest standards the engines in the Bristol were considered to be too noisy, and the vibration set up unpleasant drummings in the bodywork. In compensation for these disadvantages on the other hand, economy in fuel consumption is attained especially under relatively light running conditions, giving some advantage over London Transport vehicles. Under harder running, however, such as frequently encountered within the inner areas of London, the fuel consumptions tended to level out due to the amount of low gear working necessary on the Bristol buses. When allowance is made for the accepted fuel loss arising from fluid, as distinct from solid transmission as in the Bristol, there is nothing to choose in the matter of fuel consumption between the two types of vehicle under severe traffic conditions.

Generally smoother road surfaces and somewhat lower standards of amenity may contribute to the acceptance of the stiffer suspension characteristics of the Bristol buses which, whilst resulting in longer life of the spring leaves, produced such harsh riding as to cause complaint from both public and crews. This hard riding could not be accepted for London's vehicles; in consequence, the RT vehicles are more softly sprung, which must be paid for by somewhat more frequent spring changing, a penalty which, however, will diminish as the road surfaces are rehabilitated.

With regard to the bodywork, this is in every way complementary to the chassis; strong, rugged and devoid of troublesome weaknesses. The seating in general and the backs of the seats in particular did not compare with the London Transport standard, and the ventilation, by means of small sliding windows at the side and small hinged windows at the front, was the cause of continual criticism. These windows, however, demanded the minimum of maintenance, as did the rest of the structure and its fittings.

None of the buses was in service for more than twelve months and this appreciation of their performance is therefore based upon the service they gave when their physical condition was at its height. It is not possible to comment from direct experience on their qualities or average annual maintenance costs after extended periods in service under comparable traffic conditions, although there is no reason to expect other than that they should be capable of completing satisfactorily their expected life of twelve years in provincial service.

The opportunity to run these Bristol/E.C.W. vehicles has, however, confirmed our opinion that for operation in London the enhanced performance and simplified handling characteristics of the RT type of vehicle which was specifically designed to meet the exceptional conditions obtaining in the metropolis for an economic life of upwards of 14 years, have amply justified the policy upon which its development has been based, a policy which has already resulted in improved operation. Moreover, the maintenance experience so far obtained with the RT vehicles fully supports the prediction that substantial economies in maintenance will be secured. We are, furthermore, satisfied that the higher standard of passenger appeal incorporated in the RT vehicle is an essential factor in encouraging the travel habit, particularly in the period between the morning and evening peaks, which is of such important moment in relation to the economics of our operations in London.

J. B. Burnell
OPERATING MANAGER
(CENTRAL ROAD SERVICES)

A. A. M. Durrant
CHIEF MECHANICAL ENGINEER
(ROAD SERVICES)

B. H. Harbour
OPERATING MANAGER
(COUNTRY BUSES & COACHES)

The conversion programme using STL-type chassis to produce the SRT-class vehicles resulted in a batch of buses that looked virtually identical to RTs. Unfortunately they did not behave like the real thing and the project was abandoned after the completion of the vehicle shown, SRT160, which entered service in January 1950. The first 125 conversions had been taken from the last pre-war batch of STL buses but the remainder were based on slightly earlier chassis, this one having been STL2438 which originally entered service in December 1937. It is seen here at Staines in company with one of the first batch of T-type AEC Regal single-deckers of 1929, the life of which had also been prolonged, but by means of a more orthodox process of renovation. The SRT class buses were withdrawn in 1953-54, SRT160 being among the last to go, in July 1954, its body then going on to RT4544.

The sorry story of the SRT

As the bodybuilders for the RT programme got into their stride and material supplies became easier, output of bodies built up to a fast rate. Additional bodies had been ordered from two other builders for RT chassis — Saunders and Cravens — and although the 250 and 120 bodies respectively ordered took longer than expected to arrive, they would add to supplies by 1949 or so. By the end of 1947 about ten bodies per week were being completed but the average during 1948 was eighteen and rising, so it was forecast that, even with Leyland coming on stream to augment the flow from AEC, a chassis shortage would occur in 1949. Conversely, in the STL class the availability of enough sound bodies to match the chassis being produced by the normal overhaul process was becoming an increasing problem. In particular, a batch of 175 Park Royal metal-framed bodies that had been built on STL chassis in 1937 were found to be suffering severe structural corrosion, and an overhaul programme for them was stopped after 21 had been completed as being uneconomic.

It was decided to begin a conversion programme to modify STL-type chassis so as to accept standard RT-type bodywork as a way of overcoming the two problems, the resulting conversion being designated SRT. Modifying the chassis was intended to allow the body production lines to continue undisturbed as well as ultimately allowing the bodies to be switched to standard RT chassis, at overhaul or otherwise. It was planned to convert 300, but the initial batch of chassis chosen were the 15STL type, of which 132 had entered service in 1939. They were the final and most technically advanced version of the 'standard' STL, with flexibly-mounted engines, RP brake adjusters and automatic chassis lubrication. The original STL16 bodies on these buses were generally transferred to earlier STL chassis, mainly those which had previously carried Park Royal bodywork.

The chassis had to be completely dismantled to allow the frame sidemembers to be reshaped to conform to the RT shape in plan, but the main units — 7.7-litre engine, preselective gearbox, axles and the vacuum-hydraulic brake system — were transferred. A new RT-type radiator, steering column

(complete with gear selector housing and lever) and pedal plate were fitted, the process producing a chassis which at a quick glance looked like an RT. It was said at the time that the conversion exercise was quite expensive, but the surplus of standard RT bodies rather forced the issue.

The first SRT was completed in February 1949 originally carrying the number SRT946, the next available in the RT series in the then-current batch reserved for Park Royal bodywork. However, before it was licensed it became SRT1. The body was basically a contemporary standard RT, very similar to the RT3 type with which production had started in 1947 but which had been slightly modified. The first step had been to move the front route number down from its 'light house' position at the front of the roof, where it was vulnerable to damage, to become part of the main destination display, this type being RT3/1, coming into effect in the autumn of 1948. Not many of these were built before a change to the rear mounting points to make them suitable for RT, RTL or SRT chassis (the last-mentioned, despite all the work done, still

The warning lettering painted on to the gear selector housing of SRT buses read 'STL brakes and gears', which gave a clue to one of the major problems.

differed in this respect), this being the RT8, of which more were to be built than any other RT body variant.

Ironically, complete body standardisation was still not quite maintained. At first, it had not been fully realised that the heavier RT body would make brake performance unsatisfactory. It was decided that a bigger vacuum servo would have to be used. Clayton Dewandre, who make these items, fortunately had supplies of a suitable 200mm bore unit available — most operators outside London, other than those which had adopted the AEC Regent III, were still standardising on vacuum brakes even for new vehicles at that date. However, this fouled the RT body floor, so bodies for SRT chassis had to have a metal floor trap fitted in place of the composite floor, and were designated RT9.

The next problem to arise with the SRT concerned the gearbox. The mechanical linkage to the pedal meant that greater travel was needed to ensure that the grip on the gearbox brake bands was adequate to avoid slip, especially in the lower gears, but the RT-type pedal plate, intended to eliminate a source of draughts around the pedal stems, did not allow as much movement as that on the STL though ample for the RT's mechanism, when it operated an air valve. Unfortunately the STL-type gearbox had the old design of automatic adjuster which was slow to operate and did not always maintain the correct clearances. Hence the pedal was apt to be prevented from allowing the band to engage fully and slip was occurring.

This situation was discovered during a Works holiday shut-down period and the whole time was spent on a chassis in the Experimental Shop, playing with settings to try to ensure that the gearbox operated correctly within these constraints. It was only partly successful and in practice meant that the bus could only operate on flat terrain if serious band slip was to be avoided. This was one of the reasons why the SRT buses eventually had to be confined to essentially flat routes like the 16 (Victoria-Neasden), operated by Cricklewood garage, although at first they had been tried at other garages including Palmers Green which was one of the first to receive them in April 1949 and where drivers took an instant dislike to them, a reaction which soon became universal.

They were considered underpowered because of the extra weight, 7 tons 5cwt. unladen, compared to a typical STL at 6 tons 13cwt. or so, and even with the larger servo, braking was regarded as poor. Because of their limited performance they had to be driven hard. With hindsight, it seems clear that the psychology of producing a bus that looked like an RT but which was not even as good as that model's predecessor in braking or acceleration was unsound, and it seemed a pity that the best version of the STL became the 'bad boy' of the RT family.

This led to the premature curtailment of the conversion after 160 buses had been produced. The supply of suitable 15STL chassis had run out after SRT1-125 were completed and the last 35 of the SRT type were converted from earlier STL chassis, of which 25 were directly from the 1937 batch with Park Royal bodies. The last conversion entered service in January 1950 — fortunately chassis supply had improved by then. In July 1951 it had been agreed, after further union pressures, that they would be withdrawn as soon as all older types had been replaced and an extra 160 AEC RT chassis were ordered. Withdrawal took place between July 1953 and July 1954 — ironically most of the handful of 15STL chassis not converted lasted as long; one vehicle, STL 2584, outlasted all the SRT class!

The bodies removed from the SRT chassis reclassified as standard RT8 were fitted to new 3RT chassis, RT 4397-4556. Perhaps the only virtue of this exercise was that it prevented a stack-up of new bodies which would have been a problem to store or, perhaps more likely, a diversion of skilled man-power to other work that might have been difficult to restore. Even so, it must have been an extremely costly exercise with a poor return on the outlay.

A Guy RT

At the end of the war period, Guy had built up production of its Arab double-decker chassis to a level far greater than the small-scale involvement in the first version of a model with this name in the mid 'thirties. Demand for new buses was such that output continued with the Arab III model — virtually the same as the wartime Arab II in its final form with constant-mesh gearbox but with a lower radiator — in numbers not greatly down on the wartime build rate.

The company was naturally keen to build upon its stroke of fortune and in 1948 introduced additional options beyond the choice of Gardner five- or six-cylinder engines hitherto offered. Another Wolverhampton firm, Henry Meadows Ltd, had added a new 10.35-litre unit to its range of engine, the 6DC 630, and this was clearly comparable to the AEC 9.6-litre

The Guy interpretation of a chassis equivalent to the RT was summed up in G436, with its Meadows 10.35-litre engine, air-operated preselective gearbox and air brakes. The solitary vehicle is seen soon after entering service on the Peckham circular route in January 1950. By then it was becoming too late to justify the addition of another vehicle type to the RT programme.

and Leyland 0.600. It was very compact, fitting into the short bonnet that had been used for the Arab I in 1942-3 and now revived for this variant. Air-pressure brakes and a preselective gearbox which could also be air-operated were other new options and it will be seen that the combination of all these could be described as a Guy equivalent to the RT.

The Guy concern was clearly aware of London Transport's huge requirement for new buses and it was agreed that one Arab III with the 6DC engine, preselective gearbox and air brakes would be built, with bodywork of a metal-framed design standardised for post-war Guy chassis based on Park Royal framing but completed in Guy's own body shop. The resulting vehicle was numbered G436 at the end of the utility series and entered service in January 1950, allocated to Old Kent Road garage to run the Peckham circular route 173. It was slightly more costly than a 3RT but Guy gave technical support in view of its prototype status, mainly through their Service Depot at Paddington.

It fell to me to look after this bus and I always remember that in driving it, one got the impression of high speed from the note of the engine, but on looking at the ground the speed was considerably less. Some operators experienced trouble with the Meadows engine but it seems as if these had been overcome judging by our experience with G436, for engine life was good, conforming to the usual pattern that a big engine derated is always better than a small engine uprated.

The operation of the 173 route was transferred to Nunhead in May 1951 and G436 continued from there. This was a garage notorious for the pillars supporting the upper floor which included the canteen. The story goes that during the days of the wartime blackout, with poor lighting, no-one ever hit a pillar but come the days of peace it became quite a regular occurrence. Then in 1952, G436 moved to Enfield garage, working from there to Chingford station. Enfield had been one of the garages running wartime Guy buses, some running on that same route, these not being withdrawn until that same year. G436 soldiered on until February 1955 when sold to a company which specialised in exporting old London buses, its final home probably being Yugoslavia.

The justification for introducing an additional chassis type was becoming slimmer as vehicles already on order by the time it arrived were almost enough to cover the entire fleet replacement programme.

I have included the above information on the 'other' double-deckers which made up the bulk of the fleet at the time, although in many cases I was not directly involved with them, feeling the reader will find the subject of interest. During the period of my first position at Chiswick, 1947-1950, a selection of these vehicles would be seen at Chiswick for repair or overhaul but since the Experimental Shop was self-contained we would only become involved if there were problems to be put right or modifications to be designed and tested, as explained in later chapters.

Three Piccadilly Circus scenes (below and overleaf) convey the rapid transformation of the London bus fleet around 1950. The first, in 1948, shows a mixed collection of buses, all of pre-war or wartime origin. On the right, two of the 2RT buses, most of which dated from 1940-41, are seen with one of the 10T10-type Green Line coaches of 1938 and an STL double-decker. Among the traffic coming out of Regent Street in the background are a wartime D-type Daimler, followed by two STL buses. About to turn into Regent Street are two LT-type six-wheelers of 1931-32.

This August 1949 photograph of Piccadilly Circus, looking towards Shaftesbury Avenue, shows the effect of the huge intake of RT buses by then well under way. Six are visible, none appreciably over two years old, outnumbering the four STL-type vehicles also visible.

By 1952 (below), the fleet rejuvenation was almost complete. Some sixteen of the eighteen buses are of the RT family, the exceptions being one wartime D-type Daimler in Regent Street and one STD Leyland of the PD1 type in Piccadilly. There were at least a dozen pre-war taxis, mostly Austin, still in use however.

4. A decade of new ideas

In 1950, at the age of 24, I gained promotion within the LT organisation and became an Engineering Assistant at the princely salary of £500 per annum without any change in hours, still based in the technical section, and still working on chassis, but now I was in control of others carrying out the jobs I had previously done.

During the four years I was employed in this position many changes were taking place in London Transport and also within the bus industry, but this is an appropriate time to consider what was happening in 1950.

If anything, hours were probably longer, as we were working with the influx of RTs but still had a large number of vehicles of ancient vintage. Any experimental work had to be done without interrupting service and it was not uncommon to do a normal day's work and then report to Turnham Green, which really became our test garage, and change a defective experimental gearbox after the vehicle limped in from service, so that we had a full service the next day. Many is the time I have graced the 11.00pm train home from Victoria to Brighton and returned on the 6.25am the next morning.

There was a feeling of getting back to normal — new buses were entering service at a rate of 35 per week, never exceeded before or since. Many old-faithfuls were being withdrawn and scrapped, save for a few retained to add to those already preserved as the basis of a museum collection. There were still over 700 trams in service but as they were overhauled at Charlton Works I didn't see much of them or the 1,700 trolleybuses which were yet to reach their peak in numbers and had replaced the trams on many routes, mainly north of the Thames, in 1935-40. Postwar tram replacement by buses began at the end of September that year.

By the end of 1950 there were a total of 2,765 post-war RT, 996 RTL and 494 RTW buses licensed for service, but this volume of modern rolling stock had been achieved by more variety of body supply than London Transport normally favoured. Six bodybuilders had been involved in the 1950 intake of new RT-family buses. Although over 1,000 came from the main suppliers, Park Royal and Weymann, roundly 300 apiece came from Metro-Cammell and Leyland, both building on Leyland chassis of types RTL and RTW respectively and both conforming to RT appearance in all but minor details even though to the manufacturers' own constructional designs.

The same type of conformity applied to Saunders' contribution on RT chassis that year of 158, completing the RT1152-1401 batch), though this concern retained the 'light-house' route number box which had been current when the contract began, it not being considered worth disrupting production to change it. This also applied to a second order for 50 (which received the relatively high numbers RT4218-4267), allowing production to continue at the Saunders works at Beaumaris, Anglesey, until February 1951. Cravens, on the other hand, had finished its contract (RT1402-1521),

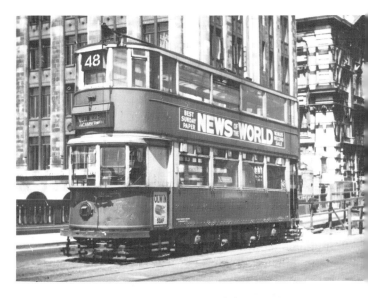

Trams were still a familiar sight in London in 1950, most of them bogie cars of generally similar design to E/3 class car number 167, seen at Blackfriars. Like most of London Transport's trams, it came from the London County Council, which had operated 1,713 trams, by far the largest tram fleet taken over by the LPTB, and indeed the largest in the country.

The Metro-Cammell bodywork fitted to 450 of the Leyland RTL buses was to standard RT outline but used the manufacturer's standard steel-framed construction. This, together with some extra weight of the Leyland chassis, increased the unladen weight of the complete bus to eight tons, half a ton more than the RT. This view of RTL707 at Aldgate in September 1954 also shows the heavy beading over the between-decks cream band which readily distinguished the type.

The inflow of new buses had been achieved partly by placing orders with bodybuilders not previously included among those supplying London bus requirements. Those for RT chassis were generally to the standard outline for that family of buses but the 120 built by Cravens Railway Carriage & Wagon Co Ltd were based on that builder's contemporary standard, though the cab, fittings and, up to a point, the interior finish were to RT pattern. The first vehicle of the batch, RT1402, is seen soon after entering service from Watford (High Street) garage in October 1948, still resplendent in green livery and yet to receive any advertisements. The first 27 of these buses went to the Country Area, and were the only new additions to the green RT fleet not to have bodywork by Weymann.

the final dozen going into service early in 1950. These were to RT specification only in cab design, trim and fittings and were the only bodies on London RT buses not to the classic outline.

Lowbridge buses

The inclusion of provincial bus companies which came into state ownership in the same British Transport Commission organisation as London Transport from 1948 drew attention to the availability of 20 AEC Regent III models with lowbridge Weymann bodywork that had been ordered by the Midland General Omnibus Co Ltd before it had been

The Saunders bodies, of which the main batch of 250 were ordered at the same time as the Cravens, were built to conform closely to RT appearance although based on Saunders framing. The batch took the numbers RT1152-1401 and RT1160, which had entered service in May 1949 from Nunhead (AH) garage, was still looking quite smart even though still in original livery 3½ years later. The 'giveaway' to the body maker was the positioning of the offside route number panel near the centre of the staircase panel instead of immediately behind the rearmost lower-deck window.

nationalised, initially as an offshoot of the electricity industry. The key feature was their lowbridge layout, for this type of body, with sunken side gangway on the top deck to allow the overall height to be reduced from that of most double-deckers, was one of which there was a shortage within the London Transport fleet. It was decided that they would not be required by MGO and, as they were based on the 'provincial' 9.6-litre chassis with preselective gearbox and air-pressure system that was the direct equivalent of the RT, they came quite close to London Transport requirements, even if the true RT chassis would probably have been preferred. There had been thoughts of developing a new low-height double-decker, but the opportunity of buying these buses killed the idea.

The provincial Regent III chassis, in addition to not having the low bonnet line that was such a distinctive feature of the RT, had a number of differences in mechanical design. London Transport preferred the air pressure equipment to be split so that the brake and 'clutch' (more correctly change-speed) valves were mounted under the cab directly adjacent to the pedal gear. The provincial version had the valves mounted on the air reservoir half-way down the offside of the chassis. On an RT it was thus only necessary to change the defective item rather than the whole reservoir, and there was no need for the rods linking the pedals to the reservoir-mounted valves.

Another important difference lay in the foundation brakes themselves—the RT had 16¾in.-diameter drums but AEC had switched from this size for the later provincial Regent III models to 15½in. drums, the aim being to improve ventilation

The RLH class came into existence as a result of a series of unexpected circumstances, but which gave London Transport a solution to its shortage of low-height double-deckers. The Midland General Omnibus Co Ltd, newly nationalised, had standardised on AEC Regent III buses with Weymann bodywork, basically not too far removed from LT's standards; 20 lowbridge buses on order were not required, and transferred to LT. One of ten similar buses retained by MGO, seen when almost new, in June 1950, shows their intended specification — for once the destination display was more elaborate than London's.

Apart from the destination indicator, and minor details such as the style of sidelamps, the original Midland General specification was retained for the RLH buses, which thus retained sliding top lights and non-London style seats. There were some mechanical differences from RT practice, too, at least one of which influenced RM design. Seen here is RLH40, one of the second batch of 56 built in 1952 to almost identical design to the first in 1952. The bodywork showed quite a strong family resemblance to that on the final batch of STL buses of 1946.

of the drums, though a thicker lining was also introduced. The RLH buses had the 15½in. brakes, in which it was not possible to fit the type of automatic adjuster used on the RT, but as we had a two-week rota at the time (later to go up to three weeks), it proved possible to keep them in service without the need for intermediate brake adjustment.

The manual adjustment was done as a matter of routine and not recorded and this fact had a Divisional Engineer stating that the RLH brakes lasted much longer without any attention at all. Based on this belief, some RTs were converted to RLH brakes but it soon became obvious that four-week adjustment was required. This also led to the RM not having automatic adjusters initially, but this was soon rectified, mainly thanks to my superior, Albert Higgins, who devised a scheme whereby the Clayton RP adjuster could be fitted externally.

Another difference between the RT and RLH was the tail-less chassis frame on the former, as rear-end collisons were liable to displace the side-members on the latter relative to each other, making repair much more difficult and expensive.

London Transport's existing lowbridge fleet had expanded during the war years and early in 1950 stood at 50 vehicles, a very small number compared to over 6,000 double-deckers of standard height, but there had been only 20 in the late 'thirties. The Carriage Office of the Metropolitan Police would not permit lowbridge buses to be used on other than the routes for which they had specifically been authorised. From a spare vehicle viewpoint, this was a nuisance and is probably why LT kept the spare vehicles very low for this category.

The most modern were ten Daimler CWA6 with Duple bodywork of utility (or in four cases, the slightly less austere

Until the RLH class appeared, the most modern buses in the small fleet of lowbridge vehicles operated by LT were the utility batches, of which the first six were also the first examples of the Daimler CWA6 model in London Transport service, dating from May-June 1944 — D2 is seen here among the motley collection of buses helping out on Derby day in 1948. Duple built the bodywork, originally having wooden seats — four more generally similar buses delivered late in 1945 (D128-131) had slightly less austere bodywork to the so-called relaxed specification.

Outlasting all the other ST-class buses were eight which had lowbridge bodies by Short Bros (or, in one case, Strachans), albeit heavily rebuilt to extend their lives. Six had been drawn from the first bulk delivery of ST-type chassis but fitted with the lowbridge bodies for operation by National Omnibus & Transport Co Ltd on behalf of LGOC at Watford. Among them was ST162, originally dating from May 1930, seen here towards the end of its days when operating from Harrow Weald (HD) on the 230 — it was one of the last five of the type to survive, running until October 1952; it had received a 7.7-litre oil engine in January 1950.

'relaxed utility') style dating from 1944-45, whereas the oldest were eight ST-type AEC Regent buses with what had been fairly typical 'provincial' bodies of Short Brothers construction, which dated from 1930. The latter had been kept in good order, having acquired more Chiswick characteristic features in the course of successive overhauls and, alone of ST types (apart from brief early experiments) had even acquired oil engines of 7.7-litre type from scrapped STL-type buses in 1949.

There were also a dozen Regents with unusual Weymann front-entrance lowbridge bodies dating from 1934 which were, again, unusual in the STL class to which they belonged in having 8.8-litre engines. In addition there were 20 standard STL chassis with the lowbridge Chiswick-built bodies mentioned in the previous chapter as being intended for 'unfrozen' chassis but fitted to whatever chassis dating from the later thirties became available from the overhaul programme as they were completed in 1942-43.

Clearly new vehicles would be welcome and so the Midland General batch was diverted, retaining most features of their original specification. They were classified RLH and entered service in 1950, beginning in June of that year. Yet there was still a shortage of lowbridge buses and almost all continued in service for a further two years. It was coincidental that the 'loaned' Bristol buses of which 135 were lowbridge, mentioned in the previous chapter, were all returned in 1950, there having been virtually no association with routes when such buses were needed, apart from ten used in the Country area. The normal objection to general use of the type had been temporarily waived. The new RLH type proved successful and it was decided to place what almost amounted to a repeat order for 56 further vehicles — slight changes to the chassis brought them a little closer to LTE standards, though still very

much the 'provincial' Regent III rather than an RT, while the bodies were identical.

The second batch included 24 buses painted in red livery, and these replaced the rebodied STL and Daimler CWA6 buses — in fact, the delivery of the additional RLH buses in November-December 1952 made it possible to replace the entire fleet of earlier lowbridge buses and even provide a margin of spares, hitherto lacking in this category of vehicles.

Other fleet developments

On the road, trials were continuing with the new wider RTW Leylands which were put through their paces in the City and central London.

As described more fully in the next chapter, a huge fleet of 700 single-decker AECs were ordered and these would begin to enter service during 1951, becoming familiar throughout Central and Country areas as the RF class. A further fifteen similar chassis were to be built to the new wider limit of 8ft. and fitted with coach bodywork for private hire and were classified RFW.

Against this background of steady improvement in the fleet, and with confidence that the development work carried out — and continuing in terms of detail items — on the RTs would mean a period of stability for some years, thoughts turned to the future and the next generation of buses. Only an undertaking the size of London Transport could afford to consider a completely new bus design from first principles but the wisdom of the policy must be judged from the life it obtained from its brain-children.

Maintenance and overhaul

Before we move to the next generation, however, let us consider for a moment the routine of keeping London's buses on the road. Day-to-day maintenance and minor repairs were carried out at the garages.

Brakes would be checked for wear and for this purpose a small hole was drilled in the side of the brake lining. When the surface of the lining broke through the hole it was time to change the brake shoes, thus preventing the drum being scored by the rivets.

Basically each garage looked after its own buses, they only going to the parent shed for an annual dock — all unit changes were carried out at the 'owning' garage. Minor accident repairs were also dealt with, but vehicles involved in major ones were sent to Chiswick, or later Aldenham. The parent shed held a float of major units and a back-up service to keep an imprest stock at the operating garage. The system was so arranged that when the parent garage returned a failed unit on the stores lorry in the morning, the evening lorry would deliver a replacement — thus a vehicle barely needed to wait for delivery of a spare unit.

Originally, the LGOC had worked on the principle of each garage maintaining its own buses, even to the extent of major overhaul work, when the vehicle would go to one of the two company's coachworks at Hammersmith or Islington for the body to be removed. It was then driven back to the garage as a

chassis and stripped down for each unit to be overhauled by a fitter before being built up again and sent to receive an overhauled body.

With the opening of Chiswick Works in 1921, both chassis and body overhaul was centralised. The Metropolitan Police were in charge of the public vehicles, buses as well as taxis, in the London area and at that time required buses to be overhauled annually, so Chiswick Works was set up to carry out this task using the latest production methods. The time taken for overhaul was reduced from sixteen days to eight days and after a few years to two days. Body overhaul took longer than chassis and the system of building 103 bodies to every 100 chassis produced a 'float' of bodies to avoid any need for overhauled chassis to be delayed in being put back into service.

An official booklet was issued in 1929, in which it was stated that the LGOC was running a fleet of 4,380 buses, mostly of the K, S and NS types, each working an average of 39,500 miles between the annual overhauls still insisted upon by the Metropolitan Police. Buses, admittedly of relatively simple design, were being overhauled at a rate of one every half-hour, or about 92 per week. In modern terms the idea of lifting bodywork and dismantling chassis annually seems unrealistic, but it must be remembered that only a small proportion of vehicles were on pneumatic tyres at that date, and many streets were still paved with stone setts, causing the wooden body framework to begin to loosen. More modern types of vehicles justified extended intervals, though the overhaul period was still only about 15 to 20 months, according to type, in 1939.

During the war, overhaul methods were disrupted. The official interval between overhauls soon becoming two years, but in practice the procedure was altered considerably — most

The SRT conversions described in the previous chapter had proved unsatisfactory but the insistence on body interchangeability meant that the bodies built on them by Park Royal could be transferred to standard RT chassis. Some, overhauled and repainted green, were fitted with interior heaters and began a more glamorous period of life on new RT chassis as Green Line coaches on the services requiring double-deckers running into Aldgate, where RT4500 of this type is seen in September 1954 — it had entered service in July, allocated to Grays (GY). All-new RT buses were still being delivered but this was soon to end, in November of that year.

Some idea of the extent of Chiswick Works is given by this view, taken towards the end of the 1960s. By that date, the large buildings were devoted to unit overhaul and associated activities. The experimental shop was the building with pitched roof to the left of the tall trees in the middle distance while the famous skid pan with its flooded surface can be seen centre right. The office block centre left was the drivers' and conductors' training school and medical centre. There were further premises, including the engineering offices, to the left of the roadway in the left foreground.

mechanical overhaul continued at Chiswick but body repairs were decentralised, at first to eleven garages though later this was reduced to four centres, of which Chiswick tram depot was the largest. The body float was largely used up to put badly bomb-damaged buses with repairable chassis back into service and the routine lifting of bodies tended to lapse, though bomb damage caused quite a number of buses, especially in the STL class, to receive bodies of types different from those previously carried.

The farming-out of body repairs during and after the war also implied sending complete vehicles, although when Chiswick returned to something approaching normality in the post-war years, body removal was generally resumed for the vehicles overhauled there.

Going back to early Chiswick days, when engine bearing life was liable to be very short, there had also been provision for feeding overhauled engines to the garages. In wartime the principle of changing engines and other units at garages on an 'as required' basis inevitably tended to grow. Improved

vehicle design, particularly with the RT type, extended the effective life of both mechanical components and the body structure — part of the philosophy of the enlargement of engine size from 7.7 to 9.6 litres was that a bigger engine need not work so hard to keep the bus to timetable.

In my early days, two years was the overhaul cycle period, but with the entry of the RT it was found possible to extend this to four years, and this coincided with the paint cycle.

Perhaps it might be permissible to relate an episode that occurred at Merton. This garage, together with Sutton, operated the bulk of the Daimler CWA6 vehicles dating from 1944-46, running them until withdrawal in the 1952-54 period. The Garage Engineer there was keen to avoid failure on the road and therefore changed his units on a time basis.

I was particularly interested in the fourth-speed mechanism of the Daimler preselective gearbox, with rolling ball activation to engage the clutch plates instead of captive, as used by AEC. When inspected at Chiswick, little was found wrong with these boxes, and I was anxious to find out how they would stand up it left to run until a failure occurred. Checking through the records at Merton, I found two vehicles that had slipped through the local net and it was not difficult to get them changed. Examination of the two gearboxes removed showed the improved performance of the Daimler top-speed arrangement which was perpetuated on later AEC boxes. This highlighted the benefit of a Central Workshop within the whole organisation, supported by a Central Technical team.

It was also decided that engines and gearboxes would not generally be replaced with reconditioned units at major overhaul, as this would often have meant dismantling units functioning well and capable of many more miles of reliable service. So these units were changed at operating garages on the basis of such indications as excessive lubricating oil consumption or failure.

We started the RM off at four years but clearly this was too short and we extended it to seven years with a repaint at four years. It proved impossible to make the paint life exceed four years — the advent of bus washing machines did not help. Brake systems have always been regarded as of great importance and, at overhaul, it was always the policy to remove the system and at least check against new specification, overhauling as necessary.

Aldenham Works

Chiswick Works had been expanded to cope with the growing fleet size and also the larger and more complex vehicles that had come into service, almost filling the 32-acre site by 1939, and quite apart from further growth of the bus fleet due to the tram conversion, was becoming inadequate.

As it so happened, London Transport had been left with large and modern redundant premises by a change of circumstances. The Northern Line tube system was to have been extended northwards from Edgware to Bushey Heath and at Aldenham, near Elstree, Hertfordshire, a large depot had actually been built for Underground cars in 1939. During the war, it was used to assemble the 710 Halifax bomber aircraft manufactured under the London Aircraft Production Scheme. The war ended and it was decided to use it for bus overhaul and repair work, conversion work to this end being completed in April 1949, although it was not until September

As Aldenham grew, it became necessary to convey staff transferred from Chiswick to points nearer their homes. Buses withdrawn from public service were selected for such duties and here STL2674, one of the two 'unfrozen' buses which had received 60-seat LGOC bodywork, is followed by one of the STD class buses with utility Park Royal body dating from the same era, during the 1951-54 period when Aldenham was steadily growing.

of that year that a firm decision was made not to carry out the tube line extension.

At first it was regarded as an overflow works to Chiswick, dealing with accident repairs and then overhauls of certain small classes of vehicles, such as the various lowbridge double-deckers of the pre-RLH era mentioned earlier in this chapter. The SRT chassis reconstruction was done there and it became the receiving point for new vehicles on delivery.

However, once it became clear it could be regarded as permanent, there being misgivings at first on the part of the Government as it was within the Green Belt, plans went ahead to convert it into the main bus overhaul works for the entire fleet, though mechanical units would still be dealt with at Chiswick. It was envisaged at that stage that the bus fleet would eventually reach the 10,000-vehicle mark and a major building programme to expand and convert the existing works began in 1952 which was completed in 1956, though operational for RT overhaul from 1955. Up to 56 buses per week could be overhauled, which would have been sufficient for the target fleet on a 3½-year cycle, though in practice it was never needed, and the peak output was 46.

The float system to provide enough bodies to allow for the additional time needed to overhaul bodywork continued, and fifteen spare RT bodies were built by Park Royal late in 1954 to provide for the beginning of the overhaul programme at

Work was transferred to Aldenham gradually. This view of the licensing shop is dated 20th February 1952 and shows in the centre SRT25, which had evidently been in for repair — the brief overhaul programme for that model did not begin until October of that year. Also visible are two new RF-type single-deckers being prepared for service after arrival from the bodybuilders. Later views of Aldenham facilities accompany Chapter Seven.

Aldenham the following year. However, this was far below the pre-war ratio, and on that basis would have been adequate for only 500 vehicles, roughly a tenth of the post-war RT and RTL fleet by then in stock. In fact, a new departure was made by delicensing 158 complete buses (including twelve of the RF single-deckers by then in service) which effectively 'disappeared' from the operating fleet and represented work in progress at Aldenham. Some of the numbers were out of circulation for up to fourteen years, reappearing when the overhaul programme for RTs ended in 1970.

The main body repair shop at Aldenham was an impressive sight, being 300 yards long and tall enough to allow a double-deck body to be lifted well above others undergoing repair in the row of bays designed for the purpose, so as to be moved to its required location. Chassis were dismantled and later rebuilt with reconditioned units on two separate moving production lines. When the integral-construction Routemaster began going through the overhaul system, it was treated in the same way, the front and rear subframes being temporarily linked to form a 'chassis', enabling the same procedure to be used.

By the mid 'sixties, the overhaul period had become four years, but in 1967 a system of carrying out a full overhaul to coincide with the Certificate of Fitness intervals — initially seven years and generally five years thereafter — was adopted, with a repaint in between. This continued until November 1987, when the national PSV inspection requirements altered. Methods altered to suit changes in vehicle design, and in particular the rear-engined vehicles called for revised procedures. Although the Daimler Fleetline had a separate chassis and thus reverted to an earlier concept than the Routemaster in this respect, it was designed so that the body and chassis were more inter-dependent than earlier generation models such as the RT, so the lifting of bodywork for overhaul ceased.

Even so, when large-scale use of the Fleetline in London was first envisaged, I had asked whether the body was to be lifted at overhaul. The answer was no and this was repeated on two further occasions. Hence it was not necessary to ensure on design that this could be done. Imagine my surprise when suddenly I was asked to make it detachable! Too late! However, the exercise was done on a vehicle with Park Royal body and the body pillars crumpled on lifting, the body tending to be weakened when the support of the chassis was removed by the two large openings for the entrance and exit doorways. With the MCW body, the pillars were of heavier section and sag didn't happen. However, the wiring, etc was so entwined that it was not thought to be economical and the idea was not carried forward.

Aldenham's full capacity was never needed, and the change of procedure in 1967 led to about one-third of the works being leased to the Leyland concern as a spares and service depot. By that time AEC had become part of the Leyland empire and the depot also took over from the AEC service department previously located at Southall. The RT overhaul programme ended in 1970, as by then withdrawal of the type was under way, and gradually more of its activities reverted to Chiswick, leading ultimately to closure of Aldenham in 1986.

Organisation

The reader will appreciate that within the vast London Transport organisation there were many different departments and many different needs. My department was a small part of the Bus Division and was responsible for research and development, and for feeding information concerning improvements to the vehicles to those who would carry out these recommendations. Also maintenance procedures would be drawn up and the provision of Maintenance Manuals for garage use had to be written. It may be that the modifications would be fairly minor in which case they could be handled by the garages, or modifications of a more major nature which would have to be handled either at Chiswick or Aldenham. Our recommendations would also affect new vehicle orders, though at this time any such orders would be for models to LT specification which would naturally incorporate the results of past experience.

The idea of Pay-as-you-board was far from new within London Transport. Trolleybus No. 61 is seen here when operating under this system soon after conversion in March 1945. The vehicle, dating from March 1933, had been the last trolleybus supplied to London United Tramways, a one-off vehicle in several respects, its chassis being the only AEC type 691T by virtue of the specially shaped frame to suit its centre entrance, also unique among London trolley-buses, which was why it was among the vehicles chosen. Note the masked head-lamp, white-painted mudguard and anti-blast netting, all typical of the war years.

Separately, of course, the Operating Division would have their own problems and in the 'fifties congestion in the streets, with the consequent delays to vehicles and disruption of services, would be very much on their mind. Increased operating costs largely due to higher wages, to the delays caused by congestion and also the difficulty of recruiting sufficient staff were also a great problem at that time.

Pay-as-you-board

London Transport had been experimenting with pay-as-you-board operation in the 1944-46 period, though retaining the conductor in the manner then often found on the Continent. Five double-deckers were converted, all based on the idea that passengers would pay their fares on, or soon after, boarding and before taking their seats. The first, STL1793, was rebuilt to centre-entrance layout, trolleybus 61 was already of this form, STL2284 received narrow front entrance and centre exit doors, while trolleybus 378 and RT97 retained the rear-entrance layout, though modified. All were found to slow down loading so much that they could not keep to time and were caught up by the conventional buses on the central area services on which they were tried. Two vehicles were selected for trial on country area services, STL2284 on a bus route and RT97 on a Green Line service, but even in these less busy conditions they proved unacceptable and the experiments ceased. Incidentally, RT97 was further extensively rebuilt as a prototype double-deck Green Line coach with conventional mobile conductor in 1949, renumbered RTC1, and although not entirely successful, incorporated some ideas pursued further in the Routemaster prototype completed in 1954.

Most of the pay-as-you-board experiments had involved some loss of seating capacity and, bearing in mind that a conductor was still required, there was a loss of revenue-earning capacity to add to the delays at stops as serious drawbacks, yet no saving of costs.

One-man operation, as it was invariably called in those days, on the other hand, had an obvious and large potential for savings, which could be set against the drawback of slow loading due to the need for passengers to pay as they boarded the bus. The more deeply rural services had been operated by 20-seat Leyland Cub buses since the early days of London Transport, but the idea of using larger single-deck buses in this

way was arousing widespread interest as the drop in numbers of passengers carried began to bite in the early 'fifties. The LTE fleet was not quite the first in this field, but the experimental operation of three specially-equipped RF-type buses (RF517, 647 and 700), the last of the type to arrive, early in 1954 was ahead of most major company fleets. They ran from Epsom to Langley Vale from 3rd March 1954—the small beginning of a major trend. However, single-decker developments are dealt with in more detail in the next chapter.

Foundations for the RM

Shortly after my promotion, and as far back as 1951, the Chief Mechanical Engineer, Bill Durrant, laid the foundations of the RM when a design study was commenced for a new bus which was to become the new standard for London. In the early stages, it was simply given the code RT12, though internally it was known as the I.M. vehicle.

Governing factors were laid down in a document dated 9th November 1951, such as:-

Box dimensions.

Maximum height.

Maximum flexibility of suspension both front and rear, giving more comfortable ride conditions, thereby extending body life.

Pioneer work on what was then called chassisless construction had been done by London Transport in the pre-war period. A prototype trolleybus of this form, with AEC running gear, was built at the Charlton overhaul works in April, 1937, followed by another built by Metro-Cammell the following year. This in turn led to an order for 175 more vehicles also built by Metro-Cammell and delivered in 1939-40, again having AEC axles and mechanical units attached directly to the suitably strengthened body underframe. The largest group of these vehicles were the L3 class, of which No. 1524 is seen, still looking very sound, on 6th May 1962, two days before the last part of the London trolleybus system ceased operation. It was in Kingston, having to pass on the wrong side of a 'Keep Left' sign due to roadworks.

Chassisless integral construction.

Maximum seating capacity.

Increased platform space with access under stairs for conductor.

To be as light as possible.

No timber without special authority.

It may seem somewhat surprising that with delivery of the post-war RT only getting under way in 1947 people should be thinking of its replacement as early as 1951, though of course work on the project that became the RT began in 1937. This was because it was always London Transport policy to keep abreast of developments and hence new ideas that appeared to have possible benefits to the business were always being tried. Regular working with AEC engineers produced a very close-knit relationship, so that they too were fully informed of the success, or failure, of new ideas. Indeed an arrangement existed that enabled London Transport to run experiments for the benefit of AEC as well as those having a joint interest to both parties. This procedure was carried on with Daimler in the Fleetline days and later with Leyland, though to a much lesser extent.

With a good deal of foresight the London Transport board realised almost 40 years ago that in the future the bus would have to compete with the private car, and it was decided that to achieve this the new bus would have to have a suspension capable of giving a more comfortable ride. From an operational point of view vehicle weight was important, emphasised by the fact that there was no rebate on fuel duty in those days and steel was ruled out for the body structure. Integral construction was seen as the way to go, so that the

body contributed to the overall strength of the vehicle. Pre-war experience with trolleybuses had shown that the chassis was not a necessary part of the vehicle's strength. Thus a small team was put together working in one corner of the Technical Office at Chiswick, subsequently working with a small team from AEC and PRV from about 1952. Various trials on RT vehicles were in progress at Turnham Green, in the main covering braking systems and the transmission, and as these had been on the go since 1947 we had a lot of experience under our belts when it came to the feasibility study.

In many studies the scheme arrived at does not become the final design but it would suffice to say that the vehicles were seen to need independent suspension to give a satisfactory ride. Unfortunately this was an area where London Transport did not have any experience, indeed, it was virtually unknown at that time among large commercial vehicles apart from a few military applications, and much of the design was based on unequal wishbones as used in cars. Steps were put in hand to obtain a scrap STL chassis and to fit independent suspension at the front. Some difficulty was experienced as it had a conventional frame and the resulting vehicle had a somewhat high front end, being nicknamed 'The Praying Mantis'. On the appointed day the chassis was started up in the Experimental Shop and was about to be driven out with the Technical Assistant who had been concerned with the project at the wheel. To everyone's surprise and horror the chassis started to sag at the front end, and gradually came into contact with the ground having barely left the Shop. It certainly lived up to its name by kneeling towards the West! One of the Fordson tractors which Chiswick boasted at the time soon pushed it back into the Shop, whence the doors closed and the chassis never moved again under its own power. Naturally an inquest was held but I don't think an acceptable answer was ever made public. Unfortunately pictures do not exist of this incident. Subsequently a very effective design was evolved.

Earlier chapters have described the development of hydraulic braking systems on comparatively new RT buses, particularly at Turnham Green which virtually became my second home. The experience of being accepted almost as one of the garage staff by not only the Engineering staff but Operating staff as well was something never to be forgotten. Some people felt this was not the time to consider developing new ideas as the fleet was still recovering from the wartime years. To have a shortage of buses for service was a crime, even if it was only one vehicle.

At the time I was concerned in making what was an aircraft hydraulic system suitable for bus operation. It offered many advantages in being virtually a sealed system requiring little maintenance, with lighter weight, more response, and with quicker build-up times giving a higher potential of reserve pressure at any time. It was because of this that it was possible to set the warning flag pressure (the setting at which a small warning device would drop a flag-shaped lever into the driver's line of sight at the top of the windscreen) well above the maximum brake line pressure that the driver ever needed. With the air system the flag could fall below service pressure due to poor performance of the compressor in keeping the air system charged. This gave the driver a get-out whereby if involved in an accident he could always say that the flag fell at the crucial moment and he therefore did not have the pressure, and hence the brake performance, he was entitled to in the situation. He therefore got away without blame for the accident. Once the hydraulic system was adopted for the RM, this excuse was no longer accepted and allegations of poor brakes soon died out.

In all development work there are problems and it would be foolish not to admit to this. An accident occurred on route 55 at the War Memorial at Greenford, the route on which the hydraulic-brake buses were rostered. On this occasion a pipe failed—the one worry on hydraulic systems—and the flag duly fell. For some reason the driver tried to restore pressure by revving the engine but omitting to bring the bus to a halt. This incident soon showed that adequately clipped seamless pipes are an essential part of such a system. Unfortunately this lesson was not fully learnt on the MCW Metrobus and brought hydraulics into disrepute, although the Titan had an unblemished record on these counts.

However as a junior I did not appreciate to what ends this work was leading—ie a bus for the 1960s. As part of this goal, transmission development was also in progress with a view to making the passenger's ride more comfortable and also to ease the driver's lot. This was to follow on from work done in 1937 brought about by the brilliant engineer from Scotland already mentioned in Chapter Two, Mr Albert Miller, who was later to become the Engineering Director of Self Changing Gears Limited at Coventry. To those interested in gearbox development I cannot but recommend a book entitled *Walter Wilson — Portrait of An Inventor*, published by Gerald Duckworth & Co Ltd. Wilson lived from 1874-1957. He was an earlier and even more famous Scottish engineer in this field, best known as inventor of the Wilson preselective epicyclic gearbox, the basic design from which not only the various preselective gearbox designs found in most London buses of the 1934-54 period but also the design from which Miller developed the direct-selection and automatic versions as used on the Routemaster, Fleetline, etc. The Wilson biography was produced by his son who succeeded to the business and whom I had the privilege of knowing very well.

To return to the development in question, the idea was to do away with the 'clutch' pedal so that the change of manually selected gears was controlled by a timing cylinder so that the speed of engagement from one gear to the next was fixed by using restrictors in the supply line. The pressure was obtained via an oil pump on the front of the gearbox so that the box was self-contained except for an electrical supply to engage the solenoid in the respective gear to allow oil to flow to the cylinder on the extreme end of the brake band in the gearbox. The four such RT buses on which development work was done were the 'One Leggers' mentioned in Chapter Two. A good deal was learnt about gear-change characteristics, in what were often full-throttle conditions, the most arduous for the gearbox internal mechanism.

It was over these four vehicles that I came to know one particular driver who has now passed away after a lifetime with buses. By some reason or other he was able to fade these gearbox linings so that the bus would hardly move. The only way was to cool the box when the friction level returned and the bus then returned to normal again. Determined to find out how he did it, I arranged for plain clothes observation but the report always came back that he was a perfect driver.

Somehow I believe he always knew when he had what we called a 'plain clothes spot' on board. I unintentionally evened the score when one wet night he rang in to say his screen had fallen out and I happened to answer the 'phone. My reply was to the effect that he was pulling my leg so would be carry on to Turnham Green where a 'sub' would be waiting. Some twenty minutes later a rather bedraggled and soaking wet driver came into the garage looking for me. Yes, indeed, his side screen **had** fallen out! After that we became the best of friends and I never had any more trouble.

These boxes also had their problems but each one was fully investigated and a reason found. These were running from Turnham Green at the same time as the hydraulic-brake buses and it was sometimes difficult to keep a full service going. On another occasion when all serviceable buses were on the road a certain driver brought in one of the 'one leggers', stating that it was slipping so badly that it was impossible to drive. I took the bus from him and proceeded to demonstrate that it would go—but what I forgot was that I was heading for the pits, fortunately covered by pit boards. Unfortunately, on braking, the pit boards flew up leaving the front wheel standing on a lone board with a gaping great hole on either side. After getting the bus off the pit the driver in question took the bus out without a murmur and the writer retired for a quiet cup of tea!

Trolleybuses peak — and plans for replacement

In 1952, with the delivery of the second batch of 50 Q1 class vehicles, the London Transport trolleybus fleet, believed to be the largest in the world at any rate at that time, reached its peak of 1,811 vehicles. The Q1 class was based on chassis supplied by British United Traction Ltd, the joint company for trolleybus and railcar business set up in 1946 by AEC and Leyland, the two companies that had, between them, built the chassis (or sets of mechanical units) for earlier London

The Q1 class vehicles placed in service between 1948 and 1952 were the final addition to London Transport's trolleybus fleet. They were 8ft. wide and had BUT chassis of AEC design with Metro-Cammell bodywork. The first batch of 77, to which No. 1800 seen here at Hampton Court belonged, replaced the oldest vehicles then in the fleet and some wartime casualties but when a further 50 were purchased there were plans to retain the combined fleet on services in south-western suburbs after the other trolleybuses had gone, which might have meant that these buses would have continued in London service until about 1970, but it was not to be.

Transport trolleybuses. In fact, they were of AEC design, even though built in Leyland's Works at Kingston-on-Thames which had also been responsible for the pre-war Cub 20-seat buses. The chassis, type 9641T, could be described as a six-wheel trolleybus equivalent to the Regent III. There had been a previous batch of 77 in 1948-49, but these two batches could be considered the swan-song of the trolleybus fleet.

As early as 1946, it had been decided that the pre-war policy of generally replacing trams by trolleybuses would not be continued and the resumed tram replacement programme that ran from 1950 to its completion, also in 1952, was largely carried out by RT-family buses — quite often of the RTL type. By 1949, it had been decided to replace the trolleybus fleet by buses, the 1952 order being partly to replace a batch of vehicles in poor condition and partly with the idea that the Q1 trolleybuses, 8ft. wide and fine vehicles, could run services in the Fulwell and Isleworth area for some years after the rest of the network, largely north of the Thames and covering most of the main roads out of central London, had gone. In practice, this did not happen as all but two of the Q1 vehicles found buyers in Spain, and of the 125 shipped in 1961, 66 were still in service at the beginning of 1975.

Apart from a small minority of vehicles, London's trolleybuses were 30ft.-long six-wheelers seating 70 passengers. Most had entered service between 1935 and 1941 and the majority had metal-framed bodywork, largely of the durable designs produced by the MCW and Leyland organisations.

The hitherto separate Tram & Trolleybus Department was merged into Central Road Services from 1950, though the overhaul of trolleybuses continued to be handled quite separately by the works at Charlton and Fulwell. The decision to replace the trolleybuses by buses was not made public until 1954 and was not actually put into effect until 1959-62, slightly behind schedule. Cuts in services were to reduce the numbers of vehicles needed somewhat even before that period, enabling 275 trolleybuses to be withdrawn before the main route conversion programme started. This enabled some selection of vehicles or classes in poorer condition to be made but the bulk of the fleet was kept smart and in good order to the end.

However, it was not known at the outset that such service cuts would occur, nor that even larger numbers of surplus vehicles would become available from the bus fleet. Even so, there were straws in the wind. By the time of the Coronation in June 1953, the vast numbers of smart bright red RT-family buses must have impressed visitors to London, there being over 5,100 in service. Just over a year later, the last double-deckers dating from 1939 or earlier in the Central Area fleet were withdrawn, ending the era of the STL except for a small number of country area examples, of which the last pre-war ones came off the road at the end of August, leaving only the 20 buses new in 1946.

It had been foreseen that there would be a surplus of new buses, but though cuts in the vehicles on order were made, some 81 new green RT-type buses and 63 red RTLs were put in store on completion in 1954. The 2RT-type buses of 1940-42 were largely withdrawn from passenger service in 1955 and the early post-war STL buses mentioned above, together with the 65 Leyland PD1 buses of the STD class which dated from 1946, also went that year, some of the stored new buses being used to replace them, though many were to remain unused until 1958 and nineteen green RTs were to stay out of use until 1959.

Meanwhile, however, the first Routemaster, RM1, had been completed in 1954. The basic principles followed in its design could be summarised as follows:-

The 27ft. overall length, given careful use of space, could give a 64-seat capacity, which was considered about right for efficient collection of fares, and it was considered that such buses could directly replace 70-seat trolleybuses, bearing in mind the drop in numbers of passengers being carried, as well as 56-seat buses.

Weight saving was important, as already mentioned, but LTE was not prepared to take the 'easy' option of adopting an austere standard of comfort or finish, so efficient use of suitable lightweight materials was the main method — notably the aluminium alloy body framing. Integral construction also played a part in this.

The RM employed two sub-frames referred to as the A and B frames. The A frames were likened to a wheelbarrow carrying the front suspension, engine, radiator and steering

As had been standard practice at Chiswick for many years, a model of the proposed design for what ultimately became the Routemaster was produced, this photograph being dated 13th August 1952. At that stage, the frontal appearance had clear resemblance to RTC1, the double-deck coach prototype and even the TF, though the body outline as a whole was very like the final design. Note also that sliding top-light windows were proposed at that stage for the upper deck.

A full-size mock-up was built, at first following the design of the model quite closely. This photograph, dated 8th December 1952, is inscribed 'Scheme 1. IM' on the reverse. Appearance is always a matter of taste, but some observers think that first thoughts are often the most effective, though practicality has to be considered. Note that at that stage the full RT-style destination display was retained.

Three weeks later, on 29th December 1952, this stage had been reached. The bonnet assembly had reached an outline closer to that on RM1 as first completed, with the slight projection of the grille panel forward of the windscreen though the grille outline was no more than a passing phase in the process of evolving the final scheme. The destination display had been reduced to the single screen as used on RM1 as first built. Though only one side of the body had been built up, it reproduced the final form quite precisely.

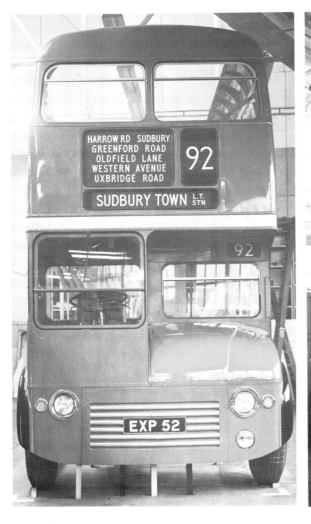

When RM1 was first unveiled in a display for the press held at Chiswick in August 1954 it bore a distinct resemblance to the mock-up as it stood about 20 months earlier as shown on the previous page. A reason for the revised profile of the bonnet top as compared to the original design is revealed in this view with the bonnet open as the clearance over the top of the AEC 9.6-litre engine was quite small. The belt drive to the dynamo and cooling fan for the underfloor-mounted radiator can also be seen.

Independent front suspension is still quite uncommon on new buses in the 1990s and in the mid-1950s it was almost unknown, especially on a double-decker. This view shows the double-wishbone assembly with coil spring enclosed within it for the offside front of one of the two Leyland-built vehicles, almost identical to the AEC version in this respect. Also visible is a manual adjuster on the brake camshaft. Automatic adjusters were later adopted for all vehicles.

column with associated pedal gear, and looked rather like the front portion of a conventional chassis though extending rearwards only as far as the first main window bay. The B frame was the name given to the rear suspension assembly, carrying the rear axle, but the gearbox was attached directly to the underside of the body structure, this form of construction adding to the weight saving.

The end result of an unladen weight of 6 tons 15cwt. on RM1 was three-quarters of a ton lighter than the standard RT figure of 7 ton 10cwt., despite the increase in dimensions from 26ft. long by 7ft. 6in. wide to 27ft. by 8ft.

Contrary to the trend elsewhere, comfort standards were improved. The need to keep up with improvements in private car suspension were realised and the independent suspension system was perfected, using unequal length wishbones and coil springs. At the rear, the need for twin tyres would have ruled out an independent suspension system in any case, but coil springs were again adopted, being housed neatly under the rear of the longitudinal seats, the axle being carried by a pair of long pressed members pivoted to the floor assembly at their forward ends at almost the centre of the floor and joined behind the rear axle by a cross-member extended at each end to connect with the coil spring units. A link running across the unit connected the axle to the underside of the body to locate the axle laterally. This system not only gave a better ride but also improved the vehicle's stability when cornering — few if any double-deckers can corner with an almost complete lack of roll like a Routemaster, even when designed much more recently.

Ease of driving, both in the sense of simplifying controls and giving the driver confidence in terms of braking (and stability, as indicated in the previous paragraph) was another aim. The 'one-legger' transmission and hydraulic brake development work done on RT-type buses provided the basis of the RM's steps forward in these directions. Fully-automatic gearbox operation was not provided on RM1 at first, though it was to follow later in the Routemaster development programme, but the direct-selection gear-change was a step towards it. Power-assisted steering was not at first fitted but was added later on RM1 — it soon became evident that with independent suspension it was a necessity.

The frontal appearance of RM1 owed a good deal to earlier unorthodox London Transport designs. The conventional radiator was removed from the front, in a manner which to some degree at least was related to the style used for the rebuild of RT97 into the prototype Green Line coach RTC1. There, the radiator became part of the heating system mounted under the stairs and the bonnet was given a rounded shape slightly reminiscent of the TF single-deckers of 1939 described in the next chapter. For RM1, however, the radiator had been moved to a different position, positioned below the offside

The destination display had been enlarged and a heating system, benefitting from the work done with RTC1, added by the time RM1 entered public service for the first time on a snowy 8th February 1956. It is seen at Golders Green station bearing the appropriate registration number SLT 56 and alongside RTL1233, also bound for Crystal Palace on route 2. It was thought that the fresh air heating system would eliminate the need for the opening upper-deck front windows which originally had been fitted — in due course this proved not to be acceptable and the windows were restored from RM251 onwards.

lower saloon floor. This allowed a slight reduction in bonnet length, helping in giving space for more seats in the lower deck than the RT, though this contribution was hardly more than marginal, with a reduction of a mere 1½in compared to the RT's very compact 4ft. 6¼in. dimension from front of the radiator to the bulkhead.

The completed vehicle was shown to the press in August 1954 and then exhibited at the Commercial Motor Show the following month, displayed on the AEC stand. In fact, it had been built in the Experimental Shop at Chiswick, though the mechanical units were of AEC manufacture; both AEC and Park Royal had been involved in their respective aspects of mechanical and body design.

This year also saw my next promotion and I became Executive Assistant in charge of the Chassis Section and was also responsible for the service trials of new vehicles. The surplus of buses was a blessing in disguise for us for it meant that we had ample time to fully test the prototype Routemasters. It was crucial that as much work as possible was carried out on testing and improving the prototypes before the large-scale orders for production buses were placed.

By mid-1955 the RTs had replaced all the pre-war and wartime double-deckers, and also the trams, and the first RTs were themselves being withdrawn. In the Autumn of 1955 there were over 7,000 buses in stock, of which just over 800 were single-deckers. It appeared at this time that London Transport's future was secure with the vast fleet of RTs and RFs, and the prototype bus of the future, the Routemaster, on the road well before the need to place quantity orders. The first vehicle, RM1, was still undergoing preliminary trials, not entering service until February 1956, by which time the original temporary destination display had been improved and a heater system added.

Meanwhile, early in 1955, a second prototype, RM2, had been completed. It looked very similar to RM1 but had the AV470 engine, a 7.75-litre unit originally introduced for the Mercury goods range in 1953 but adopted for the lightweight version of the updated but orthodox Regent V double-deck

chassis range introduced in 1954. This was more compact than the 9.6-litre engine and allowed the radiator to be fitted in the conventional position, requiring a grille in the front panel.

The reduced engine size was a reversal of the philosophy adopted in the succession of the STL by the RT, but it was considered logical to examine the overall possibilities, which included a further weight saving. This vehicle did incorporate two new features adopted as standard for Routemasters — power-assisted steering, then still quite rare on any kind of vehicle, and the fully-automatic version of the gearbox.

The original design of RM1 intended to take full advantage of the 27ft. 0in. overall length limit. However, the positioning of the radiator in an inclined position, low down to the offside of the engine, required a rather complicated chain drive to the fan, which proved noisy and had dirt problems. Then with RM2, having similar front-end dimensions but using the smaller engine, it was found possible to eliminate the remote

The second prototype, RM2, was used for stress-testing of the structure before being completed in 1955 and is seen here with temporary canvas in place of the side window glazing and lacking the lower-deck external panels. This view also just shows the original front grille used with the AV470 engine originally fitted.

By July 1956, the third prototype, then known as RML3, was nearing completion. This picture taken in the Leyland experimental department shows the front-mounted radiator position which had been adopted, this becoming possible even with engines in the 9-10 litre class by taking advantage of the increase of length which had just become permissible — RM1 was also rebuilt to this layout.

position of the radiator, together with its fan drive problems. Trials were carried out, using the Fighting Vehicle Research & Development Establishment test track at Chobham to compare the 9.6-litre engined RM1 with the 7.75-litre RM2, for which the vehicles were based at Staines garage, but these confirmed London Transport's view that a big engine derated is a better proposition than a small one uprated.

Fortunately the overall length limit for two-axle double-deckers was extended from 27ft. 0in. to 30ft. 0in. with effect from July 1956. Although, at that stage, LT did not want to take full advantage of the new limit, it was possible to put the radiator up front with the 9.6-litre engine, the length increasing to 27ft. 4½ in. A modified front grille panel was fitted to RM1 and RM2 received the larger engine with the same style of grille and radiator mounting. The latter vehicle had run in primer paint for the engine trials but was painted

green and ran from Reigate on the 406 for a few months during 1957 before moving to Turnham Green, by then in red livery.

At that stage, the expectation was that the total requirement for Routemaster buses would be comparable to that for RTs and there was also a desire to avoid London Transport being at the mercy of a monopoly supplier. It was thus agreed that two further prototypes would be built using Leyland 0.600 engines, substantially as used in the RTL, together with other Leyland mechanical units.

The body shell for the first of these Leyland-powered buses originally numbered RML3, was built by Weymann, and the fourth, finished as a Green Line coach and numbered CRL4, by Eastern Coach Works. The last-mentioned had been part of the Tilling group and at that date, as part of the British Transport Commission empire, was restricted to supplying other State-owned concerns. It had some spare capacity and could also have supplied some of LTE's needs — indeed, it had bodied the fifteen RFW coaches and also the 84 Guy 26-seat GS-class buses, as mentioned in the next chapter. Both of these further prototype vehicles were taken into LTE stock in 1957.

However, before then it had become clear that there would be insufficient volume to justify the involvement of more than one basic manufacturer of the body structure and indeed the same applied to the running gear. So the first bulk order for Routemasters, for 850 vehicles, went in October 1956 to Park Royal for the body structures and AEC for the running gear. It was decided that the standard specification would incorporate the AEC AV590 engine, still of 9.6-litre capacity but using a similar form of construction with monobloc crankcase and cylinder block and 'wet' cylinder liners in direct contact with the cooling water as in the AV470. The bonnet design was tidied up, the length increasing slightly to 27ft. 6½in. Deliveries began in the latter part of 1958.

As the 'fifties progressed it became apparent that the pendulum had swung further than had been expected or recognised. What Alan Townsin describes in his *History of the British Bus Services* as 'the Golden Age' had passed and the numbers of passengers being carried was beginning to decline. Increased car ownership and greater numbers of people staying at home in the evening to watch television were partly responsible as also were changing social habits and higher fares.

In 1958 there was a disastrous strike, lasting for seven weeks, during which no buses or trolleybuses left any of LTE's garages. Its effects were catastrophic, as many passengers, having made alternative arrangements, tended to stick with them. When it ended on 21st June, the drop in passengers being carried was marked. A series of cuts in service began in August, when nineteen Central Area bus routes were withdrawn completely. The Country Area followed with a ten per cent cut in October, a larger but more generalised Central Area reduction in services came in November and a cut in trolleybuses followed in January 1959. Overall, over

When RM2 first entered service in May 1957 it was in the Country area but from September of that year, duly repainted red, it had been transferred to Turnham Green and is seen at Hounslow West station on the 91, the traditional route where we could keep an eye on experimental vehicles. The combination of the 9.6-litre engine and front-mounted radiator required the use of a slightly projecting front grille.

The last of the four RM prototypes was CRL4, a Green Line coach, of which the body structure was built to LTE design by Eastern Coach Works and the mechanical units were by Leyland. It entered service as CRL4 in October 1957 and is seen here nearly a year later at the Green Line stopping point at Eccleston Bridge, Victoria, bound for Tunbridge Wells on the 704.

600 vehicles were rendered surplus. At first, many were simply delicensed and stored, but a major review of future needs followed.

Fortunately, the forthcoming trolleybus replacement provided a means of taking up much of the stock, and although the total of licensed buses — and in particular the RTL type — dropped sharply at the end of 1958, it recovered partially the following year. Some RT-family buses had already been sold — in particular, the 'pre-war' batch (though some were retained for staff transport) and then soon after them the non-standard batch with Cravens bodywork, sold in

1956, followed by 50 each of early RT and RTL buses at the beginning of 1958 plus 80, of both types, plus some single-deckers, for Ceylon. The period of trolleybus replacement brought more stability and it was not until it ended in 1962, allowing Routemaster deliveries to be used to replace RT-family buses, that further large-scale withdrawals followed. It was decided at that stage to put more emphasis on withdrawal of the Leyland RTL and RTW buses; when they had all gone the licensed RT fleet still numbered 3,625 vehicles at the end of 1968.

These three styling sketches were made by the late Douglas Scott in May 1956, during the later stages of prototype development. The first one comes close to the style adopted for the last two prototypes, RML3 and CRL4. Mr Scott was responsible for the Routemaster's styling though not its engineering design.

This sketch comes quite close to the production version as introduced in 1958, though the forward projection of the grille beyond the cab front is less than actually adopted and the offside headlamp was evidently to be flush with the cab front which was not the case in practice.

Easily the most radical of all the styling ideas was this version with reverse-rake windscreen, as sometimes found on mobile cranes, and a wide bonnet projecting considerably beyond it. The oval-shaped grille was in line with the trend in car styling trends of the period. Overall, it looks very strange, but would we have become used to it?

The surplus of buses led to the selling-off of non-standard types. Among them were the Cravens-bodied RT buses, offered for sale in 1956 when most were almost seven years old. Many went to independent operators who found, sometimes to their surprise, that these 'complicated'-seeming buses were very reliable. Here the former RT1514 is seen in Peterborough after purchase by Longlands (Crowland) Ltd — the 'lighthouse' route number box had been removed.

A high proportion of the RT-family buses withdrawn up to the mid-1960s saw further passenger-carrying service all over the world. Indeed, quite often they compared well in specification to much more modern vehicles, except perhaps in terms of dimensions, though London was by no means alone in favouring 7ft. 6in. buses up to the mid-1950s. London Transport's policy of tending to leave the design of its chosen vehicles largely undisturbed during long production runs might be criticised as fostering the manufacture of outdated new buses towards the end of such runs.

In fact, in technical design at least, this was not so for either the RT or RM classes, and the 40-year period between the entering into service of the first and withdrawal from regular service of the last achieved by the RT and likely to be exceeded by the RM indicates prolonged public acceptability as well as sheer durability of many of the vehicles involved. Will any of the 'off-the-shelf' models be able to achieve a similar track record?

Moreover, although outwardly London buses generally remained the same, they were continually updated by our Alteration Advice procedure. If shortcomings were detected in any unit, steps were taken to find out why and make changes in specification to put them right. Again, this emphasised the value of a Central Technical unit, which not only kept in contact with garages, but also played an important part in the Central Works. Experimental tests were always in progress to find better materials to give more reliable service. Tests were conducted on differing lubricants to reduce friction, prolong life of components, etc. So in a way, the seemingly unchanged vehicle was quietly being updated in line with modern technology.

On the other hand, changes in legislation and consequent alterations in such matters as the elimination of conductors could lead to pressure for new vehicle layout — notably the switch to rear-mounted engines.

With a certain inevitability the day approached when we would have to assess these new-generation vehicles, but more of that later.

In 1960 I gained further promotion to the position of Senior Executive Assistant in the department and I shall discuss my new responsibilities in Chapter Eight.

The end-result of our work on the four Routemaster prototypes was the production version. Here RM8, the first to be completed, is seen at Park Royal in September 1958 shortly before delivery — it was displayed at the Commercial Motor Show but was then retained by the experimental department, running there until March 1976 when it entered normal service.

The oldest single-deckers still in service when I arrived were the batch of AEC Regal buses originally built for the London General Omnibus Co Ltd in the winter of 1929-30. Originally there were 50 such vehicles with Chiswick-built bus bodies of rear-entrance layout. All but five were rebuilt to front-entrance form in the early 1930s. This picture of T31 is typical of the batch as running in the early post-war years — it had entered service in December 1929 and was rebuilt to front entrance in June 1933. Although not among eighteen renovated by Marshalls in 1949, T31 was among those converted from petrol with 7.7-litre oil engines from scrapped STL buses. It then became an instruction bus and has survived, being rebuilt virtually to original condition after purchase by the Historic Commercial Vehicle Club.

5. The single-deck scene

The typical London bus has always been — in most people's eyes — a bright red double-decker. Toyshops throughout the world sell models of Routemasters and DMS Fleetlines, and full-sized buses purchased for use overseas are often painted in London Transport livery for promotional purposes — even if they have no connection with London as in the example of the Bristol Lodekka which was exported to America carrying London Transport transfers!

Nevertheless, London has always had a substantial minority of single-deckers in its fleet, using them where it was impossible or impractical to operate double-deckers. Restrictions such as railway bridges were one of the main reasons, although it was often possible to use a double-deck bus of the low-height variety but the Public Carriage Office restricted these vehicles to special routes. Other exceptions were the opening of new routes in sparsely-populated areas which would develop as housing estates were built, for instance, and where conventional vehicles could ultimately be introduced.

At the time of my arrival at Chiswick in 1947 the single-deck fleet included a motley collection of vehicles ranging from the somewhat mixed T type which seemed to cover almost every AEC Regal variety, the single-deck LT-class AEC Renown six-wheelers and the LTC coach variant, Leyland Cubs (C), Leyland rear-engined Cubs (CR), the underfloor-engined Leyland TF and a collection of three types of the AEC Q model with side-mounted engine (Q). Finally, there were the TD-class Leyland Tiger PS1 single-deckers, which formed the most recent additions to the central area single-deck fleet.

At that date the T class could be regarded as a parallel to both the ST and STL types of double-decker. The oldest examples came from a batch of 50 with fleet numbers T1-50 (except that T38 had been completed as a Green Line coach and replaced by an extra chassis T156) that had been placed in service by London General Omnibus Co towards the end of 1929 and originally of rear-entrance 29-seat form, with Chiswick-built bodies intended for various suburban bus routes — most still survived, though they had been converted to front-entrance 30-seaters in the 1930s.

Then there were a mixed bag of vehicles mostly dating from 1930-31 and largely drawn from batches of former Green Line coaches, vehicles taken over from various independent

One of 22 former Green Line AEC Regal petrol-engined coaches of the 1931 delivery that had been converted for use as buses pre-war and then had the seating rearranged longitudinally during the war to allow more standing passengers to be carried, was T251 — it had been repainted red in 1945.

Only a minority of the early 1930-31 batches of former Green Line coaches were still with LT in 1947 but prominent among them were 31 which had been fitted with oil engines and bus bodies dating from 1935 by Weymann that had originally been on older AEC Reliance chassis. One of these was T215, of which the chassis dated from 1931, seen here at Edgware (EW) garage in July 1951.

operators and other assorted examples such as a batch of twelve buses operated by LGOC on behalf of Tilling, which had originally occupied the fleet numbers between T51 and T402. Many of these had been sold after being replaced by more modern coaches around 1938-39 and only about 67 survived in the fleet. Some had the original bodies modified to suit bus rather than coach duties, and in 1938, a total of 31 had been given 7.7-litre oil engines and newer bodies (built by Weymann in 1935, originally to update older chassis) being reclassified 11T11.

Other than the 11T11 conversions, the foregoing had petrol engines, but T403-452 were a batch of 50 Regal coaches of type 9T9 built for Green Line duty in 1937 and having the same combination of 7.7-litre oil engine and preselective transmission as the STL buses of the same period. They had bodies to London Transport design built by Weymann, and

an unusual built-up bonnet assembly which looked rather clumsy to me.

Then came the famous 10T10 type coaches, of which there had been 266 as built in 1938 — T453-718. Though having generally similar looks to the 9T9 (but with conventional bonnet design), these had 8.8-litre engines of direct injection type, marking a stage in the process of using larger-capacity engines as a means of achieving better service life as well as more refined running that led to the RT design. They had Chiswick-built bodywork and formed the backbone of the Green Line fleet, though during the war many had been requisitioned for other duties and twelve were not returned. Those still in the fleet received a thorough rebuild before re-entering service.

A first stage of post-war renewal of the single-deck fleet was represented by the 50 Regal buses of the 14T12 type with 7.7-litre engines and clash gearboxes, placed in service in 1946 (T719-768). These were central area (red) buses and had Weymann bodywork of a style then being supplied to various provincial fleets.

Still the largest single group of buses in the central area single-deck fleet were the LT-class, nicknamed the Scooters, dating from 1931. These had fleet numbers which ran from LT1001 to 1201 (except for LT1051 and LT1137), although the technical classification was LTL, which gave the clue to the fact that they were longer than the double-deck LT-class AEC Renown six-wheelers. They were on the 664-model chassis giving nominal overall length of 30ft. rather than the 27ft. of the 663-type double-deckers. Most were still in service and there were also two similar buses, LT1427-1428, that had come from the LGCS fleet. They retained petrol engines and despite their length seated only 35, no more than the 14T12 buses as built (though the latter were later reduced to 33 seats, having been found to be too cramped for the routes on which they were used, with frequent stops).

The last AEC Renown six-wheelers added to the London Transport fleet were 24 coaches on the shorter 663-type chassis placed in service in 1937 and given the numbers LTC1-24. As built, they had petrol engines that had been removed from LT-type double-deckers converted with 8.8-litre oil engines, but in 1949, towards the end of their lives, they

The 10T10 class of AEC Regal 8.8-litre coaches dating from 1938 were the mainstay of the Green Line routes in 1947 and remained so until replaced by the RF type in 1951-52, though some remained in service for a year or two longer as buses. Seen here looking almost like new after overhaul is T476, operating from Swarley (SJ) garage on the 703 and seen at the Eccleston Bridge, Victoria, stop which for many years was a meeting point for about eleven of the Green Line routes as they crossed central London. The bodies of the 10T10 class were built to this very distinctive design at Chiswick, there being 266 vehicles of which 150 were built as 30-seat vehicles and the remainder seated 34.

A batch of 50 AEC Regal buses classified 14T12 were added to the Central area fleet in 1946 for suburban routes from Uxbridge, Kingston and Muswell Hill garages. They were on the standard provincial chassis of the period with 7.7-litre engines and clash gearboxes and had Weymann bodywork also having few London Transport features. They seated 35 as delivered though this was soon reduced to 33. Seen here is T721, with one of the 1937 STD-class Leyland Titan TD4 buses in the background.

In addition to the 199 AEC Renown six-wheel single-deckers built for LGOC in 1931, two further almost identical buses were added for London General Country Services in 1932 but had been transferred to the Central Area in 1944. Apart from its high fleet number, LT1427, one of this latter pair, seen at Chiselhurst, is very representative of the whole series with their Chiswick-built 35-seat bodywork, as running in the post-war period. There were still 189 of the type licensed in 1947, forming the largest single class of Central Area single-deckers, and 98 of these, including 60 which had bodies renovated by Marshalls, were fitted with ex-STL oil engines in 1950.

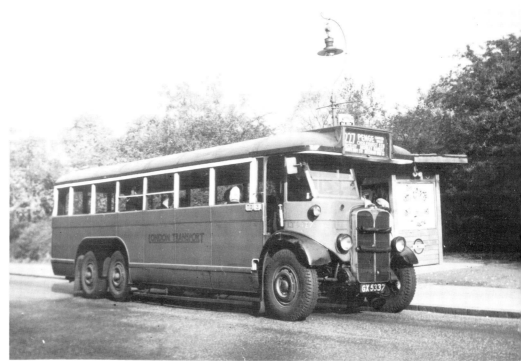

The 24 LTC coaches of 1937-38 were purchased for private hire duties and were based on short-wheelbase AEC Renown chassis on which were fitted Weymann bodies of a style very similar to that of contemporary Green Line coaches on Regal chassis. Originally petrol-engined, they were fitted with 8.8-litre oil engines in 1949-50, as shown here by LTC20.

A fleet of 100 4Q4 buses for Country Area duties dating from 1935 had been London Transport's first major order for single-deckers. The unusual sloping roof line is clearly shown in this view of Q21, operating on a Central Area bus route from Kingston garage, even though still in green livery. The side-mounted engine position of the AEC Q class is indicated by the grille behind the offside front wheel.

themselves received the latter type of engine drawn from scrapped LT double-deckers.

For a while during the mid 'thirties, London Transport favoured the side-engined AEC Q-type for its full-sized single-decker needs. The engine was mounted behind the offside front wheel, driving via a transmission line only slightly offset as the rear axle had single tyres, being set back so as to keep the weight it carried within the capability of the tyres. The first example had appeared in 1932, being a single-decker, and four double-deckers had been purchased in 1934, but the oldest examples still in the fleet when I arrived were the 100 single-deckers dating from 1935 of the 4Q4 type, intended for country area bus duties and having bodywork built by the Birmingham Railway Carriage & Wagon Co (Q6-105). Two later similar buses were Q186-187.

Then came 80 buses designed for central use, type 5Q5, which differed from the country version in having the entrance ahead of the front axle in the manner now common but then still very unusual. Park Royal built the bodies on these, Q106-185. The same firm built the bodies on the final 50 of the type, which were Green Line coaches reverting to the layout with entrance to the rear of the front axle (Q189-238). Incidentally Q188 had been an experimental double-deck Green Line coach on a six-wheel Q chassis, the only one built, but like the other double-deckers this had already been sold. All the Q types still in service had 7.7-litre oil engines and preselector gearboxes.

The Leyland Cub 20-seat buses had been purchased in the early days of London Transport to fulfil a need for small vehicles suitable for rural services. The prototype purchased in 1934 had been sold but many of the C2-74 batch dating from 1935 were still in the fleet—they had oil engines, still quite rare on vehicles of this size at that date (in this case Leyland six-cylinder 4.4-litre direct-injection units) and Short Bros bodywork to LPTB design. A further 22 built for the central area in 1936 (C77-98) were generally similar looking but had indirect-injection 4.7-litre engines and bodies by Weymann—some of these had been sold and the rest went to

For the 1936 batch of Central Area 5Q5-type buses the front axle was moved rearwards to allow the entrance to be positioned at the front, a rare feature at the time even though quite usual nowadays. Seen here is Q181, working from Cricklewood (W) garage.

The final delivery of Q-type vehicles consisted of the 6Q6 Green Line coaches, entering service in the winter of 1936-37. This type reverted to the entrance position behind the front axle, as shown by Q222 seen working on a Country bus route from St. Albans garage in 1950.

The 74 Leyland Cub 20-seat buses placed in service in 1935 were to remain a familiar sight in parts of the Country Area until 1952. London Transport had chosen the 15ft. 6in. wheelbase version of the chassis used elsewhere to seat up to 26, giving a more spacious layout for passengers. The bodywork was built to Chiswick specification by Short Bros, who had built a proportion of the body needs of the LGOC but only this one batch for LPTB as its efforts were being concentrated on the manufacture of flying boats. Shown at Rickmansworth is C60.

country routes. Some goods vehicles on Cub chassis had filled the next numbers in the series but the last Cub passenger vehicles were C106-113, the Inter-station batch of eight vehicles introduced in 1936 to provide a service connecting the main railway terminus—these were forward-control and had the petrol version of the 4.7-litre engine, no doubt in the interests of quiet running. They had bodies built by Park Royal to what was sometimes called the observation coach or one-and-a-half deck style, with raised rear seats so as to provide plenty of luggage space for the 20 passengers, and were in a distinctive blue livery.

The forward-control version of the Leyland Cub was chosen for the eight special vehicles built in 1936 to provide the Inter-station service which, as its name implies, linked London main-line railway termini. The Park Royal 20-seat bodywork was of the type with raised rear seating area so as to give generous luggage space, an idea followed up in post-war airport coaches. The livery was an attractive combination of blue and cream, C107 being seen here.

Sadly, only one of the twelve TF sightseeing coaches built in 1939 survived the war years due to wartime bombing, but this vehicle, TF9, was still regarded with particular pride in the early post-war years. The extensive roof glazing of the Park Royal-built bodywork is evident in this view of it on 'Seeing London Tour' duty in post-war days. The centre section of the roof folded and is partially open.

London Transport had followed a policy on the design of its single-deckers which was not afraid of innovation. The AEC Q was a case in point, but later in the 'thirties Leyland was the manufacturer chosen for two more designs introducing ideas which could be described as ahead of their time.

The first, of which the prototype was completed in 1937, was the TF, for which Leyland's official name was Tiger type FEC, these initials evidently signifying 'flat-engined coach', though it had very little in common with the standard Tiger of that period (of which London Transport had none, though it was broadly a single-deck equivalent of the STD-class Titan TD4 model of 1937). The key feature was the use of an under-floor 'flat' engine, basically similar to the 8.6-litre direct-injection six-cylinder unit as used in the TD4 but in many respects a fresh design to enable it to be turned on its side.

The chassis frame was basically straight and relatively high by pre-war standards, when passenger models were usually expected to have low-level frames, but more important was the fact that it was designed to have the body built directly on the outriggers with which it was fitted, producing a form of semi-integral construction.

A preselective gearbox was fitted, this being an AEC-built unit, basically as fitted to STL-type buses. However, the vehicle had air-pressure operation of both brakes and gearbox — the prototype thus predating the RT this respect. Although the engine was beneath the floor a half-cab layout was retained, there being a curved cowling to the left of the driver into which the radiator grille was set on the production version. A further 87 of these were built in 1939, TF2-13 being fitted with special sightseeing coach bodies with curved-glass cantrail windows by Park Royal. Sadly all but TF9 were destroyed when only a little over a year old in October 1940 when Bull Yard, Peckham received a direct hit in an air raid. The others, TF14-88, received Chiswick-built bodies generally similar to those on the 10T10 apart from the differences dictated by the type of chassis.

Oddly enough, when I first arrived at Chiswick and before I was able to put my little knowledge on RTs to good use, I was sent to Dorking garage where I was to look at the problems of TF vehicles which apparently consumed large quantities of cooling water. In those days new entrants had to wait for their passes, always referred to as 'stickies' because they used to have a sticky back to affix a photograph. How history repeats itself!

I caught the 414 at Redhill and was required to pay 10d for my fare to Dorking Bus Station.

The history of the TF vehicle, perhaps a potential world-beater, makes interesting reading so maybe some digression is warranted. The man behind the vehicle, in conjunction with Leyland, was Albert Higgins, then Senior Development Assistant, from whom I was to learn a lot. The project was under the general direction of E. C. Ottaway. Unfortunately the 1939 War prevented the design being exploited. Visibility for the driver was second to none and set a standard never to be equalled, although the prototype TF1 had a rather ungainly looking cab of the type without canopy to the near side, at first, though this was remodelled to bring it into line with the rest, in 1940. The Green Line vehicles had replaced the last petrol Regals at Luton, St. Albans, Grays and Dorking, but the war intervened and many of these vehicles were converted into ambulances. After the war, the Green Line services were gradually restored and some TFs found their way back to Dorking and this is when I came to know them. Unfortunately I never really found the answer to the water loss on the TF but in later years the rear-engined Titan was to play up just the same.

Apart from their construction, the air pressure braking was quite a step forward for a pre-war design. The gearbox was still of the spring-operated type but had an air cylinder on the side of it to compress the spring inside the gearbox, whereas with the RT the air cylinder became part of the gearbox proper and did away with the spring.

There is an interesting little story to tell in connection with the operation of the TFs between St. Albans and Dorking. The allocation of vehicles was such that there were not enough TFs to cover the service and in consequence a Q-type was added to the running at St. Albans — and the particular vehicle allocated was a heavy guzzler of engine oil. Certain running numbers 'slept out' at the other garage alternate nights, although unlike the railways, the driver's duties were so arranged that he came back, and wherever the vehicle slept that garage took the responsibility for it on the run out, but always ensured that it returned home that night. Dorking faithfully put the Q-type back on its home run after it slept out, but it was nothing unusual to see it changed over when it reached St. Albans so that it slept out for a consecutive night at Dorking. This developed into a game of wits during the day to keep changing

As was often the case with prototype vehicles, TF1, despite being rebuilt in 1940 to bring its appearance more into line with later TF coaches, was sold off quite early, in 1945 but oddly enough reappeared on London Transport services when independent operators' vehicles were hired in 1946-47 to help overcome the shortage of serviceable vehicles. Castle Coaches of Lewisham kept it in use until the early 1950s, but it is seen here on LT's route 1 in 1946. Note the horse-drawn railway delivery cart, then still a familiar sight.

it over so it finally reached St. Albans after the last journey had left from Dorking again! Many were the irate 'phone calls between the Engineers at Dorking and St. Albans and modesty prevents me disclosing names.

It was not until the RT arrived in large numbers that air pressure braking became the norm. Experience had been limited to the TF and pre-war 2RT. Experience with the TF brought to light a serious problem that caused the air reservoir to suddenly unload its pressure. According to how the driver applied the brake valve it could, under a particular condition, start a vibration which caused the brake valve piston to flutter violently, gradually releasing the air and at the same time creating a terrible noise which reached a crescendo, echoing throughout the coach. The natural tendency was to release the brake pedal— which was not always desirable for obvious reasons! Simple remedies were tried such as restrictors in the air line, and baffling the outlet from the brake valve, until it was found that it was due to the wear taking place on the brake valve piston on its guide. Strict control on the wear limits here soon produced a solution which was also applied to the 3RT fleet and further troubles never developed. The noise arising from this peculiarity was deafening and had to be heard to be believed.

This little investigation brings to mind an event that occurred at Dorking. Whilst a colleague was testing a TF on this assignment, he made a rather fierce brake application which caused the vehicle to lock the rear wheels. Precisely at that moment the rear wheels hit a pot hole such that the wheels left the road. When the locked wheels regained the road the shock on the springs was such that the axle twisted, broke the

The TF coaches shared with the 10T10 type the bulk of regular duties on the Green Line services in the early post-war years. Here TF83 is seen on the 714 bound for Dorking.

Only London Transport had underfloor-engined buses or coaches in regular public service in Britain in 1939. This view shows the installation of the horizontal Leyland 8.6-litre engine in TF16 when new in March of that year.

This view of the front of the same vehicle with access panels open shows not only the care taken to ensure that items liable to need servicing could be reached easily but the robust quality of the various items. Note that the main radiator faced forward, receiving its air largely through the bottom grille, but that there was also a second unit, visible behind the main radiator filler.

spring eyes, and left the axle on the road several feet behind the vehicle, with the back end of the coach on the road. The Reigate lorry was summoned from the stores round whilst those on the coach drank tea sent out from Dorking. Poor Bill Stapleton, the District Engineer at Reigate, never did see the funny side of this exploit.

A later humorous TF incident occurred when I was permitted to take the Museum TF 77 to a Bus Rally at Stratford-upon-Avon. After winning first prize the vehicle broke down on the way home at High Wycombe so, even though London Country Bus Services Limited had been formed, and as a subsidiary of the National Bus Company was thus no longer part of London Transport, I took it to the LCBS garage there and left it, the day being Sunday. On Monday I duly presented the cup to the Chief who casually asked where was the coach now? Consternation then ensued as it was suggested that LCBS might claim it in view of its Green Line livery, that section of the fleet having been transferred to LCBS. Having good relations with LCBS prevented any such action and the Experimental Shop attended and repaired the rotary compressor which was prone to bearing problems if left

standing for long periods, and we duly got our bus back!

To get back to the late 'thirties, the second unorthodox single-deck design to result from the co-operation with Leyland was the rear-engined version of the Cub, the CR. This was still a 20-seater but had a front-end design very like the production TF, with half cab and a rounded half-bonnet, even though the engine was mounted longitudinally at the rear.

An interesting feature of the design was that the engine, a 4.4-litre unit of the type fitted to the 1935 country Cubs in the prototype, drove through a special constant mesh gearbox and final drive unit to a rear axle of the de Dion type. This gave the rigid axle needed to allow twin tyres to be used, the drive from the final drive being via universally-jointed shafts. A Chiswick-built body was fitted and CR1 was completed in January 1938, in Country livery.

A further 48 vehicles were ordered, mostly to be painted red for Central area service but including five in green — all of these were fitted with indirect-injection engines. However they were not completed until after the war had begun and were put in store. One was destroyed in an air raid, but they were put into use with conductors, on rush hour relief duties

The CR was another remarkably advanced design developed jointly by LT at Chiswick and Leyland in the period just before the 1939-45 war. This view of one of the production chassis shows the engine and gearbox installation at the rear — universally-jointed shafts drive the rear wheels from the differential built into the gearbox.

Technically more advanced and certainly more robust than most modern minibuses, the CR was ahead of its time. Here CR43 is seen at the Wells Estate terminus of the 481 to Epsom Station, a Saturdays-only service. A changeover appears to be occurring, the mechanic sitting on the bonnet of the older conventional Leyland Cub evidently fitting a destination blind so that it can take over the duty — the CR has had its running plates removed. The CR was apt to be rather unreliable, suffering from inadequate time to iron out the teething troubles to be expected in an unconventional design.

The 100 Leyland Tiger PS1 single-deckers with Mann Egerton bodywork added to the fleet in 1948-49 had few of London Transport's usual features apart from minor characteristics such as the sliding cab doors and the double-opening windscreens. Two, TD104 and TD106, are seen at Edgware station.

on major routes running through central London—later they want to the Country Area. The model retained the good visibility for the driver of the TF, but the remote operation of the clash gearbox was not popular. Also the rear engine proved to suffer from overheating problems, as so often the case with other pioneer designs of this layout.

However, the newest Leyland single-deckers in the fleet were completely orthodox, being Tiger PS1 models of virtually standard design as supplied to operators all over the country, and with chassis directly equivalent to those of the 65 PD1 double-deckers added to the STD class in 1946. The single-deckers were given the class type letters TD, logical in relation to STD though oddly enough the same as had been used in early LPTB days for Titan double-deckers of types TD1 and TD2 taken over from independent operators.

The initial batch amounted to 31 vehicles with Weymann 33-seat bodywork very like that on the contemporary 14T12 class buses which entered service in the winter of 1946-47. Despite their non-conformity to London Transport standards—like the PD1 models they had constant-mesh gearboxes, the engines on both being of the 7.4-litre E181 type—it was decided to order 100 further similar chassis.

This came as something of a surprise, as already on order was a final batch of T-class AEC Regals, which seemed much closer to LT ideas on bus design. These were of the provincial Mark

III type, with 9.6-litre engine, preselective gearbox and air brakes, thus being in essentials basically similar to the RT, or to be more precise, a single-deck equivalent to the RLH, though the latter had yet to appear. A batch of 30 had been ordered, the resulting vehicles being classified 15T13, and the fleet numbers being T769-798. The body order for these vehicles went to Mann Egerton, the Norwich bodybuilder which was rebuilding large numbers of STL-type double-deckers at the time, as mentioned in Chapter Three. They were 31-seat vehicles built to a style not unlike that Weymann had used for

The last additions to the T-class single-deckers, type 15T13, were different to any of their predecessors, arriving in 1948. They comprised 30 of the Regal Mark III model with 9.6-litre engines and preselective gearbox — broadly speaking, a single-deck equivalent to the RT — and had 31-seat bodywork by Mann Egerton. All were supplied to the Country Area in the green and white livery although T798, the last and highest-numbered T-type Regal of all, had been repainted in the almost all-green style with cream relief, as seen here.

from scrapped STL-type buses was available and in addition many of the surviving vehicles from the 1929 batch of T-type and 1931 LT single-deck series were sent to another bodybuilder in East Anglia, Marshall of Cambridge, to be rebuilt. Those thus treated, eighteen T-type and 60 LT, were altered to an almost all-red livery and received updated interior trim, a remarkable transformation for buses some of which were 20 years old. There were still 31 of the 1929 T-type and 82 of the LT single-deck fleet scheduled for Central Area service at the end of 1950 — indeed these levels did not alter significantly until the veterans finally gave way to the RF-type in 1952-53.

When the Leyland-MCW Olympic was introduced, one of the pre-production batch of HR40-type 27ft. 6in.-long demonstration vehicles built in 1948-49 was painted in a version of Green Line livery but no order ensued, largely because of the non-availability at that date of the combination of fluid flywheel and Wilson-type gearbox.

Evolution of the RF

There had been careful study of London Transport's future needs for single-deckers. A survey carried out in 1949 indicated a projected single-deck fleet size of 990, from which could be subtracted the 211 post-war AEC Regal and Leyland Tiger front-engined buses already delivered, although there was some uncertainty as to the sizes of vehicles which might be available and suitable for the various types of route.

This was the beginning of the era when underfloor engines were becoming accepted as the logical choice for full-sized single-deckers. London Transport's experience with the TF was encouraging and although the major British manufacturers concentrated on front-engined models to meet the immediate post-war demand, there was widespread interest in the possibilities — the Midland Red concern had adopted this layout as standard for its post-war fleet from 1946, aided by the fact it built its own chassis in those days. Of more importance to London Transport, AEC and Leyland engineers worked on their new designs in the period from 1946 although the results were not revealed to the public until 1949.

the 1946 T and TD batches and, like those vehicle, having little if any of the general character associated with London Transport single-deck designs. The first few entered service towards the end of 1947 and the remainder in 1948, all going to the Country Area.

Mann Egerton also got the body order for the 100 further TD-class buses which expanded the class to 131 vehicles, all painted red for Central Area duties, Leyland's ability to deliver overcoming reservations about the specification. They entered service in 1948-49, and although not conforming to London Transport's usual requirements, notably in having clash gearboxes, the fact that the Central area single-deck fleet had received no new vehicles for some ten years and had so many T and LT vehicles dating back to 1929-31 made them acceptable.

Yet such was the need for buses that many of these latter vehicles were retained. By 1949, a supply of 7.7-litre engines

It should be realised that because London's requirement would be considerable the men who earned their living selling buses would be keen to get the business. There were perhaps only two serious contenders for the chassis business, AEC and Leyland, in view of the size of orders involved, and with the very close relationship which existed between London Transport and AEC it was perhaps inevitable that the AEC design department would have a better appreciation of what London wanted. It should be remembered that London Transport could not, even if it wished, place all its business with the AEC plant at Southall since the terms of the formation of the LPTB in 1933 clearly stated that a percentage of the business must be placed elsewhere.

Thus two vehicles were selected for trial in 1949. One was the AEC Regal IV, as it was to be known, and the other a Leyland-MCW Olympic. It was, in many ways, a strange choice for comparison. London was firmly wedded to a policy

The first AEC Regal IV prototype, registered UMP 227, spent some months running from St. Albans garage during 1950. This view shows the style of windscreen fitted to the Park Royal bodywork, with recessed panel to avoid internal reflections creating problems for the driver at night, but overall rather deeper than adopted for the production RF.

Two of the initial 'Private Hire' batch of RF-class coaches seen parked outside Victoria garage in company with an RT also on private hire duty. The original livery of Lincoln green with grey upperworks gave a livelier appearance than the more familiar Green Line version having only the slim band of light green relief. These 25 vehicles were the only production AEC Regal IV models built to 27ft. 6in. length. The vehicle nearer the camera, RF20, was a 'visitor' from Holloway (J) garage.

of lifting bodies off their chassis at overhaul time and yet Leyland's offering — the Olympic — was a fully integral vehicle with no chassis, although as was to be shown later, this was not insuperable. Perhaps the transmission was of greater significance for from the start there was not much doubt about the AEC's advantage of a fluid flywheel and preselective gearbox whereas the Leyland had a four-speed synchromesh gearbox with a dry plate clutch. The AEC, bodied by Park Royal, had a much sleeker look than the Olympic, of which the MCW body structure had a heavy appearance, though of course handsome is as handsome does!

Because of the transmission, tests on the Leyland were not proceeded with and after service trials the AEC vehicle was selected, from which developed the RF class. The registration number UMP 227 was used as the identity of this AEC vehicle, rather than issuing a fleet number, remaining so throughout its life with London Transport; it remained the property of the manufacturer, a break with tradition for previous prototypes for London classes. It was of the 27ft. 6in. length still current and had bodywork built by Park Royal, having been completed early in 1949, painted in a green livery similar to that of the Country Bus department. It was used for demonstration to various operators before entering service in May 1950 from St. Albans garage on route 355.

Back in the early days of the post-war RT programme, a contract had been placed with Metro-Cammell to supply 1,000 bodies on Leyland RTL chassis. This was intended to expand the existing arrangements with Park Royal and Weymann and the original intention was that these bodies would be to the same tightly standardised design. However, the need for urgent delivery caused a change to Metro-Cammell's standard framing but further negotiation led to agreement that Metro-Cammell would build only 450 bodies for the RTL class (completed as RTL551-1000). The construction of the entire body order of 700 for the RF class was part of the same agreement; the resulting RT7 bodies on RTL chassis entered service between August 1949 and April 1951, being completed just before the first RF models appeared the following month.

By the beginning of 1950, the position on overall dimensions had become clearer, it being announced that the maximum length of two-axled single-deckers would be increased to 30ft. and that the 8ft. width would become acceptable on a general basis. There was still doubt as to whether the latter would apply under the tighter rules still being used in London and it was decided to continue with 7ft. 6in. for the new RF class. The length was to be increased to 30ft. for the bulk of the order but work was too far advanced on the first batch of 25 vehicles to be coded 1RF1. These were urgently needed for the Private Hire fleet, which had nothing more modern than the 25 LTC class coaches of 1938 and the solitary surviving TF hire coach, TF9 of 1939. The Festival of Britain was to be held in London in 1951 and the first examples arrived in May of that year, just in time.

These first vehicles (RF1-25), as well as being 27ft. 6in. long, had special features to suit their Private Hire use. They had curved glass windows in the roof line and an unusual colour scheme — the familiar dark green below the waist rail but grey above, with red lining out and lettering.

I remember going to Coventry (in those days there was no Birmingham International station, which would have been very near Met Camm's Elmdon Works) to meet RF1 and to travel back with it on initial delivery, and as I saw it approach I didn't think too much of it, the upright front being unfamiliar in those days — but time is a great healer. Little did I know that in years to come I was to own RF19.

After these 25, Green Line then received their share but these were to be 30ft. long, as were the rest of the class. The Green Line vehicle seated 39, as compared to the 35 of the shorter Private Hire version, and did not have the roof-level windows but was otherwise similar. It was this type of Green Line service that soon brought to light severe problems in brake temperatures and rates of wear of linings.

It so happened that AEC had changed the design of the front axle, in line with Leyland practice, substituting thrust buttons in the king pin for the previous taper roller races in the interest of better axle life. This prevented the use of king pin-mounted brake cylinders operating through a hollow king pin. In the changeover the automatic brake adjuster became fitted to the leading brake shoe instead of the trailing, thus causing somewhat heavy wear as well as excessively high temperatures.

Someone suddenly realised this and came up with the clever solution of switching the carriers nearside to offside and

The Green Line version of the RF in its standard 30ft.-long form became a familiar sight in London by 1952, RF150 being seen not long after entering service from Addlestone garage on the 717, leaving Golders Green with its usual collection of interesting buses including RTs of various types and an STD.

turning them upside down to put things right. So a campaign change was instituted and the brake problem became a little more tenable. In particular it was the nearside front brakes that reached the peak temperatures, probably due to the influence of the entrance step, although the low overhang on the front of the bus did not help.

There were 263 of the Green Line RF types, as originally built (RF26-288) and when delivery of these was completed in September 1952, production switched to the 225 buses for Central Area (RF289-513) which had seats for 41 and no door at the entrance—this was another aspect of design which London requirements differed from those elsewhere. In a typically cautious way, the Public Carriage Office was still unhappy about fitting passenger doors to a London bus.

Because of production delays, due to Government restrictions on home market deliveries to boost exports, it took longer to obtain delivery of these vehicles than planned. Central Area drivers on single-deck routes became restive at still being required to drive 20-year-old buses with clash gearboxes, notably at Muswell Hill where there was one of the most severe climbs on a bus route in the London area. Some of the former Green Line Q-types, still in Green livery, were used temporarily following their replacement on their original duties. Some of the TD-class Leyland PS1 buses were also reallocated from elsewhere, but these moves met with little real success, due mainly to driver problems.

Finally, in 1953, came the last of the batch, 187 buses for the Country Area (RF514-700). These vehicles were again 41-seaters, but had air-operated doors as used on the Green Line. The bus versions, either green or red, featured a slim band of cream surrounding the windows, whereas the Green Line livery used pale green relief. Three of the country buses (RF517, 647 and 700) were completed as 'one-man' buses entering service in this form in 1954 and later more were adapted similarly, marking the beginning of the trend to the operation of full-sized buses without conductors.

In later years, there were various conversions of RF-type vehicles from one category to another and the blocks of numbers altered somewhat, some 24 former buses drawn from both red and green fleets becoming Green Line coaches and being renumbered to extend the Green Line numbers up to RF 313. In addition, ten of the short Private Hire coaches

Amid today's concern for passenger safety — as well as comfort in winter — it seems strange to think that when the output of RFs turned to the supply of the version for Central Area buses, the entrance was required to be devoid of doors and no interior heaters were fitted. Seen here on the 210 is the second 'red' example, RF290, shortly after entering service in September 1952.

The green bus version of the RF did at least have entrance doors — RF515 was one of the first to enter service, being seen outside the Country Area headquarters garage at Reigate in April 1953, having been allocated to the local 447 route.

(RF16-25) were also modified for Green Line use by the addition of light luggage racks internally.

On reflection, after the first initial setback with the brakes, the RF gave a very good account of itself. Unlike earlier buses, this vehicle was fitted with high deflection springs which needed a stabiliser to prevent undue roll. In the supporting links were Metalistik rubbers bonded with an outer shell. These bushes had a tendency to wear badly, and shear at the bonding, so the arm often went over-centre and caused a rattling which was, to say the least, irritating. It was then I first came in contact with Silentbloc of Crawley, who produced a cunning design so that if excessive deflection occurred the rubber bush would slip on its sleeve. It was so successful that all vehicles were subsequently modified.

It was during these early days of experience of problems with the RF that the TF problem already mentioned arose. On a high brake application a vibration would start and gradually spread throughout the bus, the whole vehicle going into resonance. Thoughts revolved around the air pressure systems but attempts here failed to control it. It was whilst I was reading a book on Automotive Chassis Design by Dean-Averns, a former senior engineer at Leyland, that I came across reference to the fact that if the brake cam operates in the direction of wheel rotation brake shudder will often develop. Just a bald statement but it was well worth a trial, which was done and was highly successful. Memory fails to record if all the fleet was done by switching back-plate assemblies, much like the RF, because the vehicles were soon withdrawn. That particular book contains quite a few pearls of wisdom for the budding Bus Engineer, some without explanation, but correct all the same.

One of the selling points of the RF was the ease with which the engine could be changed. Fitted as part of the engine suspension was a chain, so that once the engine was disconnected from the transmission shaft, fan drive and water hoses, it could be wound out of the offside of the vehicle. A time of 20 minutes was quoted to do this. However, when it came to be done, after several years of service, the chains had disappeared. It seems it was a motor cycle size and we must have employed many motor cycling enthusiasts in those days!

Another problem cropped up with the RF. In AEC's design of the steering it was decided, quite rightly at the time, to use a two-start worm and nut arrangement instead of the previous single-start. In this way it was thought that the steering effort would be lessened. All went very well until the time came to overhaul the vehicles and it was usual to buy a sufficient float of parts to have work in progress. For this, only the worm and nuts were bought, not complete columns, and somehow AEC had lost the know how of production. Reports of stiff steering kept arising and it was not for some time that it was discovered that it was these 'work in progress' parts that were continually in trouble. Attempts were made to polish the worm surfaces with metal polish, lapped with ground glass, in order to produce the right surface. After this all RF columns were subject to a stringent load reversal test, which checked that the unit would respond to a load applied to the drop arm and hence retain the self-centring capability so important on a vehicle constantly having to weave its way through traffic.

One incident comes to mind during the stiff-steering saga on the RF and this concerns one Technical Assistant and one Fitter from the Experimental Shop. For years a test procedure had been in use at Chiswick which involved fitting a second steering wheel above the existing wheel with a connection between the two connected to a pressure gauge. Thus any effort on the slave wheel gives a pressure gauge reading which the test driver shouts out to an observer on the bus. For some unknown reason two vehicles were being tested and unknown to each driver the vehicles were on a collision course. Being so intent on what they were doing a crash ensued and two vehicles were hurriedly dragged into the Experimental Shop. In such circumstances everyone rallies round and a speedy repair is effected!

By and large it should be said that the RF gave a good account of itself and gave London many years of faithful service. In particular its sterling performance on Green Line 727 from Luton to Crawley, serving both Heathrow and Gatwick airports, must be mentioned. This involved spells of motorway running and the original maximum speed of about 45 mph was inadequate. The general engine speed was increased from 1,800 to 2,000 rpm and with the axle ratio change from 5 1/6 to 4 4/7 that had been applied generally by then, about 55 mph could be reached.

The schedule of the 727 service was such that the vehicles covered 2,000 miles per week, and a two-weekly rota was instituted as against the more usual three weeks. Operation was split between St. Albans and Reigate garages, although it was originally planned to use Crawley instead of Reigate, but agreement couldn't be reached with the union.

This led to a somewhat complex operation known as 'Tango' working to cope with late running at the southern end of the route. If it was known that the southbound vehicle was running late, Reigate would put in a spare vehicle, sending it to Crawley, so that it would leave that terminus at the correct time for its northbound journey. In the meantime the late-running vehicle would proceed on its journey until it deposited its last passengers, when it would go to Reigate,

In the late 1960s, when the vehicles concerned were around fifteen years old and had already covered about a million miles each, many of the Green Line RF coaches were modified in appearance to bring them more into line with contemporary ideas, as well as adding such features as quadruple headlights. They were still well up to standard in refinement of running. Seen here in the yard of Victoria garage in May 1967 is RF103, seen in company with a Leyland Atlantean, one of the 'off the peg' models that were to give us many headaches, as described in later chapters.

where the driver would take his much needed break. On reaching Reigate the spare vehicle, now on time, would be taken over by the new driver and the Tango driver would await his next call.

This was rather an expensive system but it helped to keep the service to time. The need for it would have been avoided if Crawley had operated the route, but the drivers' hours situation was a little touch and go. Apart from this operational problem, the RF excelled itself on the arduous route.

It is also worth mentioning that a face-lift in appearance was applied to many of the Green Line RFs in 1966-68. By that date most had covered over a million miles each and some figures quoted in a *Bus and Coach* article are worth repeating—failures in service averaged one per 70,000 miles (about the mileage covered each year), lower than on many more recent types. Overhauls of mechanical units, carried out on the 'as required' basis by then in use averaged about every 200,000 miles for engines and 300,000 miles for the preselective gearboxes. Fuel consumption averaged about 8.2 miles per gallon, perhaps not all that impressive for 30ft. 39-

seat vehicles, but that included the traffic driving in repeatedly crossing central London on most routes and of course the sturdy build with unladen weight of 7 tons 15 cwt which was 5 cwt more than the RT double-decker. Alan Townsin, who wrote the article, tells me he still recalls how good RF89, which he was allowed to drive, felt even though it was reckoned to have covered about 1,140,000 miles and had been in service for eighteen months following rebuilding.

Mention should also be made of the 8ft.-wide version of the RF, designated RFW. This was a small batch of fifteen vehicles delivered in 1951 at about the same time as the first 25 RF vehicles and, like them, for the Private Hire fleet and painted in the same green and grey livery. They were based on basically standard AEC Regal IV 30ft.-long chassis of type 9821E as opposed to the 'Londonised' 9821LT used for the RF (though some minor LTE features were incorporated). The 30ft.-long bodywork was by Eastern Coach Works, London's first of that make, and closely resembled five coaches built at the same time for Tillings Transport (BTC) Limited, the last remnant of the original Tilling business, also operating coaches for private hire work in London and by then part of the British Transport Commission empire. They shared an unusual design of body of rather severe outline not repeated elsewhere but having high-backed seats and other coach features. They were coded 3RF3, the standard RF being basically 2RF2, though strictly speaking this referred to the Central Bus version, the Green Line vehicles being 2RF2/1 as built, for example.

There was also another RF deviation, coded 4RF4, the British European Airways coach. The BEA organisation had decided to put its vehicle requirements—quite large in those days when facilities at Heathrow were limited and many passengers travelled via the BEA terminal at Gloucester Road—under LTE control. Thus the 1½ deck bodywork—in principle very like the Inter-Station Cubs—was designed at Chiswick and built by Park Royal to a style which included many London Transport features. They were in two batches, the first 50 being registered MLL 713-762, delivered in 1952 and a further fifteen being NLP 636-650. No fleet numbers were displayed, but these registration number series were shared with RT and other London Transport vehicles.

Whether it was because they were heavier than the existing RF vehicles I don't know but the brake performance always

The RFW coaches on AEC Regal IV chassis broke new ground in several respects. They were London Transport's first vehicles to have bodywork built by Eastern Coach Works as well as the first, and for some time the only ones, built to the maximum single-deck dimensions introduced in 1950 of 30ft.-long by 8ft.-wide, the standard RF being 7ft. 6in. wide. Two of them, RFW5 and RFW10, are seen in Victoria coach station on Windsor and Hampton Court tour duty in September 1957.

left something to be desired. Eventually the only solution was to fit woven linings all round, instead of the moulded/woven arrangement which had become the standard. This solution was possible as the service was not arduous in that it did not involve frequent stopping.

Even before the RF programme had been completed, thoughts were turning to lighter vehicles. Single-deckers always seemed proportionately heavier than their double-decker counterparts and it is true to say that the 'first generation' underfloor-engined chassis, whether from Leyland, AEC, or Guy, erred on the over-generous side. The RFs were solid, reliable, vehicles which would give up to 27 years service, but they were heavyweights and so, for comparison, three single-deck vehicles were obtained, one each from Bristol, Leyland and AEC. The Bristol-ECW LS5G was very much the standard being produced for the ex-Tilling companies whereas the Leyland was the Tiger Cub with a Saunders Roe body and the AEC-Park Royal Monocoach was, like the Bristol, an integral vehicle, using an underframe which needed temporary bracing to enable it to be driven to the bodybuilders.

The Bristol's designation signified 'Light Saloon', and it was significantly lighter than the RF, the test example weighing 6 tons 7cwt. It had a Gardner five-cylinder engine and five-speed overdrive synchromesh gearbox. The Leyland and AEC were lighter still at 5 tons 12 cwt and 5 tons 11 cwt respectively, the Leyland having an RV16 gearbox as developed from those in the prototype 'one-leggers' whilst the AEC had a preselector, basically as in the RF.

All three were delivered in 1953 and once again went to Reigate to perform on the local 447 service and Green Line

711. It had been thought that there would be justification for an order for further single-deckers, much smaller than the RF fleet, but enough to justify the experiments. However, a survey of requirements showed that the needs would be less than anticipated so it was decided not to pursue the proposed order for lightweight single-deckers and the vehicles were returned in 1954, though the AEC did reappear in 1956-57 after receiving an example of AEC's version of the direct-selector types of gearbox. This vehicle had been registered NLP 635, a number taken from a batch reserved by LTE, although in fact owned by the manufacturer.

Of the three, the Bristol was really a non-starter, as its braking system was of the triple-servo vacuum type, as opposed to the air-pressure system by then long-established in London and which Leyland had adopted as standard for the Tiger Cub and AEC standardised for vehicles with epicyclic transmission. The choice of the Gardner 5HLW engine was probably to save weight, as this vehicle was heavier in itself than either of the other two, but again was a retrograde step as at that time it was noted for the rough idling. The alternative Gardner 6HLW was ruled out on weight grounds and the Bristol AVW, also six-cylinder, was not regarded as all that successful on the Bristol K6B — which, incidentally, had been excluded from the 1948-49 borrowing of Bristol double-deckers for London service, the vehicles taken being either 5LW or AEC 7.7-litre powered.

The Leyland Tiger Cub used a somewhat higher engine speed to obtain adequate power from its small-capacity 5.7-litre capacity, a policy which has never been popular in London, and this vehicle's centrifugal clutch could make smooth gear change difficult, as well as eliminating the useful idle drag of a fluid flywheel.

Overall, the AEC Monocoach seemed the most practical proposition as well as in my view presenting a much cleaner sleek appearance, but in the event the need did not justify any order being placed.

The GS story

It was always a pleasure to visit the Country garages and I have never forgiven the powers-that-be for hiving off that area in 1970. In some ways, this seems to have been almost accidental, for the Greater London Council seems to have been unaware of the scale of LT's activities outside the GLC area. At one stage there was a possibility of its return with the 1980 Transport Act — but that was not to be. However, as part of the London Transport duty to provide a service throughout its area, which in those days included some quite deeply rural localities, there was this fleet of 20-seat Leyland Cubs which by any standard was now ageing, the *newest* dating from 1936. A review was undertaken as to the feasibility of replacing these vehicles which served many outlying areas where the normal bus could not reach. These Cubs were unique in that one or two of them 'slept out' at night, the driver living in the village. One I became acquainted with was the duty numbered DS1 on route 412 which 'slept' at Holmbury St. Mary and was refuelled on its morning journey into Dorking. Passengers used to leave notes on the steering wheel to say — 'Don't wait for me in the morning, I am having a day

off'! This gave a good indication of the service provided by the London Passenger Transport Board and its successors up to the end of 1969, ranging from a high density city service to this personalised country service.

I believe a somewhat similar service existed in the Watford area where the driver used to collect a paper for a resident off the route who sent his dog to meet the bus and collect the paper. On Saturdays, the story goes that the aforesaid gentleman used to meet the bus and pay for the week. How true this story is I do not know but I do recall that when the service was terminated in LCBS days a duplicate GS had to be run to cope with the crowds!

The future of the Leyland Cubs had been part of the general consideration of single-deck needs. They had not built up very big mileages and a plan to rehabilitate them by major overhaul was under active consideration. Eastern Coach Works was asked to quote for rebodying to three alternative designs in 1950, but these plans were swiftly dropped when, just at the crucial moment, LT received a communication from Leyland advising that with effect from some time around 1951 — I don't recall the exact date — spares for Cubs would cease to be manufactured. Accordingly the problem was discussed with colleagues — namely our Country Area people — and after approaching Bedford, Ford and Guy a specification was put together for what turned out to be the GS (Guy Special), a hybrid of that manufacturer's Vixen and Otter.

Out of the research for a suitable design, the Guy chassis was fitted with a Perkins P6 indirect-injection 4.7-litre six-cylinder engine and front-end sheet metalwork by Briggs, similar to that being used on contemporary Thames (Ford) goods models, though with a different grille. The body was by Eastern Coach Works — LTE was under pressure from the British Transport Commission to take up some of ECW's spare bodybuilding capacity, that concern no longer being allowed to build for operators outside the State-owned group. The body seated 26 — six more than the Cub — the aim being to use it on some routes then served by 30- to 34-seat buses on which traffic was falling. Apart from the front end, the bodywork was finished in a style rather like the RF, which it quite resembled, viewed from the rear. Some 84 of the GS class were delivered, beginning in October 1953, replacing both the C and CR classes by January 1954, though these were kept in store pending various route changes later in 1954.

Like the Cub, they were normal-control, and to drive were like an oversize car. The steering turned out to be very heavy, however, and we had to pack out the front wheels to give more castor action. One slight problem arose over the front hubs in that it was possible, with a failed hub race, for the hub itself to work off over the collet washer. A larger size washer soon cured this and history repeated itself on the Leyland National where West Midlands were kind enough to bring back to our minds the problem we had on the GS many years earlier.

With the Perkins P6 engines fuel consumption was not too good and we fitted a different differential ratio to GS45 which was used as a trial vehicle in the Dorking area. Several delightful trips were made on the Dorking routes to test the hill climbing abilities, accompanied by the Garage Engineer — who I was later to meet again when he transferred nearer home to Stevenage and CRL4 was allocated to the 716 route. For some reason the powers-that-be forgot about GS45

The GS was appreciably larger than the Leyland Cub model whose duties it was designed to replace. Here GS2, newly in service from Hitchin in the autumn of 1953, is seen alongside C31 of the 1935 batch of Short Bros-bodied buses. Just visible on the right is one of Birch Bros Leyland PD1 double-deckers.

The mock-up for the GS class in the Experimental Shop in 1952. The end result was quite close to the design shown, which used the Briggs bonnet and front mudguard panels as being used for contemporary Ford goods models. The grille shape was based on that of the Guy Arab double-decker, though simplified in the production version.

This view of the rear of GS alongside an RF illustrates the way in which the detail styling was designed to give an impression of uniformity with the larger vehicle.

and it became a useful vehicle in connection with our everyday work. Judging by the returns of some of the present mini buses this consumption would hardly be criticised.

The P6 engine was not kind to its engine oil and turned it into something like black treacle in about three weeks. This highlighted itself over those garaged at Chelsham, (which although only a few miles south of the busy Croydon area is in quite a hilly part of the North Downs and incidentally was the coldest garage we had in those days) when several vehicles seized up on the run out in the morning. It should be explained that the Chelsham operation was somewhat unusual in that

The GS had a neat appearance — seen here soon after entering service in 1953 from East Grinstead (EG) on the 494 is GS58. The body was largely based on an ECW standard structure and incorporated top-sliding windows for the first time on a bus designed specifically for LT.

The three AEC Reliance buses added to the fleet in 1960 were tried out at various Country garages, including Hemel Hempstead, for which RW3 carries destination and running plates in this view. The Willowbrook bodywork was of a two-doorway type then being used by some municipal fleets but the layout did not prove satisfactory on LTE's Country routes.

the vehicles had a fairly long run to their area of operation — Oxted and Limpsfield, and it was a case of foot down hard on leaving the garage to the point of service.

With the thick, cold, oil the gears driving the oil pump wore away and the engine seized. The answer was a more frequent change of oil for those vehicles — probably with today's oils it would not have been necessary. Gradually, over the years, it was possible to replace these vehicles by RFs such that only a few were handed over to LCBS on its formation. If someone could have looked into the crystal ball and seen the need for mini buses it would have been worthwhile to have stored those GS vehicles for they would have outstripped any of the current mini bus fleet.

I must also mention their allocation to Chiswick staff bus duties, mainly from Reigate and Abbey Wood. Vehicles on such duties have a punishing time and considering the type of vehicle they gave a reasonable account of themselves. Today only a few survive in preservation.

Apart from one experimental batch, over ten years passed between the completion of the GS class deliveries and the next new single-deckers for London Transport. Indeed by 1962, virtually the whole need was being met by the 700 RF-class vehicles, the last T and TD class buses having gone and only a few GS being needed.

However in 1960, three AEC Reliance models with two-door Willowbrook bodywork were added to the Country fleet, being classified RW. Buses of similar general design were being operated by some municipal operators, it being claimed

that the centre exit aided timekeeping when one-man working was in use. The 30ft.-long Reliance had been in large-scale production for provincial operators since 1953, being the chassis version of the Monocoach of which the prototype NLP 635 had taken part in the comparative experiments of that year. The RW-class vehicles were of the comparatively rare version with what AEC called Monocontrol transmission with direct selection. Unlike other AEC models, on the early Reliance this was arranged in the so-called power-pack form, with engine, fluid flywheel and gearbox all in one unit. They proved unpopular as they moved together to spend spells at various country garages — drivers complained of difficulty in drawing up in country lanes so as to make proper use of the two doorways while the power-pack arrangement gave unsatisfactory fluid flywheel life, so after about three years the three vehicles were sold to Chesterfield Corporation.

In 1965 the Reliance Green Line vehicle appeared, initially on the 705 route, at the same time as the rear-engined double-deck XF and XA types for Central Area. The RC, as this version of Reliance was called, was an 11-metre luxury Green Line coach of which fourteen with Willowbrook 39-seat bodywork were purchased. They had 11.3-litre AH691 engines and five-speed gearboxes, giving a higher maximum speed, as well as air suspension for greater comfort, but unfortunately the brakes were not of the same quality. To all intents and purposes they were two-leading-shoe uprated from commercial vehicle brakes and as these vehicles were now covering 2,000 miles per week on the 727 route, continual brake adjustment was necessary — even so the drivers were not happy with them. As these vehicles were somewhat of a flagship for the new Green Line service it was decided to strip the foundation brakes and fit the well-tried and proven RM brakes. Even so, the Unions were not prepared to accept them without a full test with a laden bus. The Union stipulated a Saturday for the fully laden test on the first journey from Crawley at 7.30am or thereabouts.

Driver Eric Dear, the Union representative at the time, was nominated as driver, and we set out following the RF which by then had returned to the 727 route. In those days the 727 was very popular as Gatwick had nowhere developed to its present size. All went well until we left Tadworth Station, after which there is a nice open stretch of road round the side of Epsom Race Course. The RF had got away as it was not so heavily loaded and Eric decided to overtake a slow moving car in front in order to catch up with the RF. As he was overtaking, someone on the right hand side of the road decided to back his car out of his drive. If ever the brakes of a bus were called upon to stop it, this was it. The RC stopped without impact — but only just — and Eric turned to me and said he was satisfied and it wasn't really necessary to go on to Luton! The RC class then resumed service on 727 route once the brakes had been rebuilt.

History was to repeat itself with the Minibus but this is appropriate to a later chapter.

The RC-class vehicles of 1965, with AEC Reliance 11.3-litre chassis and Willowbrook body, of which there were fourteen, were of 11-metre (36ft.) length and 2.5-metre (8.2½in.) width as well as having air suspension and five-speed gearboxes among other features. They were originally allocated to the 705 route linking Windsor and Sevenoaks as shown here by RC11.

One of the problems experienced with the Leyland version of the RT was obtaining satisfactory idling with the Leyland engine's pneumatic governor, an important factor on a bus with fluid transmission in city traffic. Seen here in Duncannon Street in July 1952 are RTW 118, dating from 1949, and an RTL of the LYF-registered batch dating from 1951.

6. Matters mainly mechanical

Engine Comparisons

Because of the historical connections whereby generally AEC had built LGOC's buses, and from 1933 had a 10 year contract to build 90% of the LPTB fleet requirements, London Transport dealt with the Design side of AEC and not the Service Department. In fact the Service Department came to Chiswick periodically to hear our problems and obtain solutions. In addition AEC had the benefit of being close to London Transport and it was easy to keep up the contacts.

A joint Technical Meeting was held monthly at AEC when problems were discussed and decisions taken—and often put into operation the next morning if they were serious enough. In later years I was privileged to be a member of this Joint Consulative Committee. Usually it was led by J. W. Wicks and A. G. Higgins supported by C. E. Smith, the engine specialist and myself as the chassis expert so far as LT were concerned. On the AEC side it was led by Bob Fryers, with Dennis Hickie and George Leather, who looked after our interests on AEC's behalf.

The AEC engine was designed to a large extent around the London Transport maintenance system and, for instance, it was possible to pull down the heads without removing the rocker gear. Unfortunately with the Leyland 0.600 engine this was not the case and of course by the law of cussedness the Leylands suffered a gasket problem. The first Leyland RT—RTL501—was sent to Turnham Green and gasket failure was all too frequent. No real cause could be found and

as the trouble was thought to be due to gasket design, lengthy trials were conducted with all manner of types of gaskets ranging from sandwich construction to all-metal. A lot of the trouble could be traced to lack of follow-up of tightening the heads after running due to the difficulty of doing it. There is a lesson to be learned here.

The AEC engine had a mechanical governor on the fuel pump, giving two-speed control for idling and maximum, whereas the Leyland had a pneumatic type incorporating a butterfly in the air intake manifold. This was inherently 'touchy' as well as difficult to adjust when hot and led to many a burnt hand. The main result was that the idling was apt to be erratic, a nuisance on any vehicle, but a serious defect on a bus with fluid transmission. Modifications were made to the butterfly adjustment to make access easier but it was still difficult to get smooth idling.

Another design difference meant that should injector pipe leakage occur at the injector, the leaking fuel ran outside the engine in the AEC vehicles. With the Leyland engine the connection was inside the valve cover joint and any leakage unusually ran into the engine and contaminated the engine oil. Generally it meant that more care had to be taken on the Leyland in ensuring leak free joints. Injector pipes on both engines needed adequate clipping to prevent failure, which is still true today. At engine overhaul it is a good policy to renew all injector pipes completely.

The mounting of the AEC unit was such that the centre line of mounts passed through the centre of gravity of the engine and as the mountings were circular around the engine axis, the engine tended to twist rather than rock as did the Leyland with its suspended mounting. Generally the drivers' preference was for the AEC arrangement.

Thermo-dynamically there was little to chose between the two engines, both developing the same horse power and torque and giving much the same fuel consumption. Because of the gasket problems, life of the Leyland units tended to be a little worse. The internal design of the engine was left to each manufacturer such that the AEC had an induction-hardened crankshaft whereas the Leyland had a nitrided one. Whilst the performance was much about the same it was not possible to re-nitride the Leyland one at Chiswick and it had to be sent away.

The above relates mainly to the comparison of the AEC A204 engine as used in the RT with the Leyland 0.600 in the RTL, but it also applied to the Routemaster—AV590 versus 0.600.

In general terms, the traditional form of construction as used in the AEC A204 engine, and also the Gardner, with separate crankcases and cylinder block, made it possible to replace just the block when the need arose. It was also apt to be the case for the monobloc type of engine, with combined crankcase and block, to be noisier. There was the occasional problem with oil leaks between block and crankcase but not enough to cause serious complaint. An AV590 problem that was apt to recur was the liner being proud of the block.

One of the problems of engine life comparison between different fleets, quite apart from operating conditions, is the variation between methods. When I was with Brighton Hove & District, during the war years, we changed pistons in situ but it was still reckoned to be the same engine and the change was ignored in engine life statistics. Hence Tilling companies tended to show a better engine life figure—the fact that the bus might be off service for three days didn't count! LT changed the unit rather than do much work on it in the vehicle—anything beyond a head change was an engine change as it was possible to get the vehicle back on the road that day.

Compared with the STL, the RT engine life was excellent. I suppose an average of 200,000 miles was not uncommon, but it should be remembered that we did have the cooling problem earlier on, as well as the factors such as London traffic conditions and the preference for engine change as a means of tackling anything but minor work mentioned above.

Certainly the derating policy with large capacity engines paid off—one only has to quote the seven months life for the relatively small AEC AH505 unit in the Swift. Naturally engine life has deteriorated in recent years because the Routemaster engines are getting old and Chiswick has disappeared. Many other concerns are tackling engine overhaul work and are on a learning curve. One of the biggest problems of AEC engines of that era was 'back door' leaks, which came into prominence in later years.

Fluid Flywheels

It was as early as 1930 that the fluid flywheel appeared on the scene as an alternative to the friction clutch. The Wilson preselective gearbox was already in existence, early examples depending on use of the friction bands in order to start from rest. This was just about acceptable, though prone to judder, on a car, but was a recipe for disaster if applied to a bus with its much greater weight and frequent starts from rest.

What was at first simply called a fluid coupling had been invented much earlier, in 1905, by a German engineer, Dr H. Fottinger and developed at the Vulcan works in Hamburg. In 1926, it was taken up in Britain by an engineer named Sinclair and sometimes became known as the Vulcan-Sinclair coupling. However, it was Laurence Pomeroy, Chief Engineer of Daimler who realised that it solved the problem of smooth starts from rest with the Wilson gearbox. There is a story of him rushing to London to patent the combination of the two and royalties had to be paid to run this combination, production of cars and bus chassis so equipped beginning at Daimler during 1930.

By December of that year, three Daimler CH6 chassis with what Daimler had then christened the fluid flywheel and Wilson gearboxes were delivered to the LGOC, which fitted them with ST-type bodies and put them into service from Harrow Weald in February 1931, numbered DST1-3. The new transmission was very successful and later that year similar sets of fluid flywheels and gearboxes began to be fitted to AEC buses, at first mainly LT-type Renown petrol-engined six-wheelers based at Plumstead garage, where many were still running when I first joined London Transport in 1947. Daimler supplied the units in the early days but from 1934 AEC began making its own Wilson gearboxes, it having been decided that London Transport would standardise on the system.

Having completed my driver training on a crash-gearbox ST on joining the organisation, one of the first tasks was to take my Instructor to the Public Carriage Office at Lambeth to collect the licences. This meant travelling along Vauxhall Bridge Road with the kerb on the nearside and trams on the offside. First thing in the morning the gearbox was cold and the oil thick so it does not need much imagination to realise that by the time Vauxhall was reached, the left arm was very tired as well as the left leg. So I can well understand how the advent of the fluid flywheel for London bus work was received with open arms.

Until very recently, the combination of fluid flywheel and a gearbox incorporating the Wilson epicyclic gear train has remained standard for successive generations of London buses, at first preselective and then steadily developed through air operation and then the direct-selection principle to provide automatic operation. During the RT era virtually complete standardisation applied as both AEC and Leyland chassis employed the AEC fluid flywheel and gearbox. Mention has already been made of some of the problems and evolution of the gearbox.

The fluid flywheel was inherently simple and basically needed no attention provided the oil within it could be prevented from leaking. At the time of build of the RT fleet the fluid flywheel employed a packing gland which needed periodic adjustment. The degree of tightening to compensate for wear which occurs when idling in gear was critical—too tight and the gland burnt out very quickly, not enough and leakage occurred.

The ST was a type of bus that gave good service but its clash gearbox required both skill and physical effort when driving in London traffic, as I found when I learnt to drive one. Here ST551, originally placed in service by the LGOC in December 1930, is seen towards the end of its days — it was one of those with body overhauled by outside contractors, in this case Berkeley Caravans, in 1948. It was among the last standard ST buses to be withdrawn, in January 1950.

The London General Omnibus Company was one of the first bus operators to try out the then new fluid flywheel and Wilson gearbox — three Daimler CH6 chassis were delivered to Chiswick works in December 1930; DST3 is seen, with ST-pattern body, in service from Harrow Weald (HD). Originally, like contemporary ST-type buses, they had no windscreens because of Public Carriage Office disapproval but they were fitted later, as shown, in this case in September 1931.

It was in January 1951 that a Sub Committee was formed by Mr J. W. Wicks to look at the question of development work on fluid flywheels to overcome the problem of increasing gland failures. Out of this came the Llewellyn gland as one of the options and in December 1951 the first two glands were fitted.

A retired engineer, Stan Llewellyn, who had owned a garage on the Great West Road, brought to our attention a face type seal which he thought would provide a better sealing medium. Basically it was a bronze ring on a keyway which itself rode on a ball in the sleeve, pressed on the flywheel runner shaft. This bronze ring pressed against a steel rubbing plate gripped in the gland housing. Leakage between the bronze ring and the sleeve was prevented by a synthetic rubber gaiter. The idea looked good and so two buses were fitted up at Mortlake on Christmas Eve. Needless to say problems arose — not with the principle but the tolerances, which were soon put right, and it was not long before the Llewellyn gland became the standard for all London buses fitted with fluid flywheels and still is today. Over the years, minor improvements have been incorporated.

As in all the best regulated circumstances, trouble suddenly hit the bus business in that flywheels started to leak. The peculiar thing was that it seemed to occur as a sickness, starting with one garage then spreading to another. Naturally the gland was suspect as it was noticed that the rubber gaiter which formed a vital part of the gland showed signs of swelling. Of

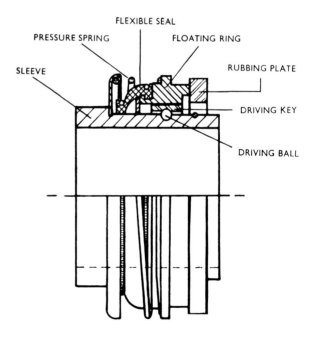

The fluid flywheel was inherently reliable provided the oil it contained did not leak. This was its likeliest source of trouble until the Llewellyn gland solved the problem in 1951. Like most good ideas, it was basically simple, coping with slight misalignment between the rotating parts.

course the neoprene rubber from which it was made was thought to be the cause, but why did it spread through the garage fleet steadily even though the gland itself had been fitted to the vehicle for some time?

I'm not sure that the solution could be attributed to a particular person but someone came up with the information that a change had been made to the fluid flywheel oil as it had arbitrarily been decided that the originally called-up specification of a highly-refined diesel engine oil was unnecessary, and a cheaper variety would be just as good!

This change had gone unnoticed and the less highly refined oil had started to appear in the new deliveries to garages. On occasions when it became necessary to refill flywheels, therefore, after say an engine change, the new oil went in. It appeared that the new 'cheap' oil contained sulphur and other harmful ingredients which attacked the neoprene. The only solution was to change the neoprene gaiter for one made from Viton, which was resistant to practically anything. Needless to say a reversion was made to a good quality engine oil as before and no change has been authorised since.

Almost all installations of fluid flywheels and Wilson gearboxes in buses up to the late 'fifties had the gearbox sited some distance behind the engine and fluid flywheel. This was partly because of the need to fit the depth of the epicyclic gearbox into the transmission line at a point which neither intruded above the floor nor ran into ground clearance problems. However, it had a beneficial effect on both fluid flywheel and gearbox temperature and the importance of this only came to light when the trend to rear engines caused designers to fit the three items together into power pack assemblies to save space in what were often cramped installations.

We had a warning of this effect in the three RW-type AEC Reliance buses purchased in 1960, which, although mid-engined, had engine, fluid flywheel and gearbox in one assembly — despite running in the Country Area, they gave enough trouble to hasten their departure after only about four years. Both the Leyland Atlantean double-deckers of the XA class purchased in 1965 and the Merlin MB single-deckers, particularly when in large-scale service from 1968, showed up the same problem. The combination of running in heavy traffic, with the inevitable heat build-up of long periods of idling in gear or with the bus inching forward, and the power-pack concentration of heat from both the engine and fluid flywheel (with the latter encased rather than being self-ventilating as previously) produced soaring temperatures. The use of aluminium alloy for fluid flywheel casings made matters worse, as the greater expansion of this material created excessive end-thrust on the crankshaft and gave rise to engine as well as flywheel failures, especially on the Atlantean.

A change to S.G. iron for the fluid flywheel overcame that problem and the charged coupling principle, in which fluid flywheel and gearbox oil supply is combined into one system arranged to circulate so as to dissipate the heat, brought temperatures under control. However, a key to much of the progress made in transmission reliability was the quality of oil. In the early days of Wilson gearboxes, the oil used in them tended to turn into something more like glue after only a few weeks of operation. Here the part played by A. T. Wilford, London Transport's Chief Chemist, must be acknowledged

— yet another instance of the specialist knowledge available to an organisation large enough to employ experts in each field. He created an oil known as SB2152 which overcame that problem and remained in use through the STL, RT and RM eras until 1968, when it proved not quite able to cope with the more difficult environment of the power-pack type of layout. Leyland became involved with oil specifications, introducing Spec E and Spec F, eventually getting it right though success rather depended in ensuring that certain constituents were not in the oil.

In the interests of economy it was once suggested that water could be used in the flywheel. Water alone could not be used as it would attack the bearings, so an additive was used, like cutting fluid. A stalled test on the bench dynamometer soon produced a tremendous pressure rise as the water turned to steam — and the test was hurriedly shut down before the flywheel reached bursting pressure.

The basic objective behind the fluid flywheel is to provide a convenient means of allowing slip during the process of starting from rest, without any need for use of a clutch pedal. It does so automatically and as the bus gains speed the amount of slip is reduced, falling to about 4% at full speed and torque. This unwanted slip at speed means there is a slight loss of efficiency compared with a conventional clutch which ceases to slip when the driver lifts his foot from the clutch pedal.

Fuel consumption was regarded as very important, especially in the days before fuel duty rebate came in during the 'sixties. Tests on means of saving fuel were frequently being carried out and there was a constant awareness of this 4% slip within the fluid flywheel at speed. With the advent of the RT the fluid flywheel had been increased in diameter to reduce the slip, but when idling in gear the drag torque increased. To reduce the drag, which occurred for a relatively large amount of time with idling in gear in traffic, a baffle plate was fitted which reduced the vortex available. Unfortunately it increased the slip when driving so its size was a compromise between the opposing operations.

Extensive bench tests were done by Self Changing Gears, Coventry, at their wartime factory at Burbage, to determine the effect of various sizes of baffle plates and eventually a compromise size was chosen. What was not realised at the time was the tremendous force exerted on this baffle which led to the failures of the bolts holding the baffle of the flywheel with somewhat disastrous results. A campaign change was effected once the calculations showed the seriousness of the position, again proving the often-quoted maxim that having analysed the trouble, it is usually easier to overcome it rather than change the design and start upon another learning curve!

Centrifugal clutch experiments

Attempts continued to be made to improve flywheel slip and a centrifugal clutch was tried, at Mortlake garage in mid-1953. The idea was that the clutch unit had a series of inclined radial ball tracks on its rear into which were fitted fairly large ball bearings. The theory was that as the engine speeded up, the ball bearings flew out under centrifugal force and caused the clutch plate to move into contact with the flywheel — making a solid drive. Unfortunately the wear products got into the ball tracks and prevented the balls from dropping back when the engine slowed down. What used to happen was that the engine would stall, the balls then clattered back and only then was the transmission disengaged. Needless to say this idea never got beyond the prototype stage.

It was on the Atlanteans that a trial was made to fit centrifugal weights in the flywheel so that at a calculated speed the flywheel was solid. This was apt to come into effect too early and thus did not allow the engine to develop full torque at start and with the hysteresis effect the weights were slow in dropping back to turn the fluid flywheel into a straight fluid unit, causing transmission rattle on coming to rest. Because the weights took the place of some of the fluid within the flywheel, fuel savings did not materialise and temperature problems did not improve.

Still in pursuit of improved fuel consumption another dry clutch was tried in the form of a pair of brake shoes which pivotted outwards under the action of centrifugal force against a brake drum which was part of the flywheel, as opposed to the ball bearing idea. Although in theory there was no slip once the 'shoes' engaged the drum, there was the absence of idling drag, which is helpful when in very slow-moving traffic, even though a source of waste when stationary, and this scheme was not popular with the drivers. Another venture was to fill the flywheel with small lead shot but this never got beyond the development stage.

Another attempt at improving efficiency was the use of a coupling based on the Hydrostatic principle, a Self-Changing Gears invention by Mr Miller. Here a series of sun wheels at the periphery acted as pumps and as soon as the engine speeded up centrifugal valves would operate and starve these sun wheels of oil so that they locked up and the drive was made. Unfortunately the coupling was not very oil tight and it was difficult to keep it in service for any length of time.

Most of these interesting experiments were carried out in conjunction with manufacturers, notably AEC, Leyland and Self-Changing Gears, and London Transport more than played its part in this important area of research. In the present economic and political climate this type of work has dwindled to a mere trickle and one has to look to manufacturers outside this country.

Fires — fluid flywheel and others

One of the first occasions that I came in contact with fluid flywheels fires was on a wartime Daimler on Putney Bridge. Its 7.7-litre AEC engine had ball joints fitted at either end of the throttle shaft, and with wear one of the balls had pulled out of its housing which allowed the engine to race away. This frightened the driver and he put the bus into top gear which slowed the engine down whilst he went for help, but set in train the process of converting energy into heat.

When he returned the bus was a blazing inferno. Naturally the moral of this story was to turn off the fuel at the emergency tap, not to put it into gear, and finally a design improvement ensured that should a throttle rod ever come disconnected, the fuel pump rack reverted to the idle position and not full load.

Another incident of this kind caused a minor redesign of the RT accelerator linkage, with a spring attached at or near the

Mechanical failures could lead to disastrous fires. Here RT85, one of the first production batch dating from 1940, which burnt out in Kensington while on route 74 on 14th May 1949. It is seen after being towed to Aldenham — in this case the reported cause was a crankcase explosion.

fuel pump lever, and was applied not only to new bus chassis of all types coming off the line at AEC but adopted on existing RT buses. It is standard on all London buses.

Occasional fires of this type had thus been known on vehicles fitted with fluid flywheels but as indicated, generally this was due to a defect developing elsewhere. It was in later years, well into the Routemaster era, that flywheels fires became a little more serious and an investigation was carried out in some depth with the aid of Ricardos, the Consulting Engineers at Shoreham-by-Sea.

Unfortunately for legal reasons the whole story cannot be told even today, but after a particular incident, the second with the same driver, I was given RTW100 (which had been involved in an accident and was for the scrap heap) in order to investigate more fully the theories I had formed. It was believed that the bus which caught fire had been put into gear and the engine deliberately operated at full stalled speed torque. In this context, the word 'stalled' means that the vehicle is stationary but the engine is running as fast as the drag from the fluid flywheel will allow. Heat build-up is rapid.

Accordingly RTW 100 was prepared for the test by fitting a pressure connection at one of the filler plug positions, so that the internal pressure within the flywheel could be taken. Provision was made so that the temperature on the outside of

A test on the effect of continuous running a fluid flywheel at maximum stalled speed carried out on RTW100, already condemned to scrap because of accident damage, produced spectacular results. Volumes of smoke resulted and then, as we walked away thinking we had taken the test far enough, it burst into flames.

the flywheel could also be taken. Cameras were stationed alongside the bus and the offside lower saloon windows were removed so that a speedy escape could be made from the inside of the bus where two of us were stationed. As a precaution a three inch hose, connected to a water hydrant, was laid outside the bus.

The test was carried out on the forecourt of the now defunct Stonebridge Garage. Our full team consisted of Terry Terrington, the Divisional Mechanical Foreman of what was the 'C' Division, Basil Holthusen, our Chief Fireman, Ralph Latter from the Laboratory, plus his photographer and the Garage Foreman, Ted Bull, who later worked for me as a Messenger, with Dick Rands, my assistant, and myself. After twenty minutes of idling at maximum stall speed, which was about 600rpm, all we could produce were volumes of dense smoke. Everyone thought that such a state of events was going too far so we shut down and decided to go and have a cup of tea.

As we walked away there was a terrific explosion and the bus burst into flames. At last we were on the right track and my theories had proved correct, but the problem was to explain them.

This was where Ricardos came in since they had investigated crankcase explosions on ships, and it appeared that the situation was somewhat similar. From test bench results it had been found that at critical temperatures there was a spontaneous ignition of the oil vapour, provided it could mix with the appropriate amount of air. In the case of the fluid flywheel fires there was always a leakage of oil from the periphery or gland before ignition took place, and it was possible to ascertain the temperature at which self-ignition took place. As a result of this, fusible plugs were fitted so that if the flywheel got overheated then the plug would fuse and let the oil out. Whilst this was not popular with the authorities it did prevent a fire. In addition it was the rule that after a plug fused the garage had to make a check on certain aspects of the vehicle and submit a return. In this way the reason for over-

heating was explained and put right. Fortunately after this routine was introduced flywheel fires became almost unknown from this cause.

In spite of this some fires still occurred and these were now being attributed largely to the electrical system. It had always been the practice to have insulated-earth-return on London Transport vehicles and not rely on earthing via the chassis. With the advent of 'standard' vehicles this rule had to be relaxed and in order to further investigate the problem the help of the Underground was sought. With two cables, one positive and one negative, it was shown that under certain environmental situations, such as hot engine compartments, there was a migration, or slow movement, of the copper conductors towards one another once the insulation, which was generally neoprene, got hot and soft. A short circuit then took place, often with disastrous results. Again it was the practice on London Transport-designed vehicles to carry the two cables in separate conduit so that migration was prevented. Although not directly related to this area of work it was found possible to demonstrate this by fitting up cables in the sub-station and pass fairly hefty currents. These tests led to the change of insulation covering to hyperlon, which resisted the effect of heat, and this was called up in future specifications.

Another interesting development in relation to fires was that arising from the air compressor. It is normal to have a flexible hose between the air compressor and its connection to the rigid pipe on the chassis. Because of the heat from the compressed air it is usual to ensure that there are at least several feet of rigid pipe before fitting the flexible hose. On the Merlin and Swift rear-engined single-deckers placed in service in 1968-72 the length of steel pipe was at an absolute minimum and much of the heat remained in the compressed air by the time it reached the flexible hose. For some reason air compressors using oil supplied from the engine for lubrication purposes have a habit of carrying over a lot of oil, often in the form of carbon particles. With time these glowing lumps of carbon blocked up the hose and gradually burned through it.

A test was conducted on a vehicle one evening in Chiswick and glowing carbon was seen shooting out from the punctured hose, setting light to anything handy. Sparks were also seen to emanate from the safety valve as the blockage in the hose caused an increase in pressure in the head of the compressor, causing the safety valve to blow. A solution suggested by the vehicle builder was to fit an armoured hose, but apart from being expensive it eventually blocked just the same. The solution adopted by London Transport was to fit a reasonable quality hose but change it annually, which was a much cheaper solution.

Of course a better solution was to fit a separate air intake for the compressor instead of taking it from the engine manifold. Naturally once a compressor starts passing oil in any quantity it should be changed. A parallel with the RM will show that a compressor with its own lubrication is a far better bet and does not suffer from any of these problems but there was a reluctance to do just this, possibly for financial reasons from the vehicle manufacturers.

With these modifications fires on buses (other than those started deliberately by passengers) are really a thing of the past, simply because the reasons for the fires were fully investigated as to the cause and the solution determined, not just a routine of changing things being implemented.

Brakes

Mention has already been made of the famous combination of brake linings that had been evolved to meet the London Transport conditions of service. Other operators have tried this combination but their conditions of service are not the same and they have found that other solutions are possible. All went well until the manufacturer of Chekko XL3 decided to sell out to British Belting and Asbestos who made the Mintex range of linings. They had planned to introduce one of their woven linings in place of the XL3 but it was found unsuitable.

So yet another crash programme of brake testing started. Three of us were involved, Dick Rands, who later left to join the Nestles organisation in charge of their fleet, Trevor Bearn, who subsequently died after a tragic illness, and the author. Dick tested vehicles at Hounslow, Trevor at Merton and yours truly at Crawley/Reigate, often on a Saturday morning in the early hours. History was to some extent to repeat itself in later years when non-asbestos linings started to appear on the scene.

It might be worthwhile to outline the type of test that was employed, often referred to as a drag test based on the Middle Row work of earlier years. The linings are first fitted to the brake shoes and then ground (or linished to use the correct term) to a newly turned brake drum. Some manufacturers seem to grind the brake drum to give a good appearance but this is not ideal and often promotes squeal due to the rapidly repeated stick/slip effect. There are schools of thought that do not see the need to grind the linings, but this is the only way to ensure a good contact between lining and drum. Failure to achieve this will result in braking taking place on parts of the lining causing local hot spots which destroys the resins in the lining. It also raises severe stresses in the brake drum due to uneven contact and can cause brake drum fracture.

A vehicle is selected which requires the majority of linings changed and the test set fitted. The vehicle is then checked out to ensure that the braking system is functioning correctly and a deceleration test carried out. At one time this was carried out on a quiet stretch of road but such things became impractical

and latterly the Chiswick Works site was used out of normal hours. A Tapley instrument is used to measure the retardation of a full brake stop at a measured pressure and the temperature of the brake drum measured. The bus is then driven in second gear with the brakes on for a measured distance to keep the speed at 10 mph and a repeat brake application made. Thus a series of deceleration is obtained against brake drum temperature and a graph can be plotted. Over the years a whole history of brake lining tests has been compiled which shows that London Transport and its successor, London Buses, have maintained an excellent standard of braking efficiency. It would be true to say that none of the approved brake linings have given cause for concern. Finally a further check is carried out as the brakes cool down to see if any 'damage' has been done to the linings and this is known as the Recovery Test.

It could be argued that this type of drag test is not representative of service conditions but it is a ready method of measuring brake efficiency at service temperature levels. Repeat tests are made during the life of the linings and finally the linings are removed and measured for wear and also to observe the condition of the surface of the drum. The most desirable condition of a drum is a dull matt surface, not highly polished as squeal will invariably occur.

Squeal is a subject which has concerned many learned people for years and many technical papers have been written about the problem. From the purely practical aspect all that can be said is that to eliminate it a stiffening flange is necessary on the mouth of the drum with an asbestos-lined band around the outside of the drum itself. It might well be appropriate to recount how brake squeal was cured on the Merlin rear-engined single-deckers — which were called 'cattle trucks' by the passengers but in the business were often called after a well-known lady Minister of Transport. These vehicles were equipped with an almost flangeless brake drum as the buses were built to a standard specification under the rules of the New Bus Grant. Squeal was abominable and the idea hit upon was to bolt on a flange in two halves to make it similar to the flanged drum of the RT/RM. It cured the squeal but absorbing the high frequency vibrations caused the nuts to unwind on the bolts holding the two halves together and the 'flange' fell off. The squeal had in the meantime disappeared!

Another little story concerns the anti-squeal band. People suggested that it was an unnecessary extra and should be discarded. The Chief Mechanical Engineer quite wisely decided that it was imprudent to be too hasty and decreed that an experiment should be carried out. It so happened that Twickenham Garage was still in existence and they happened to run, amongst other routes, the 27a at the time. As this route passed Chiltern Court, Baker Street, where the Chief Mechanical Engineer (Road Services), in those days Bill Durrant, resided, there was more than one good reason why the 27a was a good choice of location for the test. After two or three days, as vehicles were having their anti-squeal bands removed, the Chief observed that the buses were starting to squeal and on enquiry he was informed of what was going on. Needless to say the experiment was stopped in its tracks and anti-squeal bands were refitted and are still a must today. Nevertheless attempts have been made to find other alternatives but none have come up to the performance of the existing type.

Much has been written of the values of braking that a passenger can stand within the realms of comfort. A bus spends a good deal of its time braking and accelerating, with little time at constant speed. Thus any improvement in either or both could have an effect on the running time of a route. Much work has been done on improving acceleration times but the old rule of 0-30 mph in 18 seconds is about as much as the passenger can stand. To look at the braking effect a selection of staff was collected from the Drawing Office, both sexes and all sizes, and taken for a bus ride during which time stops were made at varying values and noting what happened to the seated passenger. Observations noted included such things as 'passenger started to lift off the seat'; 'forward movement'; and in the extreme 'tended to go over the seat in front'. Probably very unscientific but very interesting!

Any substantial reduction in running time can sometimes save the provision of a bus on a route. To this end recent work was carried out on Route 290 out of Fulwell where all the fuel pumps were set up to give better acceleration. However the result of the test showed little improvement as traffic congestion tended to nullify any improvement.

When I first came to Chiswick brake lining requirements were not so arduous — buses were lighter in construction and traffic flowed, which is more than can be said for today. In brake testing it is always the practice to heat the linings above the maximum working temperature — just in case there is the odd exceptionally hot day one summer. My immediate superior, Stan Beacon by name, and who, like his father, had spent his life with London Transport, at Willesden Garage, had just completed a brake test on an STL and was bringing the bus back to Chiswick via Turnham Green Terrace when the traffic lights suddenly changed and a cyclist in front stopped — but Stan couldn't as the linings had faded! The result was one crumpled bicycle — which was soon sorted out as brake testing on the public roads was not allowed!

Another incident arose when there appeared to be brake troubles around, possibly as a result of wear and tear over the war years when standards had lapsed to some extent. A little sub-committee was set up to deal with the problem and one of our Experimental Inspectors, Alf Dowden, was put on the job. The bus in question was an STL out of Norwood on which the garage claimed they had done everything possible. The District Engineer and his assistant were old servants of the Board and one was a little deaf — it was quite a comedy team of the first order to listen to them talking. However, our examination of the bus soon indicated what was wrong — the body had collapsed onto the brake rods stopping the full force being applied to the brake cams. The team was so successful that Alf became the Resident Inspector at AEC for London Transport and his associate was put into Dalston as Day Foreman when the resident Foreman died suddenly and the District Engineer retired the same week-end.

One of the tasks that came my way was the operation of the prototype Routemasters and a part of that task was to oversee the rota work. In those days there was a grade of Divisional Foreman — Mechanical, Coachmaker and Electrical. They were a grand bunch of fellows and a bond of friendship soon sprang up. It was the practice to show them how to service the vehicles at the garage and then let them teach the staff. For the prototype it was essential to make an inspection of the bus to see if all was in order and on this one occasion the regular fitter was on holiday and the one who looked after cars had to do the necessary. One of the tasks was to adjust the brakes because at this time automatic brake adjusters could not be incorporated, as on the 3RT, since the brake set-up was smaller in diameter by one inch. For some reason I did not oversee the adjustment and spinning the wheel seemed to indicate that the brakes were just rubbing. The bus went into service on Route 91 to which RM2 was rostered. Within an hour the driver, Freddie Fox, came back in complaining that the brakes were non-existent. Knowing that they had been adjusted on rota the bus was taken from him and I attempted to make a test run. Turning out of Belmont Road was simple, a left-hand turn into Town Hall Avenue and a little blip on the throttle approaching the Town Hall immediately in front of me. A gentle application of the brakes, to no affect, a grab at the handbrake managing to come to a halt gently in front of the Town Hall. A subdued driver then proceeded back to the Green at crawling pace where it was found that the brakes had been wound backwards, turning the cam on its back so that nearly all the travel of the brake cylinder was taken up. Instructions were soon issued to ensure that the brakes were wound on in the direction of the wheel rotation when the vehicle was going forwards but luckily it was later found possible to adapt the automatic brake adjusters to operate from the brake lever movement.

There are many stories like this, some of which cannot be told, but it all emphasises that bus operation and all its peculiarities cannot be learned sitting at a desk. Experience can only be gained — not taught. Those days at Turnham Green taught me a lot and many happy hours were spent there and on the road, even on Christmas Day when a reasonable bus service was operated, but with nothing stronger to drink than tea.

As is well known brake liners contain asbestos and in certain forms it can be dangerous to health. Given that precautions are taken and blue asbestos is not used, there should be little trouble. However, asbestos is a highly emotive subject judging by the somewhat unbalanced view sometimes put over by the media. Work has been going on for the last few years to find a replacement material, including glass fibre, Kevlar etc but although some alternatives started off well they have failed to stay the course. Some countries and even British bus companies have seen fit, because of industrial relations problems, to adopt such a lining. It hasn't quite given the performance of the asbestos, but work still progresses in this field.

Suspension

Until the last war, suspension on buses had been fairly standard — just rigid axles and leaf springs fitted with shock absorbers. One argument that still has not been settled even today is whether the leaves should be greased so as to reduce friction. On the other hand there were those who argued that to reduce friction would increase the deflection of the spring and cause earlier fatigue failures. Personally my support goes for the lubrication lobby.

One of the disadvantages of leaf springs is that they are mounted inside the wheel track, and indeed on a bus, with twin tyres at the rear and steering angles to be accommodated at the front, the available width is limited, which is not the best position to give a stable ride. One of the tests that a bus has to pass is the tilt test whereby, with the upper-deck loaded in the case of a double-deck vehicle, the vehicle must reach an angle of at least 28° before any wheel leaves the ground. When the post-war RT was first tilted it was touch and go and in the end side restrictor plates had to be fitted to stiffen up the springs. Before coming into action there is a bit of freedom so that the vehicle suspension has a chance to function. One occasion comes to mind on a Fleetline vehicle where a similar device known as a Fox anchor clip is employed and which does nearly the same thing. It was noted as loose by the Ministry Examiner who demanded it be tightened up. This was done with the result that the vehicle rode as if there was no suspension. A hurried explanation was made to all and sundry as to the foolishness of this action — including convincing the Examiner as to the error of his ways!

When it came to the RM, the Chief Mechanical Engineer decreed that this vehicle should seek to have the comfort of a private car. This of course spelt the end of leaf springs and a move to consider independent suspension was made. To some extent private car practice was followed by using unequal wishbones, with a spring mounted between with a concentric shock absorber.

Firstly, the internal friction of a bus leaf spring was not appreciated and therefore the settings in the shock absorber were grossly under-estimated. In fact it was soon realised that often, in a leaf spring, the shock absorbers contributed very little to the total damping effect and hence suspension comfort. It is of interest that the RT was not fitted with shock absorbers, and perhaps a commentary on the good state of repair of London's streets that they were not found necessary, though there were occasional complaints from the Country Area.

RM1 was fitted with Newton and Bennett shock absorbers, a company who were local at Acton. The tests were conducted with their Chief Engineer, Jack Rodway, whom I had known personally when he was at Clayton Dewandre, and consisted of driving over a series of planks of different thicknesses. It soon became evident that the shock absorbers were doing very little to damp out the deflections and the decision was taken on the spot to double the bump and rebound loads within the shock absorber. This was a big change and soon showed up in the life of the units and steps were put in hand to improve materials. Much of the further development work arising from service operation is described in my book *The Routemaster Bus* but it might be of interest to refer to a tyre wear problem that developed later.

To all intents and purposes the tyre can be regarded as acting like a spring which is in series with the main suspension spring. Therefore the natural frequency of the tyre is of some consequence and the effect of a radial tyre against a cross-ply can be very critical on this 'series' suspension system. To investigate this more fully a high-speed camera was fitted to an RM and the tyre marked at 90° intervals. Here the effect was shown that under certain conditions the tyre left the road at 180° intervals thus producing flats on the tyre surface which became worse as time went on. It just shows how tyre development can have an effect on other things which were not appreciated at the time.

In 1976 a suspension system had been developed by

Tyre wear can be a problem with independent suspension unless correctly designed and adjusted. This high speed camera installation on a Routemaster was used for tyre wear tests.

Automotive Products, known as the 'active ride', and had been fitted to a Ford Granada and later to one or two ambulances. My first contact with this system was when I was met at Leamington by Bob Pitcher, who was in charge of their development, and was taken for a ride in the Granada. Without warning the car was driven round a roundabout at about 60 mph and remained vertical! Further increase in speed took place until the adhesion of the tyre to the wheel became critical. Naturally it would not be desirable to allow buses to take corners at speed but it did illustrate the potential of the system. Plans were then made to equip a bus with this system and for a variety of reasons it was arranged to sell RM1, which had now come out of service, to Automotive Products, just for the duration of the experiment.

Some difficulty was experienced in getting the speed of the swashplate pump within its safe limits, but eventually a safe system was produced and it gave a very stable ride. On completion, the bus, along with RM2, was taken to Ford's test track at Dunton and put through its paces alongside the Granada. Having reached this stage it was decided to fit the system to a service bus and RM 116 was chosen, again operating out of Stamford Brook. The interest in testing this bus was for us to be prepared, should it be demanded, that the platform be lowered at Bus Stops. This could easily be achieved by forcing the strut to collapse by placing a larger cylinder over the end, rather than letting the air pressure out as South Yorkshire did on one of their 'kneeling' Leyland Nationals. This leads to delay when moving off as the pressure has to be restored whereas in the active ride the suspension pressure is still in the strut. A good deal of interest was shown in the bus when it was in service, including some from the Japanese, but in the latter case they seemed more interested in the RM design itself, judging by the clicking cameras.

Auxiliary Drives on Buses

Looking at the various auxiliary systems of a bus — belt-driven alternators, hydraulic brakes, air-operated gearboxes, electric wipers, heating and ventilating systems, with usually a combination of hydraulics and electrics, air and electric doors, the sum total of horse-power required is quite alarming. Each of the systems has its problems, at least for operation in London.

Over the years a close relationship developed with Lockheed, who were later to become Automotive Products. It so happened that they had a forward thinking department — a sort of think tank — and after looking at the problem of power requirement, I discussed it with their head, Wilf Bainbridge. Clearly it would be more economical to rationalise the type of power used since the peak of power for one source could coincide with the trough of another. Years of development had gone into the Routemaster braking system, even before the bus went on the road, and a lot of pioneer work was based on aircraft application which had to have a good safety record. Therefore it was decided in discussions which took place in 1977 to attempt to rationalise the provision of power for hydraulic services. Brakes were considered a safety-critical item and it was decided to have an entirely separate system but incorporate the pump in tandem with a swashplate which would provide all the other services. The operation was code named 'Hydrapak' and the project was approved by our chief Mechanical Engineer, Stan Smith, who was very far-sighted.

The first item that had taken our interest was the power steering. This is a closed circuit which is pumping oil around the system until power is required to turn the wheels. This is achieved by blocking the return of oil to the header tank and directing the pressure to the ram cylinder operating the steering linkage. To avoid too great a contrast with the RT, on which there was no power assistance, the system employed was not full-power but only came in after a certain wheel effort was exerted. Thus the call on the power source was somewhat limited and much of the horse-power was used in pumping the oil round the power steering system. Clearly there was an advantage to be gained by using accumulator pressure and it was found possible by incorporating a fourth accumulator, adding to those used for the brake system, to do just this. One RM was converted, operating from Stamford Brook, and it proved just possible to maintain sufficient reserve of power to operate the steering system. For a full scale trial the Plessey pump providing the pressure would have needed some modification but the principle had been proved.

With rear-engined buses it was virtually impossible to operate the 'throttle' system (or more correctly the linkage between accelerator and the engine-mounted fuel-injection pump) with direct linkage, as was proved on the early Atlanteans. A valve very much like the brake valve was eventually designed and tested — by this time on DMS1332 which had been fitted with an experimental Clayton Dewandre hydraulic brake system in 1973. It was one of several hydraulic Fleetlines withdrawn from service at the time it was decided that the Fleetline was supposedly unsuitable for London, this one being retained for the Hydrapak development work at Chiswick. More on these vehicles appears in Chapter Eight.

Door gear is another area where problems seem to arise, usually within the first month of service. Hydraulic operation of doors is not new, having been tried on some Bournemouth trolleybuses before the War, but being mounted overhead often soaked passengers when the unit failed! Nevertheless a design was produced, and one or two problems arose with manual operation on failure of the system, the law now having been modified so as to put a figure on the force required to open the doors when the power operation has failed (with further complications in recent months to cover the situation when someone is trapped in the doors). An installation was made on DMS1332, used as a test vehicle vehicle for several of these related ideas. Although not so fitted on the bus in question, in production models the motor would be placed at floor level to prevent any leakage dropping on to passengers.

One of the areas which was ripe for development was the relationship between starter, batteries and alternator. Obviously the starter has to be on the engine, whilst the alternator is usually engine-driven, and batteries are placed wherever there is a space. A good example of the latter is the Leyland National, where the batteries are placed at the front of the bus on the later versions, underneath the driver, to even the weight distribution by putting some weight on the front axle. The alternator has a run of about 36ft. to the battery, and then the battery has another 36ft. run back to the starter motor. What a voltage drop in the cable!

It was here that hydraulics would allow the alternator to be placed at the most effective suitable position by fitting a hydraulic motor to it. Furthermore, it could be driven at constant speed, rather than variable speed as it generally is when belt-driven. Additionally it offered a further advantage in that it could be smaller, and along with CAV it was found that a 5in. machine could be employed. Sperry Vickers, who were contributing to this experiment, arranged to carry out various tests on the setup at their Laboratories near Portsmouth and came up with an alternator speed of about 1350 rpm instead of 3500 rpm. Quite a saving. Unfortunately I was not permitted to take this to its final conclusions on DMS1332 but I believe there is a future to specifying the relationship between alternator, battery and starter if a more reliable response is required.

Windscreen wipers have always been a source of trouble and it is said that all the time it rains a wiper fails every minute. Whether this is true I know not, but it does give some idea of the problem. Basically the requirements have worsened with the development of screens curved in more than one plane. Added to this, screens have got bigger and blade lengths longer. In spite of this the swept area has not always been adequate and hence the pantograph wiper was developed. This was fine until the bus went through the washing machine and the brushes wrapped themselves around the blades. Again, the washing machine manufacturers were simultaneously trying to improve their product by increasing brush pressures. About this time I was dealing with Maxwell Transmissions, run by an old friend, Peter Windsor-Smith, previously responsible for bus design at Daimler, who had designed a new but much simplified gearbox which we were later to try first in a DMS at Croydon and then in a Metrobus. This firm, then located at Loughborough, was a small unit but could do experimental one-offs without all the difficulties that big organisations seem to encounter. A design was produced which would wipe a rectangular area by a vertical blade running in a track above the screen. Movement would be controlled by a double-acting hydraulic cylinder. Pressures of

Looking like any other London Fleetline, DMS1332, built as a standard Gardner-engined example with MCW body in 1972, was fitted with a prototype power-hydraulic brake system developed by Clayton Dewandre, delaying its entry into service by almost a year until August 1973. It was allocated to Turnham Green so that it could enter service under the eye of our department at Chiswick. Then in 1977, it was chosen for another experiment, the Hydropak system of operating a number of auxiliaries from a common hydraulic circuit so as to economise on power demand. As a result, it was transferred to Chiswick after Turnham Green ceased operating Fleetlines.

time needed for the gearbox work meant it was not possible to complete it. I believe a somewhat similar 'rectangular wipe' idea was used with an electric motor on some vehicles, including London taxis and various buses, in the mid-1930s.

In another area of auxilliary drives and in order to reduce labour costs it was felt that it would be worthwhile to look at self-sealing couplings so that on changing an engine it was only necessary to release the coupling rather than undo coupling nuts or hoses. Because of the cost of such components, the couplings tended to become rather large and this part of the experiment was put in abeyance.

It was intended to look at heating and ventilating, some of which work had already been done on FRM1. Here hydraulic motors reversed the direction according to whether fresh air was needed inside the bus or it was required to draw out the hot air from inside the bus. As stated this system existed on FRM1 but had the disadvantage that at constant speed the valves had some difficulty in reversing the motors, as the back pressure was rather high. However, it was decided that the system was generally satisfactory, but needed some refinement which could not be done within the confines of the work.

It was impossible to put together all this work on one vehicle, but it was anticipated that there would be savings in the horse-power required to drive all the ancillaries which are now part of the modern bus. A similar scheme for utilising electrical energy was proposed under the name of 'Elektrapak' but with all the cut backs, this and similar schemes had to be put on ice. Whether they will every be pursued in the future is debatable, but it seems unlikely. This type of research and development is one clear victim of the break-up of London Transport and as the country's other major operator — the National Bus Company — has also been broken up any future initiatives will have to come from the manufacturers.

7. Methods and alternatives

The late Mr A. A. M. Durrant

In a book such as this, it would be impossible to omit reference to the career and influence of someone who, at the time of his retirement, was the longest-serving chief officer in any sphere of London Transport, and more directly relevant here, the person who guided LT's bus design and maintenance policy from its beginning in 1933 until his retirement in 1965.

A. A. M. Durrant, unofficially known as 'Bill Durrant', joined the London General Omnibus Co Ltd in 1919 and in 1929 became Assistant Superintendent of Rolling Stock, then Assistant Chief Engineer in 1931, Engineer in 1932 and Chief Engineer in 1933.

On the formation of London Transport he was appointed Engineer (Central Buses), His counterpart as Engineer (Country Buses) being Mr W. A. C. Snook. Mr Durrant was appointed to the new post of Chief Engineer (Buses and Coaches) in 1935. In the dark days of May 1940, when the German army was sweeping through Europe and Britain was soon to find itself fighting alone, Mr Durrant was asked to switch his expertise from buses to tanks and departed to join a Tank Board that had been formed, becoming Director of Research and Development and Controller (Tank Design).

Returning to London Transport with the end of the war in 1945, his position took the new title Chief Mechanical Engineer (Road Services), which he held until his retirement on 3rd July 1965. Overall, it was a remarkable career which could be measured on one scale by the fact that the bulk of three of London's most successful bus chassis, which each earn them place among the all-time greats, the STL, RT and RM, had been developed under Mr Durrant's direction. Yet his vision and influence had a much wider impact — many of the ideas and principles which were eventually adopted by much of the industry as a whole — the generously proportioned but derated engine in the interest of long life and reliability, air-pressure brakes and the progression to automatic transmission, were three examples which he was pursuing in 1937-38 and much later generally accepted, even though it took 30 years or so in some cases!

Much of the following information has been gleaned from official Annual Reports and one or two official histories, but I was privileged on two occasions after the Chief's retirement to have interviews with him at his flat in Chiltern Court. He was always held in high esteem by the staff, and I had the conviction that the work he pioneered in London Transport and that carried out on his secondment to the Government Research establishment at Chobham, would make interesting reading.

I put the idea to him of producing a book on his life but he declined, stating that with the passage of time inaccuracies would no doubt creep in due to the quirks of the memory, and he did not want that, but in discussion so much interesting information came to light, so I was reluctant to give in. A little later I returned to Chiltern Court with a suggested ghosting of a book, one chapter of which covered his time at Chobham. The Chief was still reluctant and there the matter rested.

In the senior positions he reached from 1929 within the LGOC he was already involved in an important stage of the development of the London bus. The adoption of the compression-ignition oil engine (very few people called it a diesel in Britain in those days) was a key element in this, and the LGOC was not only one of the pioneer users but from 1931 had the largest fleet of oil-engined buses in experimental service in Britain. Much the same was true of the adoption of the fluid flywheel and Wilson gearbox.

At a meeting of the newly-formed London Passenger Transport Board on 6th June 1933, three weeks before the LPTB came into life in organisational terms on 1st July that year, Mr Durrant recommended that the compression ignition engine be adopted for the next batch of 100 double-deckers being built. Although his recommendation was accepted in principle, in practice, it did not work out quite as simply at first, for, at that stage, AEC did not have an oil engine that would fit into the STL-type double-decker (by then the LGOC and hence the Board's standard) without requiring some shortening of the body to keep within the 26ft. length limit. This did not apply to the LT-class six-wheelers and so the 100 8.8-litre engines went into existing vehicles of that class, releasing petrol engines which were fitted to the STL chassis, a sequence of events that had been adopted for a batch of vehicles already on order.

However, the essential point was that no further petrol engines for use in double-deckers were purchased by London Transport, and only a handful of petrol-engined single-deckers (the Inter-station Leyland Cubs, mentioned in Chapter Five). AEC was developing its 7.7-litre engine, originally introduced for the Q, of which eleven of the first examples in the A171 form for orthodox chassis, were fitted from new in STL342-352, entering service early in 1934.

These buses also had Wilson preselective gearboxes and it was also decided to standardise on this feature, again virtually from the beginning of the LPTB era—the combination of the 7.7 engine and Wilson box was standard from STL609 which appeared, complete with improved body design, in November 1934. Yet he did not rest content and experiments with air-pressure brakes and gear-change and then automatic transmission were made in 1937, the RT design was developed to prototype stage by 1939 and was in production by the time he was called upon to devote his knowledge to tanks. Even this omits the technically advanced single-deckers with which he was also involved—Q, TF and CR as well as the more orthodox but fondly remembered 10T10.

In 1939 the Board's organisation was changed, with its functions divided into five groups:- Corporate Engineering, Operation, Commercial and Staff. All forms of transport services were put under the control of Mr T. E. Thomas, General Manager (Operations) with Mr V. A. Robertson as Engineer in Chief, to whom Mr Durrant reported.

Much of the information on Mr Durrant's wartime career has been provided by Colonel Hugh W. B. Mackintosh of Royal Armament Research and Development Establishment, perhaps rather better known by its old name and initials, Fighting Vehicle Research and Development Establishment (FVRDE) at Chobham, to whom I am very grateful.

One thing I did learn from discussion with Mr Durrant was his reluctance to leave his beloved buses to go to Chobham, or more correctly, Staines, for that was where the Department of Tank Design resided, at Roverbank Flats until the purpose-built camp on Chobham Common was completed in 1942. At the beginning of the 1939 war, the British Army found itself with limited numbers of tanks, many of those in service obsolete, but with a multitude of experimental tanks not passed for production.

British tank design had been entrusted to a number of agencies, and without much cohesive policy direction from the War Department, they tended to go off in their own particular directions. The Tank Design Section of the Royal Arsenal at Woolwich was also involved.

Mr Durrant was summoned by the Government, evidently on the basis of the highly successful manner in which London

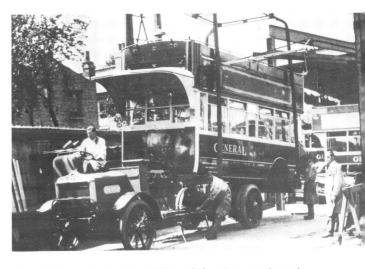

A. A. M. Durrant joined the LGOC in 1919 and among the early advances he witnessed was the NS-type, with its low frame. Here the chassis of NS1458 is united with its body, probably when new in 1924 though this was an annual process as overhauls were carried out at this interval in those days at the insistence of the Metropolitan Police.

Transport conducted its own evaluation trials of new bus types before buying fleets of the successful designs. He was asked to take over the equivalent task in regard to tanks, but resisted the offer, saying that there were far more experienced people in that field than himself. The interview ended on the basis that Mr Durrant would provide a list of such suitable people and return within one month. He duly reported with the list and was told that the only suitable person was not on that list—himself! Hence his secondment as Director of Tank Design.

On 29th May 1940, a Tank Board was formed, of which Mr Durrant became a member, together with representatives of Vickers-Armstrong, Rolls-Royce, Leyland, BSA (at that time the parent company which included Daimler among its subsidiaries) and Nuffield (the name then given to the group of which Morris Motors was the largest member). A directorate of Tank Production was also set up. In the pre-war period, only Vickers-Armstrong had any experience of tank production and in 1939 was concentrating on the Matilda, but the onset of war brought in such diverse concerns as

Mr Durrant's career ran through several generations of London bus. He had been Assistant Superintendent of Rolling Stock when ST160, in the centre of this picture, had been new in 1930 and, as Chief Engineer, was responsible for both the standard STL type—represented here by STL919 of 1935 on the right—and the RT, of which RT104 of 1940 appears on the left. All three were on learner duty when photographed at Hounslow in 1950.

The pressure of war led to Bill Durrant's expertise and organisational ability being diverted to tank development. This scene in the workshop of the Fighting Vehicle Research & Development Establishment at Chobham gives an indication of the nature of the work carried out. Some of the tanks and armoured cars in use at that time had engines similar to those in contemporary buses and what is thought to be an AEC unit is seen on a test rig in the foreground.

locomotive builders Vulcan Foundry and North British, rolling stock builders Birmingham Railway Carriage & Wagon Co, Metropolitan-Cammell Carriage & Wagon and, for the Cruiser series of tanks (Covenanter, Crusader, Cromwell, etc), Nuffield Mechanisations Limited, English Electric, Leyland Motors and the LMS Railway workshops at Derby. Vauxhall Motors was brought in for the Churchill.

The Department of Tank Design was quite small, comprising about twenty professional designers and technical officers, part military and part civilian, in what ought to be described as somewhat unsuitable premises at Staines. Much of the time at this stage was concerned with the shortcomings arising from rushed production, and competing with the Ministry of Aircraft Production for resources in labour, machine tools and materials.

It would appear that Mr Durrant was beset with continual changes in the Ministry, especially when Lord Beaverbrook became Minister of Supply. In August 1941 he was appointed Controller General of Research and Development, together with a new post, Controller of Tank Design. Added to this the Tank Board suffered a fourth change in Chairman.

In his notes Colonel Mackintosh then mentions the problems arising from purchasing tanks 'off the shelf' from the United States under Lease Lend. I had always thought that the bus business coined the phrase 'off the shelf' for buses to Bus Grant specification after the RM production was curtailed but I now know differently.

I can do no better to complete this section at Chobham than to quote from Colonel Mackintosh's notes:- "When Mr Durrant left the Department in 1945 to return to London Transport it is certain that he left an organisation which at long last was extremely healthy and properly constituted and to him must go much of the credit for that. It is perhaps a fitting illustration that the year he left saw the roll-out of what is probably the most successful British tank ever—

Centurian—designed and developed in-house by his Department—but too late for the War." A fitting tribute to a man who was to achieve much the same results in the design of London buses.

It was not unusual to find tanks in the Experimental Shop at Chiswick to help in solving problems experienced at Chobham during Mr Durrant's reign there.

In December 1945 Mr T. E. Thomas retired and Mr Geary was appointed General manager (Road Services) with Mr Durrant appointed as Chief Mechanical Engineer (Road Services). He was appointed CBE in that year. Following on this appointment Mr E. C. Ottoway was appointed to the post of Works Manager (Buses and Coaches) who took under his wing a lot of the development work with Mr J. W. Wicks as the Assistant Engineer—Development. Mr Ottoway was appointed to the Board in 1963 and took over Catering responsibilities, Supplies (1958) etc. Unfortunately in January 1967 Mr Ottoway suffered a heart attack when travelling by air and died. This was a great loss, for he had made some significant contributions to the various posts he had held.

While detailing the work of Mr Durrant it might be worthwhile to quote his answer given to a question that was continually being posed and it was this. "Why does London Transport, a nationalised organisation, spend thousands of pounds on designing and developing a special bus of its own? Why does it not go out to the bus industry and let them spend the money on the project, so as to save London Transport all that expenditure? This was quite a sensible and pertinent question but it has a clear answer. The justification rests on two fundamental factors which are, I think, clearly established. The first is that the size of London Transport's fleet is such that, assuming the organisation of a reasonably considered programme, the numbers of vehicles involved are sufficient to enable a specially-designed vehicle to be produced efficiently and economically. The second is that the operating conditions—the degree of traffic congestion and so on—are peculiar to London, and there is no doubt that if a vehicle can be designed to meet these conditions closely, then there is going to be economy in operation."

The foregoing was taken from a talk given by the Chief Mechanical Engineer to Divisional and Garage staff on 18th December 1957 at Chiswick Works and is still true in principle today. One has only to look at the record to see the performance of vehicles purchased after the cessation of the RM build.

At the end of the War London Transport found itself with a very time-worn set of vehicles and a return to the policy of standardisation was made. Although the vehicle was still classed as RT it was much changed in the construction of the body, in particular, from the programme that had started in 1939 and was terminated due to the War. During the War London Transport had become involved in building Handley Page Halifax bombers at its Chiswick, White City, Leavesden and Aldenham factories, in conjunction with Chrysler Motors Limited, Duple Bodies and Motors Limited, Express Motor & Body Works Limited, and Park Royal Coach Works Limited, each being responsible for building certain components. This achievement constitutes a story in its own right.

The method of building aircraft caused a rethink and the post-war design of RT was created. Each component was carefully jigged so that fitting was not necessary and therefore each part was interchangeable. This was to have enormous advantages in the procurement of spares later in the operation of the vehicles. Body and chassis were carefully jigged so that a particular body was not tied to a particular chassis, a point which was to be of great value when the vehicle came to be overhauled. As mentioned in Chapter Two, bodies usually took a week longer to overhaul than the chassis so in theory the chassis never received its own body back at overhaul. This in itself was a resumption of the policy of standardisation that had been established in LGOC days. As far back as 1920 it was decided by the LGOC to centralise the overhaul of the fleet rather than do it at garages, and this led to the opening of Chiswick in 1921. By 1939 the fleet of buses had reached 6,000 vehicles and Chiswick no longer had the capacity to deal with these vehicles totally, though the 1939-45 war intervened before any major change could be made.

Under the direction of Mr Durrant, alternative or additional sites were sought, including a piece of land at Ickenham, but permission was refused by Parliament when powers were sought. As explained in Chapter Four, what at first were auxiliary body shops were located in existing premises at Aldenham which had been built before the War for eventual use as a railway depot to form part of a scheme to extend London Transport's Northern Line.

Then the decision was taken to build a bus and coach overhaul factory on this land, using the existing buildings as a nucleus, construction starting in May 1952 and finishing in 1956. The factory was built on a flow line principle enabling a vehicle to be overhauled over a period of three to four weeks. In addition, Aldenham also produced body parts, leaving the overhaul of all mechanical and electrical parts to be dealt with at Chiswick.

The transfer of the overhaul work to Aldenham then allowed a revamp of Chiswick to be carried out. In this case production had to be maintained as it proceeded whereas Aldenham was virtually a new venture. Naturally space was available to manoeuvre because of the setting up at Aldenham. Again under the guidance of Mr Durrant a modern factory was

The organisation of overhaul procedure for London Transport's fleet of buses, about to exceed 9,000 at the end of tram abandonment in 1952, called for volume production methods. This is the assembly line for overhauled engines at Chiswick, seen in April 1950. The three nearest engines on the line are AEC 9.6-litre units as used in the RT, while the engine hoisted overhead for movement out of the shop is a 7.7-litre unit, probably from an STL.

(Below) Aldenham Bus Overhaul Works was designed to provide the most efficient system for dealing with a fleet of up to 10,000 buses, and was larger than many manufacturers' plants.

(Right) The Aldenham chassis strip and assembly line was of the moving table type. Seen in the April 1956 view are the chassis of an RF, an RT and an RTL.

This view of the High Bay gives some idea of the vast scale of Aldenham's facilities. It was taken in September 1956, when the fleet was almost standardised on the RT family double-decker and the RF single-decker.

set up to give smooth and controlled flow of work with proper facilities for storage of items awaiting attention. The theory of the exercise was propounded in an excellent paper presented to the Automobile Division of the Institution of Mechnical Engineers in 1948 by the late Mr E. C. Ottoway.

Thus the design of the post-war RT had completed the work started on the pre-war RT to introduce a standardised type of bus with two factories planned to meet its supply of units on a day-to-day basis and give the vehicles a four year overhaul, all based on up-to-date lines. It was with this design that some interesting work was carried out during the 1948-50 period in conjunction with the Motor Industry Research Association which was written up by one of their staff, Mr P. Metcalf, and released for publication in March 1957. No doubt Mr Durrant was aware of the Association's previous work on large passenger chassis frames and a commercial vehicle in the period 1947-1948 and felt that being committed to a large scale fleet of buses it was as well to carry out similar dynamic stress tests on the post-war RT. The conditions under which the stress measurements were to be taken were clearly laid down by London Transport and included:-

1. Bumping, cornering and braking tests with the body structure as a framework only.
2. The same tests were repeated with the body panels fitted.
3. A further repetition of the tests was made with the body completely panelled and glazed.
4. The same tests to give the stresses in the rear part of the body with a heavy passenger load on the platform and stairs.
5. Further tests covering tests with the rear roll stabiliser fitted.

Some 150 gauges were fitted, many of them during the build of the body at Park Royal. Clearly the tests had to be carried out during the build stages and my small part was to take the uncompleted vehicle to the premises of the Motor Industry Research Association, which was situated on the Great West Road at the time, and collect it each evening to garage it at Chiswick; later the MIRA premises at Lindley, near Nuneaton, were opened and the later stages of testing continued there. Naturally only an organisation such as London Transport had a standard type of vehicle in large enough numbers to justify such a test being conducted. The report gives full details of the stresses involved in the RT body under all the likely service conditions and indicated that the design was sound—as was to be proved by many years of service operation. At the end of the tests, the wires to the strain gauges were cut and the actual stress gauges left in position and the body entered service retaining the fleet number RT 769 originally allocated in February 1951, though mounted on a later chassis, that originally used receiving a standard body and becoming RT2533, entering service in May 1951. The actual report contributed an extensive amount of knowledge in respect of stress levels in a modern double-deck bus.

The next important phase in Mr Durrant's life with London Transport was the RM design. Much of this was covered in my book—The Routemaster Bus—to which Mr Durrant contributed a Foreword and I can do no better than quote his last paragraph—"Many Routemasters will have their normal lives extended. This will present no technical or cost problems because the Routemaster was built for long and economical life and will most assuredly give it". How true were those words written in 1981, and the reasoning is still valid today.

It was following the 1964 Phelps Brown Committee of Enquiry into the pay and conditions of London Bus Crews than one-man-operation came to be introduced on a large scale in London. Further details of the new types of vehicles introduced appear in the next chapter.

At that date, one-man operation of double-deckers was still illegal and the extension of the maximum length permissible for single-deckers to 11 metres (36ft.) that had come into force in 1961 had focussed attention on such vehicles, designed to carry more standing passengers than hitherto usual in Britain as a means of extending one-man operation to cities. However, there was some interest in the possibilities of extending the idea to double-deckers and London Transport had included drawings of the single forward-entrance Routemaster in London Transport's fleet, RMF1254, built in 1962, and of a rear-engined model as well as standee single-deckers in its submission to the Phelps-Brown Committee.

Although forward-entrance front-engined double-deckers of similar layout to RMF1254 were quite common by then in provincial fleets, there was a general resistance by drivers of such vehicles to turn round and face the passenger, even though this had been quite common on omo conversions of older single-deckers. Even when similar working of double-deckers became legal in 1966, only a few operators made successful conversions of front-engined double-deckers — though Brighton Corporation was one, using Leyland PD2 models with manual transmission!

Not to be beaten, in 1964 Mr Durrant authorised the building of a rear-engined Routemaster, which became the FRM. Originally several prototypes were to be built by Park Royal to a design evolved by LT, AEC and Park Royal, including provincial examples — there was talk of one being planned to appear in Sheffield livery at the 1966 Commercial Motor Show, but Leyland, in whose group AEC was by then a member, decided against proceeding with the project and only one prototype was built, being taken into stock in July 1966. Later I acquired one set of parts as spares for this vehicle.

Mr Durrant had retired a year previously, but the prototype, FRM1, passed through acceptance trials and entered service from Tottenham garage in June 1967 to run on the same routes as the Leyland Atlantean buses which had been taken into service by then. It gave an excellent account of itself. It was so popular with the drivers and conductors that they almost refused to book it off for fear of losing it. Once the twin-door Fleetlines entered the fleet in 1971 it became difficult to operate the FRM and it spent a somewhat quieter life on one-man-bus routes operating from Potters Bar and Croydon, followed by a spell on sightseeing tour duties. It has now been transferred to the London Transport Museum and makes occasional appearances showing what might have been.

Mr Durrant died in August 1984.

Test procedures for new vehicle design

As the reader will appreciate, there was always a good deal of testing of various components on existing buses with a view to future adoption if successful, and, of course, cost effective. This did not cause a lot of hassle and the general public were not really aware of the setbacks that were often encountered. There is no satisfactory equivalent to real service testing, although the next best thing is to do simulated testing by following a service bus if one has any doubts. The public at times must often have wondered what a second bus marked PRIVATE following a service vehicle was doing. Even so, having developed a component to be reliable by such means it cannot be assumed that when fitted alongside other components in a new design that all will be well. It was a maxim of our Chief Mechanical Engineer that evolution was the order of the day, not revolution. How right he was.

The procedure was for a new type vehicle to be put through its paces on closed ground and in later years the Army Test Ground at Chobham was used. The original contract related to A. A. M. Durrant's appointment as Director there during the War, as described in the first part of this chapter. In more recent years the Chobham facilities have been made available to manufacturers and others requiring to carry out vehicle tests on a commercial basis. He was so highly regarded that one of the roads is named after him — Durrant Way. London Transport is similarly honoured in my home town of Crawley where the road by the bus station is known as Ashfield Way, after one of our greatest Chairmen. At Chobham the braking, acceleration was checked, turning circles etc. to see that the vehicle met the specifications.

When Mr Durrant retired, the Routemaster was firmly established as London Transport's latest standard. Here RM2020, one of those with illuminated external advertisements, is seen in service in April 1965. The contrast with the open-top B-type bus that had been standard when he joined the LGOC could hardly have been more striking.

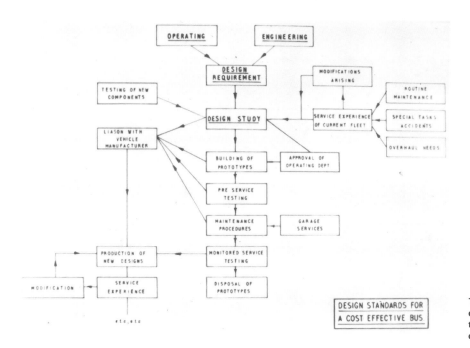

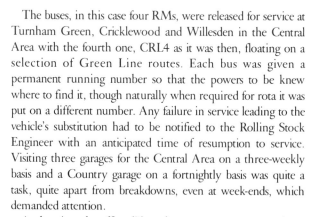

DESIGN STANDARDS FOR
A COST EFFECTIVE BUS

The combination of new ideas and operating experience require to be brought together in a logical sequence to produce a cost-effective bus, as shown on this chart.

The next stage was to instrument all the components on the bus and carry out simulated service runs behind a service vehicle both laden and unladen. The routes used have covered the 6, 11, 65, 88, 406, 705 and 715, although in later years the 220 has been used to investigate the effect of one-man-operation, as it was then. Journeys were done at the peak and off-peak and enabled full documentation of the vehicle to be obtained. This was discussed fully with the vehicle builder, in many cases AEC. This enabled any shortcomings to be ironed out before letting the prototypes into full service.

Before the release date a further exercise was arranged in conjunction with the Divisional Foreman. The prototype bus was brought into the Experimental Shop and any task that was thought to present problems was carried out. Naturally at the design stage all these things should have been foreseen but no one is perfect. One small example can be quoted. It was difficult to remove the rear cylinder head as a piece of fairing on the body stopped it being lifted upwards sufficiently to clear the studs. The offending material was soon removed to everyone's satisfaction.

The buses, in this case four RMs, were released for service at Turnham Green, Cricklewood and Willesden in the Central Area with the fourth one, CRL4 as it was then, floating on a selection of Green Line routes. Each bus was given a permanent running number so that the powers to be knew where to find it, though naturally when required for rota it was put on a different number. Any failure in service leading to the vehicle's substitution had to be notified to the Rolling Stock Engineer with an anticipated time of resumption to service. Visiting three garages for the Central Area on a three-weekly basis and a Country garage on a fortnightly basis was quite a task, quite apart from breakdowns, even at week-ends, which demanded attention.

At that time the office did not have a permanent car and one had to be borrowed out of the Pool. This was not always successful, apart from the regular visits which could be planned and arrangements were made for the last van to be removed from service to be on loan for six months. I don't think I am giving any secrets away when I say that one of the vans was in dark blue and had been used by the Board's police.

Instrumentation of vehicles to obtain data used to involve fitting pressure or temperature gauges to relevant items and the observer had to note down the readings by hand, an arduous task when behaviour in repeated stops was being noted.

Modern electronics made it possible for much of the recording of pressures and temperatures to be automatic. Here a Titan is seen with recording equipment installed.

In order to obtain experience on the operation of the standard Routemaster running units in advance of completion of the first production body shells, the first three sets were fitted to specially made mobile test rigs which could carry appropriate loading. They were very 'basic' but incorporated RM cab features. The three sets of units were later built into buses RM459, 341 and 398.

During its lifetime it had received at least three registrations and it was quite a thrill to be saluted by the police when using it for the first few weeks! But then I think someone let the cat out of the bag when I was pulled up for speeding attending an incident with CRL4 at Windsor. Eventually the Central Distribution Service took pity and decided that we should have the permanent allocation of a vehicle.

The idea was to run the prototypes for an eighteen-month period when the decision would be made to go into production. Fortunately during this period nothing really serious happened although there was a suggestion that the load pinion race in the differential might not be man enough for the job and it was found possible to substitute in the same space a race with greater carrying capacity.

The decision was made to start production and the first 50 or so were monitored to see if all was well. One or two changes had been made in production techniques which were to give trouble but this never occurred on the prototypes.

Alternative power sources

It was always thought that London Transport had a duty to provide a service for London and with this in mind, it always looked to the future as to what would be available in the way of fuels. Thought was being given to this even before the outbreak of war in September 1939, when it was realised that supplies of diesel fuel and petrol, in those days all imported, would be liable to disruption as tankers came under attack from U-boats.

Within the first weeks, a Country Area AEC Regent ST1100 dating from 1930, was running experimentally with a producer gas plant mounted on an extension to the frame immediately behind the rear platform. This seems to have proved unsuccessful and the vehicle was converted to haul the plant mounted on a trailer within a couple of months, and this

was the system later adopted generally on a larger scale in 1942-3.

The producer gas system required anthracite to be burned in the plant to make the gas which was then fed to the engine, being mixed with air in a valve replacing the usual carburetter — generally petrol engines were used for conversions, retaining the ignition system to fire the resulting mixture. Some operators used town gas stored in a balloon carried in a suitable frame on the roof of a single-decker.

My first contact with producer gas vehicles was when I was with Brighton Hove and District. This concern had also produced an early AEC Regent conversion in November 1939, with a built-in gas plant. In this case the open-staircase body, almost identical to those of the ex-Tilling ST-class buses in London, allowed an installation under the stairs. Explosions of the gas plant were not unknown and it is said that this experiment ended in November 1940 when the staircase was blown off.

My own experience was during the later period when most operators had been asked to convert some buses. On test with a Regent with gas trailer, easing back the throttle on the downgrade past the Brighton Football Club ground caused an enormous back-fire and the emission of a huge cloud of soot which smothered the screen of a following vehicle! Needless to say, a hurried return was made to Conway Street garage.

In London Transport's fleet, a total of 252 ST-type buses plus nine T-type single-deckers were converted to run on producer gas during 1943-44, though only 146 of the STs are known to have actually run on gas. Hill-climbing performance was poor and the whole exercise time-consuming when skilled men were scarce, so it was dropped as soon as better fuel supply allowed — even so, it provided experience which would have been valuable had normal fuel supplies been more seriously disrupted, as had seemed quite likely during the worst days of the War.

When the fuel oil crisis started in the mid-1970s, London Transport looked at all the alternative forms of energy and the famous single-deck RM1368, converted from being a standard double-decker following its top-deck having been burnt-out in December 1973 and used thereafter as a research vehicle, was fitted out to run on liquid petroleum gas — LPG.

London Transport, in conjunction with AEC, was experimenting with producer gas as an alternative fuel in the early weeks of the war. This photograph of ST1100, one of a batch of AEC Regent buses with bodies built to LGOC design by Ransomes, Sims and Jefferies that were originally operated by the East Surrey company, dates from October 1939, and was taken at the AEC works at Southall. It shows a producer gas plant mounted on an extension to the frame. Later a trailer-mounted unit was substituted.

Although a reasonable alternative, it created difficulties on starting in cold weather and the Department of Transport was never very keen — ultimately we were told that it would not be allowed for public service vehicles. In any case the world supply had been mortgaged!

Other feasibility studies were carried out, including looking at battery buses, but although the sodium sulphur battery was always 'just around the corner' it never seemed to appear. Existing lead-acid batteries were far too heavy and, for example, a four-ton battery would give only about 40 miles running. The Alkaline battery gave a good life but had certain technical shortcomings.

In connection with alternative transmissions I found myself as a member of the 303 Committee whose job it was to look over, or rather hold a watching brief over, a hybrid bus design which was basically an electric vehicle with a diesel engine as well. When overhead wires were available the vehicle ran as a trolleybus but when environmental pressures prevented the overhead wires, the diesel engine came into play and with a generator provided an electrical supply to drive the trolleybus motor. The idea gained some popularity on the Continent, particularly in France, Germany, and Italy and also in the USA in Seattle. On a visit to Lyons I was able to see fairly old examples in operation but their speed was somewhat limited in the diesel mode. At Essen I was able to take part in a trial of the Italian attempt, which was quite impressive. As the bus approached the end of the overhead wires, the trolley poles automatically came down and secured themselves on the bus, reversing the exercise when the wires were regained, the trolleyheads finding the wires with the vehicle still running. In addition the bus was fitted with a guided system so that it was unnecessary to steer except when road intersections were reached. This system was similar to that employed in Birmingham and had been installed on a tramway route in Essen. The interest shown in this system in Essen was that there was a tunnel through which the buses had to pass and it was not high enough to permit overhead wires.

A visit to Seattle in 1986 indicated an interest in such a system, often referred to as the 'Duo Bus', again with a tunnel under a river but there were other factors influencing the decision to try a dozen or so of these vehicles.

The only British interest shown in this type of vehicle was in Yorkshire, where the South Yorkshire PTE set up an experimental track alongside the Doncaster race course, using a Dennis vehicle fitted with an Alexander double-decker body and West Yorkshire PTE proposed a scheme for Bradford. Once the various continental countries had produced their vehicles the watching brief of the 303 Committee ended, and the Bradford scheme was not pursued. From an efficiency point of view the vehicle was very heavy and expensive due to the two systems of propulsion. Nevertheless it was an interesting diversion to the day-to-day problems and widened one's circle of colleagues.

The next serious consideration of alternative fuels centred on methane. Italy had a large natural supply of methane, particularly in the River Po valley and a feasibility study was carried out as to what it would mean to adapt a vehicle. One of the big disadvantages was that the volume of gas needed for a day's work was about eight times that of the corresponding amount of diesel fuel and presented problems when trying to apply it to an existing vehicle. It was not possible to run the engine on methane alone at idling, it needed something like an 80% diesel 20% methane mixture, but as the speed increased the diesel content was reduced until it was using methane alone. Naturally the exhaust was much cleaner and the general engine noise level was much lower. Filling had to be done under pressure which required special plant in garages and needed a good deal of co-operation from the local Gas Board. A visit was made to Florence where two vehicles were operating, and the result was quite impressive.

Quite large numbers of cars use methane and a visit was made one evening to a filling station. Here the car was driven to the pump and the driver and occupants left the vehicle and retired to a waiting area. The attendant then fitted a connector to the storage tank on the car and recorded positively how much gas was left in the tank. The tank was then filled and the pipe disconnected. At the cash desk it was then possible to calculate from the readings how much gas had been put in and a charge made by reference to a chart. Not a very speedy operation, and hardly suitable for a bus garage. Discussions took place on the possible conversion of the single-deck RM1368 to run on methane stored in a bottle on board and to see at first hand all the problems, but support was lukewarm and it did not proceed in my time. Discussions with the Department of Transport indicated that regulations did not exist for the running of buses carrying methane on board but they promised their support in passing regulations if and when the test progressed.

About this time I was invited to attend a gathering at MAN in Munich, where a presentation was to be given to all the Chief Engineers of the West German transport organisations involved in the work that had been carried out with Government funding in the MAN organisation. Little did I know that I was to be asked to give an 'off the cuff' review of the work that had been done in London on the Volvo Energy Storage City Bus! That part of the story on that project is worth telling in another chapter. The main item at Munich was their version of an energy storage vehicle but what did impress me was the level of funding that was provided to assist manufacturers in research — thus ensuring that their industry was in the forefront of innovation. As can be gathered, I had made acquaintance with MAN on previous occasions and it is a friendship that I have come to value. A degree of trust had developed and much was shown to me but the one item concerning this chapter is the work that has been done on the use of methanol as an alternative fuel. All the work was made available to me and the fact that over 100 engines had been built and are running on this fuel was proof of the soundness of their work. Vehicles were running in Australia, West Berlin and were about to do so in America. Unfortunately for London Buses it was a flat engine design which would not fit into one of our rear-engined double-deckers. There is still hope that one might become available!

There are many advantages of methanol and it is MAN's view that it is a better proposition than methane. It requires approximately twice the storage volume but it can be made from coal. What a wonderful use for our abundant coal supplies in this country, but this again failed to raise any enthusiasm with our Government. One of the pieces of equipment that MAN had made was a marvellous chassis dynamometer attached to the engine test bed. This enabled an engine to be run with any load, simulated gear changes, braking and so on. A most marvellous piece of equipment that any manufacturer would be proud of in this country. On 'driving' the methanol engine it was noticeable how early up the torque curve it was possible to change gear, especially as the torque curve reached its peak much lower down the speed range. Hence fuel saving would be possible with lower noise levels. Interest is gradually being shown in this country but it is making a slow start. At the end of my stay I was invited by the Research Staff to attend the customary dinner that is given by the Management to all the staff who have worked on the project. This took place at the nearby Brauerei Schlossberg Hotel, with a built-in brewery next door. As you can guess, an enjoyable evening was spent by all, including a presentation of a German beer glass, complete with lid, to the visitor.

The Leyland O.600 engine was London Transport's chosen alternative to the standard AEC units for both the RT and Routemaster families of buses. This example, dating from 1956, is one of the engines adapted for use in the two Routemaster prototypes built with Leyland running gear. Among many differences, the repositioning of the water pump and dynamo to the offside and the low-mounted fan (driven directly by the crankshaft) are evident. The modified dipstick and oil filler designed for ready access from the front can also be seen. The mounting arrangement followed AEC practice.

Alternative engines

It was always London Transport's policy to have two sources of supply for major components to cover against possible disruption of supply, such as strikes, as well as maintaining a competitive edge to those involved in purchasing duties.

It was with the post-war RT family that two different types of engine were employed in buses otherwise intended to be largely similar — the AEC 9.6-litre and the Leyland O.600 (the latter designation referring to the swept volume as 600 cubic inches, equivalent to 9.8 litres). The 'pre-war' fleet of RT buses had the earlier A185 type of 9.6-litre engine which had been deliberately intended to have quite a low output in relation to its size, 100 bhp, using the same type of direct-injection combustion system as on Leyland engines of that period.

Experience had shown over the years that a bigger engine derated was a far better proposition than a smaller one in terms of longer life and, in London conditions, better fuel consumption. The RT's 9.6-litre engine as compared to the 7.7-litre unit used in the STL had shown the way to go and hence the larger engine was judged to be the right choice for the post-war programme.

AEC had been developing its own direct-injection system during the later 1930s, using a toroidal (in non-technical terms 'doughnut-shaped') combustion chamber in the top of the piston rather than Leyland's version of that period, which had one shaped more like a flower pot. It had been used on the final pre-war batch of 7.7-litre units for STL buses, of type A173, and during the war many of the earlier ones had been converted to this system from the original indirect-injection A171 type. When applied to the 9.6-litre, the toroidal system allowed the power to go up to 125 bhp at the same 1,800 rpm governed speed used for most types of AEC direct-injection engines of those days, but London Transport, in line with its general policy on engine ratings, adopted 115 bhp for the A204 engine used in the post-war RT — and indeed this continued to be the setting favoured for the later AV590 engine as used on most Routemasters. When the chassis of RT19 was modified to act as a prototype for the post war fleet, its engine introduced the new design and subsequently the

engines of the pre-war RT buses were modified from 'pot' to toroidal, losing their original rather deeper engine note in the process.

When it was realised that AEC were going to fall short of London Transport's needs on the supply of RT chassis, it was arranged that Leyland would be invited to supply a similar chassis which could be fitted beneath the RT body. It was considered that what were substantially standard Leyland units for the engine, axles, and steering were acceptable but it must have fluid transmission and air-pressure brakes. As Leyland only made constant-mesh or synchromesh units at that time, it was arranged that AEC would provide the fluid flywheel, preselective gearbox and change-speed units. As described in Chapter Three, the result was the RTL and basically similar but wider RTW chassis delivered from 1948.

For its post-war engines, Leyland had also adopted the toroidal-cavity direct-injection system, and the O.600 was thus almost directly comparable to the AEC 9.6-litre in output and fuel economy, though as explained previously, LT's experiment was of a greater tendency to gasket trouble due at least partly to the fact that tightening down the cylinder head after a few days was carried out more easily with the AEC design. Altogether, the Leyland O.600 engine was fitted to 30% of the total RT family.

When the Routemaster came along, the main choice was the then current AEC 9.6-litre engine known as the AV590 though once again a comparative trial was made with a smaller AV470 engine, roughly corresponding to the old 7.7-litre, which only served to confirm that the larger unit was the better proposition. There had been interest in Leyland being a supplier of the mechanical units as a whole, hence the prototypes RML3 and CRL4, but even when it was realised that the numbers needed were not going to be sufficient to justify this, the supply of alternative engines for production buses was still in mind.

Trials were conducted with the Leyland O.600 engine in RM632, followed by RM870 and RM1009, and it was agreed that batches of vehicles would receive this engine, still rated, like the AEC units, at LT's usual 115 bhp at 1,800 rpm — those involved were RM1255-1452, RM 1521-1719 and RM1811-1985. In one sense, the idea of an alternative supplier had faded, as the merger of AEC into the Leyland organisation which occurred in 1962 meant that there was no longer true competition between the two, and no further Leyland-engined Routemasters were built for London service.

On the other hand, it was considered that the availability of the Leyland engine might encourage other operators who were not AEC minded to try the RM design — indeed this did occur, as Northern General Transport took 50 examples with the O.600 unit in 1964-65, these being forward-entrance buses of similar layout to RMF1254, which was also fitted with a Leyland engine when sold to NGT in 1966. I understand that NGT obtained good results from the O.600 engine in its Routemasters, with overhaul life of nearly 250,000 miles compared to under 100,000 for the same engine in Atlantean buses of the time, though it is fair to comment that the NGT Routemasters were used largely on inter-urban routes with much fewer stops than a London bus.

The next series of vehicles to have alternative engines were the Fleetlines, of which the story is told in Chapter Eight. When the model went into production after its introduction in 1960, the Gardner 6LX engine was standard with the similar but higher-rated 6LXB available from 1969 and chosen for the London DMS class buses, as well as many others built in the 1970s. The British Leyland Motor Corporation had been formed in 1968, bringing Daimler into the Leyland empire.

Gardner was having difficulty in coping with the demand for its engines, particularly for the Fleetline, being built in very large numbers, and Leyland was naturally keen to use its own engine production. So a Leyland O.680 engine was fitted to DMS132, this 11.1-litre engine being a large-bore version of the O.600, both units being set to develop 170 bhp for use in the DMS class buses. It was agreed that 1,600 further DMS-type buses, to follow the initial batches totally 367, were to be split so as to have 850 Leyland and 750 Gardner engines. It so happened that, although some early buses planned to be Leyland-engined received Gardner engines pending the overcoming of a noise problem, Gardner ran into some prolonged industrial trouble. In the event, the numbers of Leyland engines was increased further and only 280 buses of this batch received Gardner engines. Indeed, in order to keep production going at Coventry, Chiswick supplied a few overhauled Gardner engines from its overhaul float.

Fleetline production was transferred to Leyland Farrington Works, the declared aim being to allow Jaguar expansion at Coventry. Ever mindful of impending legislation on noise levels, tests had been conducted on DMS88 to reduce the noise emission, and then DMS854 with O.680 engine. The air inlet and outlet for the engine were formed as two chimneys either side of the engine pod. This led to a somewhat complicated installation, so much so that London Transport was not keen to proceed. However, the view was taken by Leyland that so much had been spent on the development of this scheme that a large cancellation charge would be incurred so what was to be the B20 was the Fleetline of the future. In the case of the Gardner engine, noise levels were well within the new proposed limits so the B20 design was not necessary.

Always mindful that it was prudent to have more than one supplier, especially after the Gardner hiccough, when overhauled engines had to be supplied to fit new vehicles, a Rolls Royce Eagle engine was tried in one Fleetline, eventually extending to six. After these trials it was decided that this engine could be considered as an alternative to the Gardner but it did not rank in the same league for fuel consumption.

With the Leyland decision to drop the O.680 engine as the tooling had been fully amortised, the question of a direct substitution for the Gardner still existed and it was during the early days of the Metrobus that an approach was made by Cummins Engine Company. They put forward the L10 engine, a 10-litre six-cylinder in-line turbo-charged engine which had been developed to a reliable stage for commercial vehicles in the United States and now in Great Britain and were keen to adapt it for bus work. Such an attitude was quite encouraging in that Cummins recognised that bus operation was different from haulage work. In conjunction with MCW a visit was made to Cummins plants in the States, and this indicated a very highly organised engine builder.

The MCW Metrobus demonstrator was fitted with a Cummins L10 engine and subjected to the usual route tests which indicated that, apart from fuel consumption, the L10 was an alternative engine. It was decided to have 22 vehicles fitted with L10 engines, and that these would form the Brixton allocation of Metrobuses. In fairness to Cummins, it should be stated that because of the unusual fuel system of the engine, it was not designed that the fuel tank could be filled to the maximum extent since the fuel was subject to a temperature increase in service and expansion had to be provided. Thus the actual consumption figures obtained were not as bad as first thought, but nevertheless it did need some improvement. Modifications were made to the fuel pressure and to the degree of turbo-charging which brought the consumption to the Gardner level. After two years operation it was declared as an alternative to the Gardner.

One of the interesting points arising from the Cummins was the fact that it was much more oil-tight than any other comparable engine; also it did not burn oil, so oil topping up was a thing of the past. As a result it became obvious that oil changes had to be carried out at the stated intervals but improvements in oils have allowed an extension. This helped to being about a change in oil specification, bringing in multigrade oils for the fleet.

Further visits were made to Cummins to discuss future developments and a highly satisfactory rapport was built up. Both parties have learned a good deal of useful information on bus operation which has no doubt helped with the success of the L10 in British vehicles.

For the rear-engined Leyland Titan, Leyland had produced the T11 engine as a replacement for the O.680. All the time it was London Transport's belief that unless the turbo charger was carefully matched to the engine, there was always the problem of excessive smoke when moving off from a stop. Thus it was stipulated that a non-turbo version would need to be tried and ultimately six Titans were fitted with TL11 and another six with the non-turbo L11 engine. Although the engine performance matched the Gardner, it did not fit exactly to the transmission requirements and some modifications had to be made to the gearbox control panels. Problems arose over spare parts and it was ultimately decided that neither the TL11 not the L11 could be considered as alternatives to the Gardner in the Titan, for London service.

It is perhaps interesting to note that DAF had an agreement with British Leyland to manufacture the O.680 under licence and produced what amounted to an improved O.680. Such an engine has been fitted to an RM which was operated out of Norwood on Route 2 with a high degree of success. The cost of maintaining the AEC engine for many years beyond its designed life has naturally become expensive and as it has been decided to retain the RM for Central London operation, the continued use of the AEC engine was becoming uneconomic and it was thought, therefore, the DAF engine could be a highly suitable alternative. At least it followed the well proven principle that a large engine derated is a far better proposition than a small one uprated. Other developments are taking place in this field such as trying the Cummins 'C' series engine,

which is a smaller L10 but maintaining many of its features.

The Cummins 'C' series engine, an 8.3-litre unit, was more suited to the RM than the L10 in derated form, and on my first visit to that firm, the question of its possible use was raised. At that time Cummins was fully committed and the cost of matching it more closely to the RM was thought prohibitive. However, since then the money has been made available and 230 are on order at the time of writing for fitting to RML buses.

Alternative engines based on the Leyland O.680, made in Poland and India, have also been tried but apart from cost benefits did not come up to the requirements.

Another engine, the Iveco, made in Italy and previously unknown in British bus applications, has also been tried. It had been fitted to Fleetline vehicles mainly in what was the Wandle district. Just before I retired, one was fitted in an RM but with the fuel pump on the wrong side and other problems, I did not consider it was a satisfactory choice. However, it was decided to fit more in RMs, again in the former Wandle district, which is now South London and London General. A batch of 193 of the Iveco 836/1, of 8.2-litre capacity, has been ordered.

Despite being of smaller capacity, the Cummins and Iveco engines are set to give rather more power than the original AEC units.

Poplar garage, October 1959, shortly before the first major entry into service of Routemasters to replace trolleybuses — there had been limited numbers put on the road to gain operating experience earlier in the year but this was the first large-scale use of the type. In front are RM62, 103, 66 and 82 — note the trolleybuses filling the other bays of the garage.

This line-up of vehicles placed in service in 1965-66, posed within Chiswick Works, pinpoints the transition between the old 'bespoke' order and the new 'off the peg' regime. On the left is XA50, the last of the 50 Leyland Atlantean buses with Park Royal 72-seat bodywork to largely the manufacturers' standard designs. Next to it are two Routemasters of the 30ft. variety — RCL2235, a Green Line 65-seat coach, and RML2396, a Central Area 72-seat bus. Beyond them is XMS5, one of the first batch of AEC Merlin rear-engined single-deckers with Strachans bodywork designed to carry 73 passengers (of which only 25 were seated), for the Red Arrow services. At the end of the line is RC4, one of the AEC Reliance 11-metre Green Line coaches with Willowbrook 49-seat bodywork. Significantly, Routemasters are still a familiar sight but the other types have long since disappeared from the London scene.

8. Off the peg and on the hook

Routemasters in production

At the beginning of the 1960s, the Routemaster was in production and the methods and procedures with which London Transport arrived at the types of bus it needed and arranged for them to be built were much as they had been since it came into existence in 1933 — indeed there were obvious parallels going back much further to the early days of motor bus operation by the LGOC.

Yet within a few years all was to change, and much of what had been built up as a result of learning from experience began to be lost. At first though, the work we had done on the Routemaster prototypes was rewarded by a relatively trouble-free large-scale entry into service. The first production examples went into ordinary service in June 1959, when RM14 ran on route 11 from Riverside and RM24 began operating on route 8 from Willesden. However, these and others over the following months were pre-service development trials and the large-scale entry into service did not begin until November of that year when Stage IV of the trolleybus replacement programme used RMs at Poplar and West Ham — the earlier stages were carried out using RT and RTL buses.

One of the problems that arose with the early production RM was that they were not fitted with automatic brake adjusters. This was a conscious decision by those above me,

misled to some extent by the alleged success of the 15½in.-dia brakes on the RLH vehicles mentioned in Chapter Four. The greater clearance between the road wheel and brake drum and thicker lining were beneficial as expected, but it was an unreported fact that adjustment had been required every three weeks.

It soon became clear that automatic adjusters were still needed, just as previously, and as there was insufficient space to fit the adjuster to the brake shoe, as on the 3RT, my boss at the time, Albert Higgins, devised the scheme where it was fitted on the brake camshaft. This worked well until bad winter weather led to fantastic amounts of salt to be put on the roads, but better sealing overcame that problem and a refit programme was arranged. Incidentally, present-day council policy of waiting until mornings to see if salting of roads is needed, rather than taking preventative action based on no more that a risk of ice or snow as indicated by weather forecast the previous night, has reduced the salt problem.

A lot of time was spent on training staff to ensure that they were used to working on power hydraulic brakes and the drivers found them more responsive and hence safer, with the added advantages of freedom from freezing in cold weather and corrosion from the condensation formed in air systems. Overall, the teething troubles were quite modest, especially in relation to the advanced features the type incorporated, showing that thorough development of a design tailored to

The solitary forward-entrance Routemaster to be supplied new to London Transport, RMF1254, new in 1962, proved in the event to be of more interest to provincial operators — Northern General Transport ordered 50 similar buses, though with Leyland engines, in 1964-65 and then purchased this one, suitably re-engined, in 1966. It is noteworthy, however, that the possibility of one-man operation of such buses was considered for London in 1964.

London conditions could give reliability of a kind which was not obtained with the 'off-the-shelf' buses which followed.

The trolleybus conversion was completed on 9th May 1962, by which date over 1,000 RMs were in service. What was to prove a more important event took place just under a month later, when it was announced on 5th June that a merger between the Leyland and ACV groups had been agreed, subject to stockholders' agreement, which was given, of course. The Associated Commercial Vehicles group included not only AEC but Park Royal — thus the Routemaster became a product of the Leyland Motor Corporation, as the new combined group was called, the following year.

It may have seemed appropriate that the first production Leyland-engined Routemaster, RM1255, entered service

later that year. Yet the main reason for buying Leyland engines — to preserve an alternative source of supply — had vanished, and although further examples were delivered over the next two years, as explained in the previous chapter, all Routemasters entering service in London after August 1964 had AEC engines.

At first, AEC continued to operate with little, if any, outward sign of the change of ownership. The company remained separate within the new group and a new model was announced only a month after the merger was agreed, though of course this had been planned entirely by AEC. This revived the model name Renown, but this time was a low-floor double-decker, giving conventional seating layout on both decks within a 'lowbridge' overall height. The front-end of the

There was no compromise on interior finish despite the lightweight construction of the Routemaster. This view inside the lower deck of RML2692, when new in 1967, reveals finish well up to the standards of the best of today's buses. The illuminated panel at the front is for advertisements.

Motorway running with a luggage trailer called for more power and thus, although the coaches for British European Airways were of the standard RM 27ft. 6in. length, they had the larger capacity AV691 engine with 175bhp power setting and revised gearing to give 70mph speed capability.

chassis was similar to the conventional Regent V model of the time and, as the driver sat lower, his vision over the wide bonnet was severely restricted by comparison with the RM or RT. We operated one vehicle, taken into stock briefly on hire to allow evaluation as a possible replacement for the RLH class, fitted with the standard Park Royal forward-entrance body designed for the model. We gave it the number RX1 while it ran from Northfleet Country Area garage, but it did not find favour with LT, being nicknamed 'Hardwick's Horror' after the driving instructor responsible for training staff on it, and the model gained only limited success with other operators.

The Routemaster itself began to appear in various forms other than the standard 64-seat rear-entrance bus. First to appear were 24 buses with length increased to 30ft. by inserting a short extra bay into the middle of the body structure, giving a 72-seat capacity. These were originally to be classified as ER but instead RML was adopted, the vehicles in question, RML880-903, entering service from Finchley garage—which had operated 70-seat trolleybuses, previously, of course, (despite which the staff sought extra money for the

increased capacity over the 64-seat standard RM) mainly in November-December 1961. However, the standard length continued to be 27ft. 6½ins. until 1965, the highest-numbered such bus being RM2217.

There was one further early 30ft. vehicle, RMF1254, of forward-entrance layout, with 69-seat capacity. This was displayed at the 1962 Commercial Motor Show, but never entered service with LT, although it was used as a demonstrator, visiting the Manchester and Liverpool Corporation fleets and that of East Kent, as well as being used to try out the idea of using a vehicle of this layout with a luggage trailer for British European Airways to replace the Regal IVs. In 1964-65, Northern General Transport purchased 50 buses of similar layout and length but with Leyland engines and RMF1254 was sold to that company in November 1966, a Leyland engine having been fitted before sale to match the existing NGT examples. By that date BEA was taking delivery of 65 Routemasters also of forward-entrance layout but of standard RM length, this being considered preferable with the luggage trailers.

Before then, however, there had been two batches of

The additional bay inserted in the centre of the body to produce the 30ft. Routemaster is evident in this view of RCL2226, one of the Green Line coaches of this length on the 721 service to Brentwood at the Aldgate terminus in May 1967. This was one of the routes that had been double-decked since early post-war days.

Routemasters for Green Line service. The first 68 were the RMC type, of 27ft. 6in. length and with more comfortable seats for 57 passengers, entering service as RMC1453-1520 in 1962. A 30ft. equivalent, the RCL, appeared in 1965, this time with 65 seats. Both had power-operated doors, air suspension at the rear axle and twin headlamp assemblies, the RCL also having the larger AV690 engine of 11.3-litre capacity. There were 43 of these, RCL2218-2260, and following on from them came the final 500 Routemasters supplied to LT, RML2261-2760 — all RML-type 72-seat buses, of which 100 were painted green and delivered to the Country Area. The last ten of the type entered service in 1968.

By then, the climate of opinion on bus design had changed radically and both legal and political factors were important in this.

Merlins and Swifts

The reader will appreciate that everything which happened in R&D up to the time I joined London Transport had been directed towards improvements and development of the fleet. The further work which had gone into the RT, GS, RF and RM classes has been chronicled in earlier chapters.

All this work was part of the policy of designing and developing bespoke London buses, using the expertise and

drawing on the experience amassed over the years since 1933, and indeed even earlier into well back in the LGOC era. As the cost of such design work escalated — partly due to the more sophisticated vehicles being put into service — questions were raised about the wisdom of, or need for, such bespoke vehicles. Finally the Government took the view that large scale investment for new buses designed specifically for use in London was inappropriate.

Market forces changed with the gradual elimination or absorption of all Leyland's competitors — including AEC with whom LT had always shared a very close and successful relationship, and for the first time for many years London was faced with the prospect of having to buy very large numbers of 'off-the-peg' buses.

Those who would argue that such vehicles performed satisfactorily elsewhere, and should perforce do similarly in London, have not drawn the full lesson of the earlier chapters. Horses for courses was never truer than in the bus industry and if a vehicle was to be universally acceptable it seemed that it needed to be quite basic. The Bristol K, favoured by the Tilling Group, was such an example, well suited to the less severe traffic generally to be found in the provinces in the early post-war years, but on-the-street experience during 1948 and 1949 showed that this vehicle was not suitable for London operation.

By the mid 'sixties the industry generally was moving towards high specification vehicles. Power steering, power-operated doors, fluorescent lighting, windscreen heaters, saloon heaters, automatic transmission, power-operated ticket issuing and cancelling equipment were just some of the options increasingly likely to be specified by operators. All these items could and did affect the reliability and availability of vehicles.

In London there was the added requirement of good acceleration and smooth easy-to-operate transmission to enable buses to keep up with the ever-increasing speed of private motor cars whose numbers were steadily growing month-by-month.

One-man-operation was also coming into urban services, albeit with great union opposition in many cases. It came to London's full-sized buses with the introduction of the Red Arrow service using large single-deckers to link main-line rail termini to business and shopping centres in 1966, though the planning stage and thoughts on choice of vehicle had begun in 1964. That service was clearly unique in many ways but this fact was not fully recognised; the implications on the actual service life and performance was not appreciated. Horses for courses again.

The law did not at that time permit one-man operation of double-deckers, though this was about to change. Indeed, another batch of vehicles ordered at about the same time as the initial batch of Red Arrow single-deckers consisted of eight Daimler Fleetline double-deckers for the Country area, on which it was planned to conduct experiments in part-time one-man operation with the top deck closed-off. Indeed by the time the first Red Arrow entered service on 18th April 1966, changes in the law to allow one-man working of double-deckers were in the pipeline, coming into effect on 1st July that year.

However, there was of course no experience in Britain of the operation of double-deckers without a conductor, even on country routes, and it took some time before the full implications of this change were widely accepted in the industry. Trade union attitudes to any increase in driver-only working tended to be adverse, especially where large-capacity buses were concerned — there had been enough trouble getting approval of 72-seat as opposed to 64-seat double-deckers even with a crew of two.

The thinking of the period up to the mid 'sixties was that a single-decker built to the 36ft.-long by 8ft. 2½in-wide dimensions which had come into effect in July 1961 could carry more passengers than a traditional double-decker provided it was designed so that most of them stood rather than sat. The original Red Arrow vehicles had a seating capacity of 25, all in the rear part of the vehicle, and up to 48 further passengers were permitted to stand, giving a total capacity of 73, at least in theory, and thus one more than even an RML (or one of the batch of 50 experimental Leyland Atlantean double-deckers also bought in 1965-66) seated,

though a little short if the double-decker's capacity was counted as including five standing passengers.

More importantly, shortage of drivers and conductors was seemingly a never-ending problem in the capital, especially in those days of virtually full employment and other types of employer able to offer higher rates of pay. To the west of London, Heathrow airport was proving a magnet for labour as the use of air travel expanded. A change to o-m-o would kill two birds with one stone, it seemed — reduce the platform staff requirement (and therefore the shortfall) and secondly allow payment of a higher rate to drivers, thus aiding recruitment.

Much contemporary thinking saw the rear-engined single-deck bus as the answer to all the industry's problems. Following the Leyland-AEC merger of 1962, a new range of single-deck models with rear-underfloor engines was introduced in 1964, Leyland and AEC versions having some features in common though the engines and most mechanical units continued to be of the respective makers' own designs. The model which appealed to London Transport was the heavier duty 36ft. (11 metre) version of the AEC Swift, which had an AH691 11.3-litre engine, rather than the AH505 8.2-litre unit being offered as standard on home-market models. We in London Transport always referred to the resulting type of bus as the Merlin.

Although in very broad terms the specification conformed to previous London Transport vehicle policy in using a larger-capacity AEC engine and the automatic version of the Wilson gearbox, many of the features which had been regarded as essential on earlier generations of London buses were lost as this move to an off-the-peg vehicle progressed. The extent to which it was tailored to London's requirements was clearly insufficient, as shown by the problems experienced when the vehicles finally entered service in quantity after determined efforts by the unions to extract a high price for one-man-operation.

Nevertheless, with the swing of the pendulum towards the single-decker fostered by the one-man concept, large numbers were added to the fleet. As originally planned this was to go far beyond the replacement of the RF single-deck bus fleet, although the first experimental order was for a mere fifteen vehicles with bodywork by Strachans — the first six were numbered XMS1-6, these letters signifying 'experimental Merlin standee' vehicles, and were the initial Red Arrow fleet. The other nine, originally numbered XMB1-9, were completed as 46-seat country buses though having a similar front-entrance centre-exit layout to that of the Red Arrow version. The success of the Red Arrow services soon led to all but one of these latter being converted, repainted and renumbered XMS7-14, leaving only one vehicle in green (it later became XMB15).

London Transport's Bus Reshaping Plan, announced in 1966, provided for much wider use of single-deckers and orders were placed for 150 and then a further 500 Merlin buses with various body layouts but all having basically the same design of body structure, built in Birmingham by Metro-Cammell Weymann, which by that date had closed the Weymann works at Addlestone. They varied from 25-seat plus 48-standing buses for further Red Arrow or surburban routes, 45-seat country buses (all of them having the front-entrance centre-exit layout) to 50-seat central area buses with

The production Merlin buses had bodywork built by MCW to a revised design which, with minor modifications, was to be used for the subsequent rear-engined AEC single-deckers for LT. Here MBS568, dating from 1969, is seen in later years.

a single-doorway layout. Deliveries began early in 1968 (though union problems delayed the introduction of the planned suburban services until September of that year) and were completed in October 1969, bringing the total number of Merlin vehicle to 665. The basic class letters were MB, with MBA indicating the Red Arrow and MBS the suburban equivalent.

Effectively, the whole of this fleet had been ordered with very little practical experience. Initially, a vehicle had been made available for inspection, but there was no full-scale evaluation trial and it was not a design over which we had any great measure of influence. The body design was also more 'basic' than had been usual in London, quite apart from the reduced provision of seats.

There had been little time to develop suitable vehicles following the Phelps Brown Committee's recommendation that one-man single-deckers be more widely usesd, and therefore it was decided at a Board level that standard manufacturers' chassis designs and a body only partially in accord with LT's ideas had to be accepted, though the front end in particular was modified from the Strachans version of the XMS batch, adopting the 'barrel' windscreen seen on FRM1 and to remain an LT standard through the 1970s.

In several ways the specification of these, and also the subsequent Daimler Fleetline double-deckers, represented a step backwards. The light-weight integral construction of the RM gave way to separate chassis and bodywork; despite their lack of seats for most passengers, the MBA Red Arrow buses weighed 8 tons 4 cwt unladen compared to the 72-seat RML's 7 tons 15 cwt. We were back to beam front axles and there were leaf springs, with their tendency to breakage, once again. The brake systems reverted to air pressure instead of benefitting from the advantages we'd demonstrated with the Routemaster's power-hydraulic system.

Despite this greater weight, the Merlins were by no means free from structural problems. The positioning of about a ton of engine plus gearbox under the long rear overhang, with nothing of comparable weight ahead of the rear axle, made the chassis subject to severe bending stresses. Considerable

deflection occurred on a bare chassis driven over even a moderately uneven road surface and this, in turn, put considerable stress loading into the body structure, itself not helped by the extra aperture of the centre exit, and even MCW's normally reliable construction was unable to cope. Forms of construction that had proved satisfactory with mid- or front-engined models proved inadequate, and cracking of the roof framing on the production machines soon began to occur. Oddly enough the Strachans bodywork on the prototypes had not given this trouble, as the rear end of the body had not been directly tied to the chassis at the extreme rear and this cantilevered construction allowed the chassis to deflect without imposing damaging stress on the body.

An investigation of just what was happening, and the reason for it, was put in hand and one vehicle was sent to the Motor Industry Research Association's proving ground at Lindley, near Nuneaton, when it was sent round the very uneven track designed to resemble a Belgian pavée road and stopped after each three circuits or so, when MCW engineers placed a ladder against the side and went up on to the roof to check what, if any, damage had occurred. Eventually the portions of roof needing reinforcement were identified and the problem overcome.

So far as the chassis was concerned, the air pressure equipment was, in the main, of the type then being used in very large numbers on goods chassis—air brakes had become almost universal on models in the heavy-duty classes, illustrating the benefit of London Transport's pioneer work of over a quarter of a century earlier. Although there had been isolated earlier applications, it was not until the RT had proved so successful that British makers and users of such vehicles—goods as well as passenger—began to adopt air brakes as standard. Unfortunately mass production, or more correctly efforts to cut costs to make the equipment price more competitive, had lowered the quality of some of the components.

The first 150 production Merlin chassis, taking the fleet numbers to MB165, incorporated AEC fluid flywheels and gearboxes. They gave comparatively little mechanical trouble considering the use of the power-pack layout, with these units grouped together with the engine. However, the low driving position, similar to that on early Atlanteans, was very unpopular with the drivers as the view of the road was poor.

The fruits of the Leyland take-over of AEC began to be evident in regard to the mechanical design at the beginning of the next 500 vehicles, at MBA166. On the positive side, LT was able to have the driver's floor level raised to its acceptable standard and LT's preferred type of brake and accelerator pedals were fitted instead of the organ type.

The disaster was to incorporate the Leyland rationalised fluid flywheel, which had an aluminium casing. With the exceedingly high temperatures reached in the combined engine and gearbox unit, the aluminium casing distorted, much as had happened with the Atlantean.

The failure situation almost got out of hand and attempts were made to manufacture a steel casing but nobody seemed able to achieve this. So SG iron was adopted and this ran into manufacturing problems with blow holes in the castings, but these were overcome and a conversion programme was immediately put in hand. I became deeply involved in rationing out supplies as new deliveries arrived.

The AEC gearbox was replaced by the Leyland/Self Changing Gears rationalised unit, which also gave trouble, but we soon put that to rights by substituting AEC brake bands of the type used on RM first and reverse gears plus a few more modifications.

Fluid flywheel fires, to which the high temperatures made these vehicles prone, are covered elsewhere, but another fire risk in LT's view was the adoption of earth return elecrical wiring in place of the system of providing a two-wire system, with insulated return. High temperatures caused the pvc covering to soften and allow short-circuits and although LT pioneered the use of hyperlon and/or silicon, the real answer would have been a return to previous practice. There were also fires in the air system due to the use of an engine oil supply to the compressor with air taken from the engine inlet manifold.

It was soon found that 11-metre single-deckers suffered difficulties in manouvering, particularly on suburban routes routed through areas where the parking of cars on street was a growing problem. A car parked near a junction could create serious difficulty on a corner which could be negotiated without difficulty when clear, disrupting services in an unpredictable way. Accordingly, soon after the first production MB-family buses entered service, it was decided that a switch should be made to the 10-metre (33ft. 5in.) length.

This made it impossible to fit the AH691 engine within the rear overhang, so a switch was made to the AH505-engined Swift, which was available in this shorter length, with a 16ft. 6in. wheelbase rather than the 18ft. 6in. as used in the Merlin version. These vehicles were numbered in a fresh series coded SM or SMS, the final S indicating 'standee', beginning with SM1-50, which were 42-seat front-entrance buses with bodywork by Marshall and SMS51-100 which had Park Royal two-doorway bodywork seating 33 and with space for 34 standing passengers. These were delivered in the early months of 1970.

Further batches, all of two-doorway layout, took the fleet numbers up to SMS838 and all the vehicles involved were delivered by February 1972, though SM101-148 (Park Royal 38-seat buses) and SM449-538 (MCW 41-seat buses) which had been ordered for Country Area use were delivered direct to London Country Bus Series Limited, which had taken over the 'green' sections of the fleet from 1st January 1970. The remaining vehicles, all SMS 33-seat plus 34-standee buses, were bodied by Marshall (SMS149-223), Park Royal (SMS224-448) and MCW (SMS539-838).

Thus a total of 1,503 rear-engined single-deckers had been ordered and although the 138 delivered to LCBS can be subtracted from this total, some 1,365 red single-deck buses of the two rear-engined types represented a huge increase over the 225 RF buses plus 49 surviving TD-class Leyland PS1 models that were all that were needed for Central Area services, at the

The shorter AEC Swift model was adopted from 1970, SMS58, with body built by Park Royal, is seen in the main drive of Chiswick Works before entering service in April of that year. The canteen clock can be seen reflected in the windows of the drawing office.

end of the 1950s — indeed there had never been so many single-deckers in the Central Area fleet. In many suburban areas new networks of routes run by MBS or SMS buses had replaced double-deck services.

Originally it had been planned that this process would go much further and single-deckers would be in the majority overall, with double-deckers only on the main 'trunk' routes. Yet by the time the first big deliveries were being made in 1968, the pendulum was already beginning to swing back to the double-decker, with the prospect of one-man operation of this type, too, now given full Government backing. But when you are a big user, you become like a gigantic flywheel which runs for some time after the decision to switch off had been taken.

It was just as well that no more of the SM/SMS class were supplied, for they proved if anything even more troublesome than the Merlins. Although a little lighter at just under 8 tons, they confirmed our distrust of smaller-capacity engines for failures were frequent. The large increase of engine failures resulted in AEC having difficulty in supplying sufficient spare parts for Chiswick to overhaul them. Overheating, leading to seizure, was a serious problem.

Taken together, the Merlins and Swifts were far from successful and hardly had the last arrived before their future was put in doubt. Certificates of Fitness for the Strachans-bodied prototype batch were due to expire in 1973 and MBS4 went to Aldenham for a pilot overhaul to assess the extent to which work would be needed. It emerged after eight months in January 1973, but had revealed that overhaul costs would be very high. The body contained much wooden construction which needed replacing and the riser (step) in the floor to the rear of the exit door needed strengthening to eliminate cracking. The matter went to the Greater London Council, which from January 1970 was the authority to which London Transport reported on policy decisions. Replacement of the whole Merlin fleet was authorised in August 1973.

Withdrawal of the class as a whole began in 1974, and by July 1975 it was necessary to hire space at the former Radlett Aerodrome to park withdrawn buses, some 350 buses had been taken there by the end of that year. By October 1976, the only Merlin buses remaining in use were the Red Arrow fleet.

Much the same story applied to the SM-family Swift buses. Similar pilot overhauls were carried out on representative early examples of the three bodybuilders' products from October 1974, and although in this case an overhaul programme was begun, only 20 SM-class and four SMS were given full overhauls before the decision was taken to replace the class as soon as possible. In this case, however, it was decided to carry out sufficient work to allow some of the vehicles to be recertified for three years rather than the usual five. Even so, withdrawals began in 1976 and over half the fleet had gone by the end of 1978, with only 174 out of the 838 still scheduled for service. By that date the Merlin fleet had shrunk to 70, with only 57 Red Arrow buses still scheduled for service. Many vehicles of both classes saw further service, notably in Northern Ireland and Australia, often after overhaul by dealers, but many more were scrapped.

Thus this fleet of vehicles had largely come and gone in a period of not much over ten years, and many buses were withdrawn after about six years' service or even less. Ironically, though the bulk of RF-class Central Area buses had been withdrawn by then — often after a very honourable quarter-century of service — some 25 were given an overhaul as late as 11977, when the Merlins and Swifts were well on the way out, for use on the 218 and 219 routes running from Kingston, the last not being withdrawn until 1979.

Rear-engined double-deckers

As the popularity of rear-engined double-deckers grew during the early 1960s, it was sometimes suggested that London was out of step with the rest of the country in that it was still building front-engined rear-entrance buses, whereas elsewhere, at any rate in city fleets, almost everyone seemed to be moving to rear-engined models. The question of the single-

The rear-engined Routemaster was the last major design project put in hand during Mr Durrant's period of office as Chief Mechnical Engineer (Road Services). It is seen here outside AEC's works at Southall before entering service. At that stage, FRM1 had no opening windows except for the driver's side window, the intention being that the heating and ventilating system would make them unnecessary.

This view under the right-hand portion of the engine cover of FRM1 shows the layout, with part of the AEC AV691 engine visible on the left, and the fluid flywheel linked by a drive shaft (hidden by a safety cover) to a gear train on the right. The automatic gearbox was driven by this, and could thus be at a lower level and easily removed separately. The coiled electrical lead was for a test gauge temporarily fitted for proving trials.

decker versus the double-decker was related to one-man-operation, but even among those loyal to the double-decker, rear-engined models were being favoured.

This trend had begun with the introduction of the Leyland Atlantean. Early prototypes had combined a rear engine with the traditional rear platform, but the production version introduced at the 1958 Commercial Motor Show had the entrance ahead of the front axle in the manner by then almost universal for single-deckers. The Daimler Fleetline, introduced in 1960, was also of this layout. They impressed operators by their capability of seating up to 78 passengers but the trade unions were suspicious for precisely the same reason. Getting acceptance, even with a crew of two, was far from easy and although a few far-seeing pioneers discussed the possibility of one-manning such buses, it was generally seen as no more than a remote possibility, especially on busy city routes. It was, in any case, still illegal at that stage and the Government gave no indication of willingness to change this position until after the whole question of wider use of one-man operation was brought to the forefront by the Phelps Brown Committee of enquiry into the pay and conditions of London bus crews, in the spring of 1964. By June of that year it had been agreed, along with other things, that if the law was amended, part-time one-man working of Atlantean or Fleetline style double-deckers might be tried in off-peak periods with the top deck closed off.

This led to the development of the rear-engined Routemaster, as mentioned briefly in the section on Mr A. A. M. Durrant in Chapter Seven. The basic concept was to retain as much of the Routemaster design as possible but with the engine mounted transversely at the rear and the entrance at the front, ahead of the front axle. By that date, the overall length limit was 11 metres (36ft.) and so it was possible to use the standard RM wheelbase of 16ft. 10in. with a full-length extra bay to give an overall length of 31ft. 5in. About 60% of the body was built up from standard Routemaster components.

The engine was the AV691, the vertical version of the 11.3-litre unit used in the Merlin, but the rear-end mechanical layout was differently arranged from those of either the Atlantean or Fleetline, with the aim of being able to remove any component from under the 'bonnet' without the need for removing the engine. The suspension, brakes and steering were similar in principle to those of a standard Routemaster, but there was no need for the front sub-frame and hence the front independent suspension assembly was attached directly to the body underframe.

Plans were made to build five vehicles at Park Royal — one for service, one for AEC experimental purposes and three as demonstrators, but unfortunately the Leyland group management decided against proceeding with the project and only one vehicle was completed, as FRM1, being taken into LT stock in July 1966, entering service in June 1967. In the process of editing this book, Alan Townsin told me that he recalls being allowed to road test the vehicle for 'Bus & Coach' magazine, which he then edited, just before it entered passenger service. Even after 23 years, it stands out in his memory as a remarkably impressive vehicle, with standards of braking, suspension and steering far ahead of its time as well as attention to detail in such matters as the placing of **all** controls so that they could be reached easily from the driving seat — an obvious-seeming merit but one he found remarkably rarely.

Meanwhile, however, it had been decided to buy 50 Leyland Atlanteans for the Central Area and eight Daimler Fleetlines for the Country Area. All had Park Royal bodywork, basically of that firm's standard steel-framed design of the period and seating 72, the same as the RML, and a figure also adopted for FRM1. The Daimlers, XF1-8, were sent to East Grinstead for operation on the 424, entering service in September 1965, and as they were Country buses they did not have the automatic gear control as fitted to the Atlanteans. The Atlanteans, XA1-50, began entering service in November and most were on the road by January 1966, operating out of Chalk Farm on the 24 and Highgate on the 271, in comparative trials with RML buses, at that stage on a crew-operated basis.

The two models had generally similar overall layout, with conventional chassis frames, although designed so as to make up a rigid structure in combination with the body, and like the AEC single-deckers of similarly 'off the peg' design, reverted to beam axles, leaf springs and air-pressure brakes. The Atlanteans had the Leyland O.680 engine, an 11.1-litre larger bore version of the O.600 familiar in the RTL and some RMs. The XF-series Fleetline had the Gardner 6LX unit, of 10.45 litres, an engine introduced in the late 1950s, having many design features in common with the LW-series engines last seen in London in 5LW form in the wartime Guy buses, but updated and with larger cylinder bore size. Both had their makers' respective versions of the direct-acting Wilson epicyclic gearbox.

However, the two models differed widely in their transmission line, the Leyland having a power pack, ie engine, flywheel and gearbox assembled as one, with the problems described in Chapter Six, whereas the Fleetline had a trailing-link coupling between the engine plus flywheel and the gearbox. To make matters worse the Leyland flywheel was made from aluminium and not only got exceedingly hot but expanded and caused excessive thrust on the engine crankshaft, leading not only to flywheel failure but engine as well.

On the other hand, the Fleetline flywheel remained very cool, being exposed, and I well remember on a Saturday evening in the wilds of Copthorne checking the flywheels for temperature and finding them so cool that it was possible to put a hand on them without discomfort. Although this was a good benefit, the trailing-link coupling was a headache as it was essential to keep the engine and gearbox in line; being separately mounted, this meant keeping an eye on the condition of the mounting rubbers. It was possible also, if anyone so desired, to wreck the coupling by changing down with the engine speed and the road speed badly mismatched. This did in fact happen on one occasion at the bottom of Stonequarry Hill where there was a Halt sign and although it was never admitted, I was sure in my own mind that the driver in question did change down rather than apply the brakes. Much development was carried out, including alternative designs, but nothing satisfactory could be found.

It was at East Grinstead that the one-man-operation of double-deckers was tried on the part-time basis that had been proposed in 1964. The route in question used to run from East Grinstead to Reigate through the town of East Grinstead itself, Horley and Reigate with fairly quiet areas between such as Copthorne, Smallfield and Burstow. It was felt that there was some economy in converting the bus to one-man-operation in the quiet parts by shutting off the top deck. The economy was that after leaving East Grinstead the conductor would change to the incoming bus so there was a total reduction in the conductors needed. Naturally this sort of operation demanded a very sympathetic timetable and any late running could cause havoc.

Because the reliability of the Fleetlines was so good it was arranged at a later date to move the Fleetlines into the Central Area on route 271 out of Highgate, and eight Atlanteans to East Grinstead. Later the Fleetline buses returned and three were allocated to the then Blue Arrow service which was started at Stevenage in December 1969 in the last days of the old London Transport regime. They were painted blue and at the time carried the London Transport legal name but on 1st January 1970 all changed and the London Country Bus legal name was substituted. To cover the three Fleetlines at Stevenage three Atlanteans were drafted into Grinstead and were ultimately painted green and three Country RMLs were sent to Central area in exchange.

Even after the handing over of the Country Bus Department to the National Bus Company, these buses were still looked after by London Transport as far as spares were concerned, and regular journeys were made to Grinstead or items put on a bus at Reigate on the 424 if I was unable to call in on my way home. Now Grinstead has gone and with it many happy memories. One or two of the staff transferred to Crawley on closure and at least two still remain at the time of writing.

Before ending this section it is worth mentioning one small point. Concerned about the stability of rear-engined buses, it was desired to see how these compared with a front-engined bus especially when in rear-wheel spin. The idea was to get a vehicle into a rear-wheel skid, which usually means that the rear end starts to swing and if the skid lasts long enough the bus will gyrate. Naturally there was some concern as to whether it would turn over. It so happened that when the XA Atlanteans were running at Croydon one conveniently had a severe accident but was still driveable. One of my staff struggled in from Croydon with the bus and the skid patch was cleared.

The comparative trials in which 50 Leyland Atlantean buses were run on selected routes in central London soon revealed that bus operation in the capital will show up design weaknesses to a degree not often experienced elsewhere. Seen in Trafalgar Square on route 24 when newly in service in November 1965 is XA12, in company with an example of an earlier generation of Leyland, RTL589 of 1949, one of those with bodywork by Metro-Cammell, most of which were withdrawn in 1966.

However hard it was driven the rear end was so heavy that it was almost impossible to even start the rear end to spin, and of course, the twin rear tyres meant that the oversteer effect found on some rear-engined cars did not apply. Everyone was happy that in this instance the rear-engined bus was very stable. The bus then went to Aldenham for repair.

The choice is Fleetline

When it was decided that the one-man single-deck bus was not for London, attention turned once again to the double-deck vehicle. Effectively, the choice therefore lay between Leyland Atlanteans and Daimler Fleetlines.

The change of policy from that in the Bus Reshaping Plan of 1966 had begun almost immediately after the latter's increased emphasis on single-deckers was going into effect, in 1968, but such was the 'flywheel effect' I have already mentioned that the big influx of single-deckers continued until early 1972.

Fortunately, there was the experience of both the XA Atlanteans and the XF Fleetlines on which we could draw.

The Fleetline was reckoned to be much the better of the two models on the basis of experience and when further double-deckers were decided upon, an order for seventeen for delivery in 1969 was placed with the idea of gaining further experience of the model as produced to the specification chosen for the

new-generation vehicles. These were to adopt some of the ideas adopted at Manchester under the general managership of Ralph Bennett, who became a member of the London Transport Board in September 1968. By that date, Manchester had received all but one of its initial batch of Atlantean and Fleetline double-deckers designed for one-man-operation introduced earlier that year. There were 48 of each, all having Park Royal-built bodywork with seats for 73 passengers and standing room for a further 21 produced to Mr Bennett's specification and given the name Mancunian appropriate to a citizen of that city.

Much the same principles were applied to the new version of the Fleetline, also bodied by Park Royal, for London, but in this case there was seating for 68, again with 21 standing, giving a total passenger capacity of 89. Weight was considerably greater than that of previous generations of London double-decker, at 9 tons 15cwt. unladen — a source of some subsequent problems. They had the uprated Gardner 6LXB engine, capable of giving 180 bhp but derated to 170 bhp for this application, and the gearbox had automatic control. It was publicised as The Londoner in exactly the same way as the Manchester equivalent, even its square shape being quite similar, but somehow the name never really caught on and was gradually dropped. Those of us in the business had another name which rather described the shape!

Demand for Fleetline chassis was very high and Daimler was unable to meet the original planned delivery. To avoid further delay a follow-up order for 100 was placed before the first were delivered, and then another 250. The first vehicle, DMS1, was completed in time to be displayed at the Commercial Motor Show in September 1970. Entry into service began in January 1971, and the combined batches to DMS367 completed before the end of that year.

It has to be said that at these early stages, Daimler fell over backwards to help in providing what LT wanted. My contact was largely with Peter Windsor-Smith, Chief Engineer, and Bob Crouch, Bus Sales Manager. At that stage, the New Bus Grant system was in its infancy and, in theory at least, vehicles eligible had to be a standard product of the manufacturer, as any deviation could nullify the Grant. In our discussions with Daimler, provided we could convince them of the need for a modification, they immediately offered it as a standard option so as to avoid any problem with the Grant.

In addition, once it became clear that demand was going to be large, Daimler set up a special line in its Radford Works in Coventry to build the LT version of the Fleetline chassis, thus allowing the assembly staff to become thoroughly familiar with the specification as well as improving output.

The initial reaction to the vehicles in London service was quite good but when they had been in service for a year or so gearbox troubles began to appear. In order to carry the increased load and torque, and overcome the full-throttle gear changes, it became necessary to increase the gearbox line pressure but scope for this was very limited as it was comparatively high anyway, and one had to be sure that this pressure could be maintained at all times. This increase in pressure helped considerably but did not completely arrest the top speed slip. It was impossible to increase the toggle setting for fear of overshoot so a different top speed clutch plate was employed. This was a sintered variety and there are many variants available, including coarse to fine grain sintered bronze.

The plate was changed on DMS6 which had been returned to Daimler at Coventry and the occasion comes to mind where a visit was made to test the bus. The Experimental Engineer there was George Fabel, whom I came to know well over the years. I took the bus on a Coventry city route and showed George how a London bus driver would expect to drive it. In the early part of 1971 traffic was nothing like it is today and it was possible to really drive the bus, with full throttle changes and anticipation of traffic behaviour, ensuring that the bus did not hold up traffic but, on the other hand, was able to keep up to schedule. I can see poor George sitting there now, holding his head in his hands, and saying that I should ease off the throttle as it changed gear, and apply the handbrake every time the bus came to rest. Although a change to Ferodo SN51 material from SN1 for the gearbox band linings did the trick, there was later to be another series of events which nearly put us into deep despair.

Whilst these changes did a good deal to improve the life of the gearbox, it was very nearly on its limit. Also, and without going into too much technical detail, the box employed a feature which was considered highly undesirable for London operation. It is customary in the planetary gearbox for the incoming gear to have a servo action when changing up and a trailing action when changing down. This makes the gear change much less noticeable and this is very desirable with automatic control. For reasons best known to Daimler, they had arranged matters the other way round by the brake band configuration. Added to this, on grounds of safety, it was required that when the doors were opened the bus went into neutral. On closing the doors, the gear re-engages but this takes a little time (about two seconds) and the driver naturally does not wait so long before putting his foot down on the throttle. This causes an unacceptable degree of slip to occur, leading to heavy band wear on second gear and severely reduces the life of the gearbox. With the help of my good friend Stan Burnett, who had previously been Chief Engineer, Self Changing Gears, before Leyland took them over, we devised a simple way of welding up the second speed inner band so that when put on the opposite side it took a servo action and considerably improved the grip of the second speed.

To improve the matter still further London Transport arranged to fit throttle inhibition so that the throttle remained at idling until the door had fully shut, but with the dodge of engaging the gear when the 'door close' button was depressed. As the door took up to two seconds to close this time was adequate for the gear to engage fully so that when the air was restored to the throttle the engine could not race away. This arrangement did a good deal to improve the life of the box but the fleet was not fully converted as the improvement could not be proved, due, in my opinion, to inadequate records being kept at garage level.

When the modification of throttle inhibition was proposed there were a few qualms at the Department of Transport since the regulations stated that the bus must not be able to be driven with the doors open. However, the Senior Area Mechanical Engineer of the Department at the time, Ken Wakefield, was a very reasonable person with whom I had developed an excellent working arrangement and he agreed that as the bus could only idle until the doors were fully shut, it could not, in the accepted sense, be driven and thus he gave his approval. In all my dealings with the Ministry I found that if one was honest and straightforward, a good relationship ensued.

One of the initial attractions of the Fleetline was that the engine and gearbox were separately mounted, and not as a complete assembly sandwiching the fluid flywheel as on the Atlantean. However, this presupposed that the engine and gearbox were always correctly aligned. Unfortunately the engine mountings on the Fleetline suffered from oil contamination which allowed the engine to settle and thus introduced a misalignment which had to be taken by the trailing link coupling which connected the two items. In the extreme this led to failure of the link coupling such that the links failed and cut through everything in range, and in particular the gearbox casing, resulting in a very expensive failure. A picture of the coupling is illustrated.

The increased demand for the already popular Fleetline resulting from the London orders created engine supply problems and as already mentioned it was decided to offer the model with the Leyland O.680 engine. By the time the first DMS buses had entered service in January 1971, orders for a further 1600 similar vehicles had been placed. The intention was that 750 would have Gardner 6LXB engines and 850 would have Leyland O.680 units—the body order was also to be split—Park Royal 880 and MCW 720. In practice, practical considerations disrupted the actual deliveries and the batches were not as tidy as originally planned. One problem was that of meeting new legal requirements on noise levels.

Preliminary work had been done on DMS88 to reduce its noise level to what was to be the impending noise legislation. The idea was to move the air intake above the engine pod, taking the air from beneath the upper deck. This had been found to be a notoriously dirty place and the filters soon became very dirty. Since the noise level reading was taken at the side of the bus, this new position did tend to reduce the level. With the Gardner installation it was not necessary to do anything special with the engine, but when the Leyland O.680 engine was fitted it had to have a slight degree of turbo-charging to help in meeting the requirement. This played havoc with the exhaust run, there being hardly any room to

Achilles heel, almost literally, of the Fleetline was the trailing-link coupling between engine and gearbox. Alternatives, including a doughnut or tyre-type coupling and one using rubber bobbins, were tried but did not stand up to London operating conditions.

Later vehicles included batches with Leyland engines and MCW bodywork, including the vehicle shown which entered service in June 1975 as DM1827, being one of those equipped for operation with a conductor during a period when plans for one-man operation of central London routes were abandoned for the time being. However, it was later converted to permit driver-only working becoming simply D1827 and being seen here with 'Pay driver' sign.

take it between the front of the engine and the side of the bus. Unfortunately leakage from overfilling the steering header tank just above the turbo-charger caused a few fires. Part of the over-filling was due to the sight tube getting discoloured whereby the level could not be determined and usually some oil was put in for good measure. Eventually it was proved that there was no need for the turbo-charger and the components were removed, but leaving the casing. This did not help the exhaust pipe run so a new one was designed which eliminated the casing altogether. Unfortunately the garages were slow to see the advantage and it was only introduced on Chiswick overhauled engines.

The original intention was to fit DMS1248 upwards with Leyland engines and MCW bodywork but the noise problem led to Gardner engines being diverted to complete vehicles built without Leyland engines. Then a prolonged strike at the Gardner concern had the reverse effect as described in Chapter Seven. A further complication was that, following difficulties with one-man operation on major central London bus routes, it was agreed that 460 buses would be completed without the fare collection equipment. These were designated DM rather than DMS, and it is noteworthy that the class code was also DM, the first 117 vehicles being 1DM1. The DM buses had seats for 73 passengers.

Further disruption to production and more mechanical problems followed Leyland's decision to transfer Fleetline production from the Daimler factory to Leyland's own factory. This took effect when the second batch of 400 chassis (all with Leyland engines) from the 1,600 vehicle London order was going through and one of these chassis was temporarily delivered from Radford Works to Leyland rather than a bodybuilder in May 1973 to allow development of production methods. Briefly, both works were delivering chassis but long delays occurred before Leyland production really got under way and then some attempts at rationalising

production methods brought more trouble. In addition, the effective liaison with Daimler gave way to a much more remote attitude from Leyland.

In particular, a change to the grooving of the gearbox brake drums brought a recurrence of slip problems and put new buses off the road until they were rectified. Unfortunately, the fuel crisis that followed the 1973 Arab-Israeli war brought delays in producing spares due to the three-day week imposed on industry to conserve electricity.

Despite — or perhaps as an indication of — its good efficiency, the Gardner engine employs a very inefficient water pump, the impeller often referred to as a paddle. If there is any small shortage of water in the system — not uncommon on a rear-engined double-decker with a typical rather complex heating system — and the pump virtually ceases to work. On the other hand, AEC always designed their engines so that they could still perform even with a gallon of water short. This had become taken for granted by drivers so it was not surprising that engine failures occurred on the Fleetline.

There were also spares problems and I think it was true to say that Leyland was not organised to cater for the volume of Fleetline spares required. Trying to fit the Fleetline into Leyland's own production at Farrington works did not help and in later years the manufacture of epicyclic gearbox parts was put out to Avon Transmission. Overall, Leyland's name suffered considerably.

Meanwhile further orders for what were to be the final deliveries of Fleetlines to London were placed, due for delivery in 1975/76. This time the total number of vehicles ordered was 679, of which the last 400 were of the 'quiet' type also known by their Leyland development code, B20. The Leyland engine would not meet proposed new noise legislation which we were told would become law before they could be delivered. We tried to bring forward production but this was not possible and even tighter standards were to follow later, so something had to be done, and in any case the price to be paid for the work already done and material made was considered too high.

The body contracts continued to be split between Park Royal and MCW — both building to similar though not quite identical appearance but each concern using its own framing. Gardner supplied 6LXB engines for 139 of the standard models, but Leyland O.680 engines were used for the remainder, including all the B20 type. The latter, numbered from DMS2247 upwards (though the final 120 buses were of crew-operated type and thus numbered DM2527-2646) had greatly altered rear-end appearance due to the pair of rectangular 'chimneys' with angled grilles for air inlet and outlet which meant that the corner shroud panels fitted above the engine pod on earlier London Fleetlines could not be used.

Delivery of the final batches was completed in August 1978, the B20 vehicles (for which DMS854 had been used as a prototype) arriving from early 1977. Before then, however, the troubles we were experiencing had become public knowledge and later in 1976 it was announced that no more Fleetlines would be ordered. However, pilot overhauls were already in hand and as mentioned in Chapter Four, the overhaul procedure had to be altered without separating body from chassis. Heavier lifting gear to cope with the complete vehicle was installed at Aldenham.

Even so, the future of the class — one of London's largest — was already in doubt, and in 1979 large-scale withdrawals began. Many of the vehicles saw further service elsewhere in Britain as well as abroad, proving quite successful in a different environment.

In relation to the size of the fleet, experimental work done by LT on the Fleetlines was limited, beyond that dictated by troubles of one kind or another. However, XF3 of the 1965 prototype batch was fitted with a Cummins V6 engine of the type used in the Roadliner single-decker, but after a number of failures it was decided to be uneconomic to pursue the matter further. The Rolls-Royce Eagle engine was tried in DMS864 from December 1974 and led to five more such engines being acquired in 1976 and fitted in DM1199, and DMS1968, 2059 and 2120, with one spare unit. They proved quite reliable but not as economical on fuel as the Gardner.

Perhaps the most significant work was that on hydraulic brakes, DMS1332 being fitted with an experimental system made by Clayton Dewandre, in 1973. This was related to Leyland's intention to use a Lockheed hydraulic brake system on its new B15 double-decker (subsequently named Titan), then being designed and intended to replace not only the Fleetline but also the Atlantean and the Bristol VRT (this last-mentioned being widely used by the National Bus Company though not by London Transport). Clayton Dewandre, as the main air equipment suppliers, could see their share of the business shrinking. Further sets were fitted to DMS2161, 2162, 2170 and 2224 in 1976-77.

These hydraulic brakes were to be the forerunners of those used on the Metrobus, and with the higher pressures compared with the Lockheed system, pipe joints were very critical and oil losses were a problem. They ran from Turnham Green until DMS buses were withdrawn from there and ended their days at Thornton Heath. Two (DMS2170 and 2224) ended up with Hampshire Bus but DMS1332 was retained for the Hydrapak development work carried out at Chiswick, as described in Chapter Six.

Single-deckers again — the Leyland National

A study of bus market prospects towards the end of the 'sixties had led Leyland to the view that, in future, the major demand would be for single-deckers. This was no doubt influenced by the order position at that time, based on the linking of one-man operation with single-deck vehicles, as well as such factors as London's Bus Reshaping Plan of 1966. A mock-up of a proposed single-decker was built up at Leyland in 1967 and, although that eight-wheeled design was not pursued, a subsequent exercise provided the basis for a joint venture set up with the newly-formed National Bus Company in 1969.

The objective was to build what became the standardised Leyland National single-decker to supply not only the majority of NBC's needs but, it was thought, the greater part of those of most other major operators in Britain and, in addition, it was hoped that it would attract big orders from abroad, too.

So far as London Transport was concerned, most of the requirement for new buses had switched back to double-deckers as a result of the capability of one-manning them, too,

Large-scale withdrawals of Fleetlines began in 1979. Many of them found new homes such as the former DMS1354, a Gardner-engined example with MCW body, both features which suited West Midlands PTE, which purchased it in December of that year, building up a sizeable fleet of similar buses, which were basically quite similar to its own standard vehicles of comparable age — this one dated from 1972. The centre exit was not favoured and was removed before re-entry into service. Many such vehicles were to spend longer with their second owners than they had in London.

long before the Leyland National got into production in 1972. Even so, there would be some continued need for single-deckers and as already indicated, there was growing dissatisfaction with those recently purchased. In addition, there was interest in some features of the design should a double-decker have been built on similar principles.

There had also been a short-term experiment with a Metro-Scania single-decker demonstrator in the early months of 1970. This was a version of the integral single-decker already being produced by the Swedish Scania concern, but with body shell constructed in Birmingham largely to Scania design by Metro-Cammell Weymann. Orders for six each of the Metro-Scania and the Leyland National were placed in 1972. The Metro-Scania buses, MS1-6, were delivered beginning in May 1973 and entered service in August from Dalston garage on what had been the 208 route, now numbered S2 and nicknamed the 'Wall of Death', remaining on the route until 1976, when they were stored and subsequently five of them were sold to Newport Corporation, which already had a fleet of the type. Their main function from a technical viewpoint was to act as a pilot study for the MD-class Metropolitan double-decker, the story of which is told in Chapter Ten.

To return to the Leyland National, it might be interesting to relate a little about the concept of the bus itself. It was of integral construction with a leading frame at the front carrying the axle and with a trailing 'A' frame at the rear carrying the rear axle.

The factory at Workington, owned jointly by Leyland and NBC, was purpose-built for Leyland National production but it never reached the design volume for the premises. To some

The majority of the Leyland National buses added to the fleet in the 1970s were 36-seat two-door vehicles purchased mainly for use on suburban services, all being of 10.3-metre length. The vehicle seen here at Kings Cross in November 1980 happens to be the ill-fated LS186. Three months later it was to be involved in an accident at Archway, its destination in this view, giving rise to a major investigation as described in the text and illustrated on the opposite page.

extent this was due to a change of policy in LT, as has been indicated. The factory was really an assembly plant putting the bus together, rather like a Meccano exercise. There were no trained fitters employed on assembly work as everything was planned to fit together, being jigged at the point of manufacture, i.e. Leyland for the front and rear sub-frames. Anything that did not fit was cast aside and dealt with at the source of manufacture. This enabled a semi-skilled workforce to be employed, many of whom had been employed in the local industries, such as coal mining which even then was suffering from cut-backs. In all a very good idea which assembled a bus to a good standard of quality, though offering little scope for deviation from the 'standard'.

Our friends at Midland Red had had experience of the Leyland National and had found weaknesses in the region of the trailing 'A' frame where it joined the body — a modified design was fitted to the London ones as a result of this. A further innovation was that LT's first six were fitted with noise suppression shields which produced a very quiet bus but were soon left off through maintenance difficulties.

London's vehicles were unusual in another respect. The National plant incorporated many advanced production techniques and its paint spray booth was — by any standards — a masterpiece of technology. This hi-tech extended to the paints themselves and the result was Henry Ford-like — any colour so long as it was National Poppy Red, Leaf Green or, to allow operators to apply their own paint schemes(!), white. My masters conveyed to Leyland that London Transport buses were painted LT Red , or not at all, and LT Red was added to the shade card at Workington.

The length chosen for these and subsequent batches was the shorter 10.3-metre option, marginally longer than the SM/SMS Swift, the layout favoured having the front entrance and centre exit doors and giving a seating capacity of 36, with space for 27 standing passengers. Most features of the design were Leyland National standard practice but a rear route number box was provided. The body construction using pressed-steel components was intended to give strength, but the unladen weight, at 8 tons 13cwt (the same as the Metro-Scania figure) was greater than that of the Routemaster rear-engined double-decker, FRM1. The engine was the turbo-charged 8.2-litre Leyland 500-series unit (to be precise the 510), with fixed head. The class letters chosen were LS, which

to old hands brought back memories of the twelve LS-class ADC six-wheel buses of 1927-28 which had preceded the LT-class AEC Renown six-wheelers, some surviving as breakdown tenders until 1951.

In due course six vehicles for London were built on the production lines at Workington, and then converted at Leyland to fit the then new close-ratio version of the Pneumocyclic gearbox with a charged coupling. The charged coupling idea was a means whereby the flywheel and gearbox oil were common and in contrast to the ordinary fluid flywheel the oil did not reach such a high temperature as it had the benefit of the surface area of the gearbox to cool it. This would have almost enabled London Transport to use the basic gearbox oil that it had developed with the oil companies in the late 1930s, but not quite, and hence a new generation of oil had to be developed. Trials on this coupling had been carried out on some MB vehicles at Hanwell with a good deal of success.

It was usual to carry out certain other trials on new type buses including a lift and tow exercise — particularly for the benefit of the Fire Brigade. Unfortunately at the time there were industrial relations problems in the London Fire Brigade and they were unable to turn up. Hence when they went into service in November 1973 alongside the Metro-Scanias on route S2, this training had not been given, which was to prove unfortunate. One of the Nationals decided to take a motor cyclist into a fish and chip shop, somewhat unintentionally, especially as he was caught up under the bus. When the Fire Brigade came to jack up the bus the lack of training soon became obvious, but many hands made light work in lifting the bus to extricate the motor cyclist.

In 1975, it was decided to order a further 51 Nationals, these being among the first production examples of the Phase II design, with forward-mounted battery. They were intended to cover for the large numbers of SMS buses by then out of action but all were allocated to Hounslow garage. The opportunity was taken to set up a stores system direct with Leyland and Hounslow. The set-up became known in the organisation as the Hounslow Bus Company, perhaps as a forerunner to what we have today with Westlink etc. The six buses from Dalston soon joined the Hounslow contingent and subsequently a further four batches were ordered for more universal use but unfortunately they differed in many niggling

116

little ways which tended to cause minor problems.

Ultimately a total of 437 Leyland Nationals with the 510 engine were placed in service in the period up to 1979/80. Then it was decided to modernise the Red Arrow fleet with 69 Leyland National 2 models (LS438-506), these being of the extensively revised design with Leyland O.680 engine and length slightly increased to 10.6 metres to accommodate a front-mounted radiator.

One of the things which was noticed right in the early days of the National by those of us at London Transport was that the brake pedal and throttle pedal were identical instead of using the more conventional different types. In London, we had always favoured a 'mushroom' pedal for the throttle. What was also disconcerting was that the pedals were much closer together than one would expect and London Transport insisted that those for London should have the spacing increased to the standard accepted distance and the throttle pedal be changed to a mushroom. The point was to become very important in the light of future events.

There were odd cases of drivers reporting so-called runaways, allegedly without their having touched the throttle, and then the brakes apparently failed to stop the bus. At the outset the question of 'wrong footing' was thought to be the cause—especially where it occurred on provincial vehicles where the London Transport modification had not been incorporated as it had not been asked for by the customer. Another factor was that the driver was apt to turn somewhat in his seat to take fares and hence the risk of his right foot landing on the wrong pedal as he turned back again seemed to be increased. Naturally the matter was discussed at our meetings with the PTEs and, of course, Leyland, and CAV, the fuel injection manufacturers. London's incidences were considerably less and it was not until the disastrous accident at Archway on 26th February 1981 that matters became clearer. This involved LS186 on route 239, the driver concerned having taken the bus from Holloway garage to Junction Road, where he stopped to pick up his first passengers. On moving away, the bus seemed to accelerate on its own, careering into a Routemaster bus in front of the LS and pushing the rear of the RM across the road. The LS then hit a Volkswagen car coming in the opposite direction and both vehicles then ended up in the window of a Co-op store on the opposite side of the road. Unfortunately an old lady was killed in the Co-op shop window.

As a fatality was occasioned there had to be an inquest. It was decided this incident had to be examined in minute detail and the vehicle in question, LS186, was taken to the Experimental Shop at Chiswick and gradually the engine, gearbox, etc were checked and then built into another vehicle so that they could be fully tested. All this was done in conjunction with the Coroner's officer and in the end a satisfactory explanation was found for the incident.

The vehicle proved to have been in a very satisfactory condition except that the throttle (accelerator) actuator clevis

The accident involving Leyland National LS186 at Archway in February 1981 resulted in a long and painstaking investigation of the cause and a programme to eliminate features that might have contributed to its occurrence. This view of the damaged vehicle was taken after its return to Chiswick.

pin had worn a flat on one side which sometimes prevented the throttle from releasing fully. Secondly, the retaining clip for the cold start facility (not normally used for London) had become displaced and gave a high maximum fuel output. When these two defects acted together, it could surprise the driver.

As a result, a series of eight modifications were proposed. A spring was added at the throttle lever on the fuel pump to ensure that it returned to idling in the event of linkage failure, the pedal pads were modified to standard LT design and various other minor changes made to eliminate possible causes of unintentional over-fuelling or slow release of the throttle as well as making operation more progressive. So important was it considered that Turnham Green garage was re-opened and, under my Experimental Shop Foreman, the whole fleet was sent there at the rate of about five per day and suitably modified. In this way the Ministry was satisfied that every attempt had been made to eliminate the possible repeat of such an incident. It can be said that the incidence of this complaint has virtually been eliminated as far as London is concerned.

Generally speaking, for what it was, the National gave a fairly good account of itself, but so far as the 'headless wonder',

The last additions to the Leyland National fleet were of the National 2 type, with O.680 engines and front-mounted radiator. Seen here is LS494 on Red Arrow route 501, soon after entering service in June 1981.

the 500 series engine, was concerned, it did not lend itself to overhaul after about an initial five year life. The Mark 2 National with the horizontal O.680 engine was a far better vehicle and it was a pity that Leyland could not be persuaded to fit this at the beginning — especially as it was naturally aspirated. Turbo-charging engines always presents problems since on start-up the driver, in line with normal custom, will always put his foot on the throttle; this does not give the turbo-charger time to get its oil supply and heavy wear can take place. Then, on shut-down, the engine is stopped and the oil supply to the rotor of the turbo-charger, which is still running at a fair speed, is cut off. During take-off it is difficult to eliminate the puff of black smoke. There are ways of overcoming these problems, but it all adds up to complication of vehicles.

Production of the engine has now ceased and many operators are carrying out conversions with Gardner and Cummins engines. Some, like Western SMT, were adamant that until the Gardner engine was available as an option on new vehicle, no Nationals would ever enter their fleet. Others swore by the 500 series and wondered what all the fuss was about. There is a moral here in relation to working practices, driving techniques and size of fleets.

Mini buses

In the period before the formation of the London Passenger Transport Board in 1933 it would be true to say that the only serious adventure with what would be described nowadays as mini-bus operation was the fleet of 42 Dennis Dart buses, mostly with seats for eighteen passengers, placed in service by LGOC in 1930-33. There had also been smaller numbers of other types, such as Lancia and Guy buses operated by National, a solitary Bean taken over from an independent and known unofficially as the Pinner Six, eight Morris-Commercial Viceroys for East Surrey and two for Green Line and six Commer Invaders, also for Green Line but which passed to East Surrey. Acquisitions of independent operators by London Transport also brought the prospect of a varied collection of small buses.

Fortuitously, not long before the new Board began considering a suitable choice of small bus, Leyland had introduced a new model in this class, the Cub, and in 1934 the first for London Transport, C1, was added to the fleet. By 1936, there were 98 in service.

The Cubs gave yeoman service and many were still in service when I joined London Transport as mentioned in Chapter Five. The intention of replacing them by the rear-engined CR-type developed jointly by London Transport and Leyland was stopped by the 1939-45 war — the 49 CR-type buses built spent most of the war laid up at safe outer garages — obtaining spares for these unique vehicles became a problem. The development of the GS-type Guy buses to replace the Cubs has also been covered in Chapter Five.

With the loss of the Country area in 1970 the need for such small buses seemed to have disappeared, but in 1971 a request was made by the GLC to provide a specialised service including one Dial-a-Bus operation. The interesting point was that London Transport would operate these vehicles on a 'no loss' basis. Since it was to be an experiment it was not worth putting out a specification, but instead to accept what was standard in the market place. This was logical since the experiment was to last for six months when a decision would be taken as to its continuance. In the event of its cessation the vehicles would have to be sold, and a standard vehicle would fetch a better price in the open market. It so happened that a review was not made, and the service continued, the vehicles being replaced as and when they wore out.

Four routes had been decided upon by March 1972, and sixteen Ford Transit 16-seat buses ordered — later the batch was increased to twenty, numbered FS1-20, delivery being made in 1972-73. The chassis was the version with Ford 2.4-litre diesel engine and synchromesh gearbox, the body being basically the standard parcel van as fitted with windows and seats and modified to public service vehicle standard by Strachans at their works at Hamble, where the first experimental Red Arrow bodies for Merlins had been built. Subsequently, similar body conversions came from Dormobile. Eventually the Finchley ones were replaced by Transits with automatic gearboxes, but these were more thirsty on fuel. It was here that the Experimental Shop at Chiswick came to the rescue by converting the fuel tanks to a greater capacity.

The two Transits operating on the PB1 service were replaced by two Dodge S56 type buses with Rootes (Maidstone) 20-seat bodywork, numbered A1-2. This was quite a sturdy vehicle to drive with its automatic gearbox, but it suffered a series of brake problems. Being a van derivative it had the infamous two leading shoe brakes which, although they had automatic adjusters, worked only when the vehicle was reversing with the brakes applied. Unfortunately buses do not often reverse and it was quite common for the pedal travel to gradually increase. Many problems were discovered on the foundation brakes and after much experimentation by the local service agents, with little success, I made contact with a former colleague who was now a Director at Renault and arranged for the vehicle to go back to Dunstable in their Experimental Shop. After a lot of work a reasonable situation

Typical of the earlier generation minibus was the Ford Transit, which generally had bodywork of a design derived from the parcel van version of this model. This one, FS25, was one of a batch of five with 16-seat body conversion by Dormobile dating from 1979.

was arrived at and the vehicle eventually returned to service.

The maintenance of these small buses was somewhat different from normal buses in that dealers and agents were used who were not necessarily part of the parent organisation—especially where Factors were concerned. One case arose whereby replacement brake shoes were obtained which did not have the right lining material fitted, although the shoes were correct as they were common to many other types of vehicles. Added to that, they were badly rivetted such that squeal developed. This problem had been voiced at the PTE engineering Sub-Committee, of which I was Chairman, and vehicle manufacturers had been asked to use nominated Factors who were approved by the manufacturer. How this is working I do not know, but it did at least identify a problem.

With the so-called autonomy of the satellite companies that were set up within London Buses, there was a period when the Districts went off and bought their own vehicles in the mini-bus field. No one was really sure that autonomy went that far as it was always said that the vehicles were owned by the Centre. Be that as it may, a variety of types was bought and some were even maintained on outside contract.

Experience was obtained on the Victoria Volkswagens as they happened to be maintained by Bus Engineering Limited (the Chiswick organisation of Frontsource). In the case of Westlink (the Stanwell Bus Company) good co-operation was maintained between the Centre and that organisation where we soon found that on their Metroriders the same Girling two leading shoe brake had been fitted prior to that used on the modified Dodge. I remember when shown the earlier designs of the Metrorider that I expressed my fears in the use of this brake. The modifications were quickly put in by MCW but trouble still persisted. Tests were conducted at Kingston on service vehicles which showed the inconsistency of the brake from wheel to wheel even throughout the day.

In order to relieve the foundation brakes, MCW started fitting a retarder. Two types were considered, one the well-known Telma and the other the Maxwell. For a variety of reasons outside the scope of this book the Telma was the popular choice and some experimental observations were taken on some vehicles so fitted. Naturally brake temperatures were reduced but it did nothing to alleviate the inconsistency problems.

The provision of a frequent service was popular with the public and this was put down to the use of mini buses. My own personal view was that whatever bus was used, provided it was frequent enough, the public would use it.

Nevertheless, loadings had increased beyond the mini bus stage and the stretched vans, which many of the mini buses were, showed their shortcomings. Fortunately with the late entry of MCW to the mini bus market their design was capable of stretching, whereas the Transit, Sherpa, Volkswagen etc had already been stretched to the limit of the basic design. With the brake problems looming on the mini MCW Metrorider, they wisely decided to go for disc brakes all round on the midi version. Temperatures taken seemed to indicate that there was far more consistency, and with it improved life of the pads. Time will tell. On these smaller type buses it does seem expensive to fit a retarder at an overall cost of about £2,000 when the whole exercise is to cut costs. On the mini and midi buses a retarder was non-obligatory. Who knows, the single-deck bus may even make a come-back, followed later by one with an upper-deck!

Whilst at first sight the running costs of mini and midi buses may seem much higher—through shorter vehicle life and poor engine life—it would appear that the financial situation with the current high interest rates makes the borrowing of smaller amounts of money for shorter periods a better proposition than larger amounts over a longer period.

Whatever the eventual outcome, I shall always find it difficult to accept these converted vans as buses.

The Bristol single-deck interlude

A paradox of the minibus is that when most successful in attracting passengers, it lacks the capacity to cope with the resulting numbers. A case in point among the original set of routes requested by the Greater London Council and introduced in 1973 was the C11. Alternative slightly larger buses examined included a Seddon from SELNEC Passenger Transport Executive but the choice fell on the Bristol LHS,

In 1975, the demand for a slightly larger vehicle than a minibus for the C11 service linking Willesden Green Station and Archway Station led to the purchase of six Bristol LHS buses with ECW bodywork, BS4 being seen on that route in 1977. Eleven more were added to the fleet in 1976.

which was a shortened version of the LH model originally introduced in 1967 as a light 30ft. single-decker intended mainly for rural services.

The LHS was 24ft. long but its units were basically as used for the longer version, with the Leyland O.400 engine given an easy time in so small a vehicle. The body, seating 26, was similarly a short version of a standard Eastern Coach Works product. Six were placed in service in 1975, numbered BS1-6, and these were followed by eleven more in 1976, taking the numbers up to BS17.

Although the short wheelbase of 12ft. 6in. did not permit a fluid transmission, the Turner spur gearbox provided a fairly easy gear shift. To cater for the full range of operation of National Bus Company (Bristol having been a subsidiary of NBC and its predecessors) the gearbox was five-speed, the bottom gear being a crawler gear for the Devon hills and the like. In view of the London operation this gear was blanked out, turning the box into a simple four-speed box which was very easy to operate. A few minor problems with the clutch were soon ironed out and the BS was a reliable creature, putting to shame many of the current mini buses today. What a pity these were not kept instead of being sold out of service when replaced.

The RF vehicle was generally replaced by the MB and SM but problems arose (in addition to the reliability ones) in respect of the 8ft. 2½in. width. The Licensing Authorities refused to accept this width in certain areas and demanded a 7ft. 6in. wide vehicle. The Bristol LH series of vehicles was built in three lengths — the LHS (short), LH (medium) and LHL (generally a coach but longer), and they could be provided in the 7ft. 6in. width.

A visit was made to Ulsterbus who operated some of the Bristol LH vehicles but these had a manual gearbox which would not have been acceptable in larger scale use in London. Discussions with Bristol enabled a fluid transmission to be fitted with a generous torque capacity. Unfortunately as standard the vehicles employed a two-leading-shoe brake which had been proved unsuitable for bus duties in London. Added to that, brake adjustment was manual which again is not acceptable in this modern day and age. Bristol chose a brake arrangement which was still two-leading-shoe but did have automatic adjusters. When the first vehicle was built extensive trials were undertaken at Bristol by one of my staff and the usual non-progressiveness of the brakes arose. After some more extensive tests amongst the brake lining manufacturers, only one liner arrangement was found acceptable. Again the 95 buses (BL1-95) built in 1976 proved to be sturdy and well equipped to deal with the rigours of London service. A few are still running, others having been sold to PTEs, Jersey, etc, as it was found possible in the interests of standardisation to convert the routes to Leyland National operation with some diversion to allow wider vehicles to be used.

The Dennis Domino was a heavier-duty midibus concept, inevitably more expensive than a van-derived vehicle. This one, with Northern Counties body, was given Abbey district insignia for operation on the C11, being borrowed from Greater Manchester Buses.

9. The XRM project

To the layman it may seem surprising that the next generation of buses is being considered soon after the current fleet is introduced. Yet this is essential if enough time is to be given for adequate study and development. Thus it was in 1974 that thought was being given to the replacement of the RM, the project being code named XRM. It was visualised as the successor to what were then the coming generation of double-deckers typified by the Leyland B15 (later the Titan) and the MCW Metrobus, to come into production in the 1980s. For an in-house developed vehicle, it is an advantage from the point of view of manufacturing costs if it is also attractive to other operators.

The co-operation with AEC over the RT had provided the basis for the Regent III, with almost as many 'provincial' examples (with most major parts of basically common design to the RT) sold at home and abroad as supplied to London Transport — the proportion was higher if the single-deck Regal III is included. The Routemaster suffered from a division of the types of double-decker being offered by AEC, not being marketed to other operators until its declining years. It was essential that a new design be cost-effective and easy to maintain, as well as attractive. The RM's higher initial cost doubtless discouraged provincial users and the power-hydraulic brakes were unfamiliar, although when Northern General purchased its fleet, their advantages were underlined by the freedom from trouble in a colder climate with more snow, salt, etc than experienced in London.

In all these feasibility studies it was customary to draw up a chart of existing vehicle details and compare them with the projected new vehicle. Such a comparison is reproduced. Then came a Development Programme to act as a guide to the timing of the project, as indicated. Naturally at this stage it could only take into account the information already known and in the light of further knowledge would be subject to considerable change. Behind each heading on the chart is a separate development task, sometimes of a fairly large magnitude, and I hope in this chapter to give an outline of these programmes showing how changes in direction were brought about by service trials.

By that period there was growing pressure for low flat floors with shallow entrance and exit steps and more internal headroom. To achieve this, it was desirable to have small wheels, and the only way this could be done was to have a multi-axled vehicle. The nearest thing readily available to this concept was the Bedford VAL with its twin steering axles, then recently out of production, so what better to obtain one second-hand, which I did, and thus a 1967 example with Plaxton coach body, RUW 990E, formed what must have seemed a surprising addition to the fleet. As made, it was fitted with a retarder — and it did not take long to find out why, for the model was notorious for poor brake life. Tests showed that, without the retarder, it could not meet LT standards.

Apart from this, the other worrying point was the steering

There was only one 'voluntary' provincial customer for the post-war RT — St. Helens Corporation, which took 40, complete with Park Royal bodywork to London Transport specification — the vehicle shown was one of the first batch of fifteen dating from 1950. However, several others operators received RT-type chassis as a result of immediate post-war allocations.

AEC's version of the Regent III and the single-deck Regal III as sold to provincial and overseas operators had a considerable following and although visually quite different had much in common in fundamentals. The standard version had 9.6-litre engine and air-operated gearbox and brakes, like the RT, helping to spread the manufacturing and development costs of many of the main components. This Sheffield Corporation example of 1949 had bodywork by Cravens to basically similar design to those supplied to LT on RT chassis, even though finished differently.

geometry. Good rapport with Vauxhall Motors, makers of Bedford vehicles, suggested that it was virtually impossible to set the steering to avoid excessive tyre wear on one wheel. It was hinted that the only way to set it up was to treat each bus as an individual. Help was sought from Cranfield Institute of

An unlikely-seeming purchase for London Transport in 1976 was this Bedford VAL coach with Plaxton bodywork, nine years old at the time, from the fleet of Sampsons of Cheshunt. I chose it to gain experience of vehicles with small wheels and twin steering axles, and much was learnt from it.

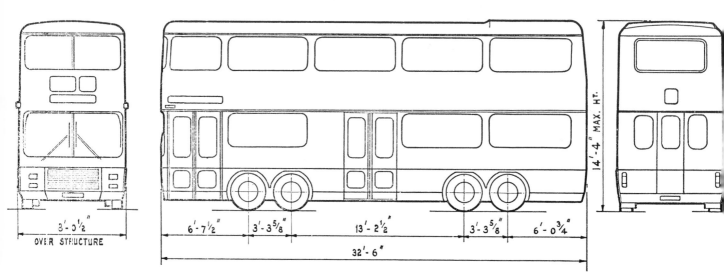

This comparison of the XRM with Routemaster Fleetline and B15 (Titan) indicates that despite being the longest, it was to have been even lighter than the RM.

This drawing reveals that the XRM would have been 32ft. 6in. (9.9-metre) long.

ITEM	XRM		RM		DM			B15			
OVERALL DIMENSIONS.											
LENGTH	32'-6"		27'-6 9/16"		30'-11"			31'-4 5/8"			
WIDTH	8'-2½"		8'-0"		8'-2½			8'-2 7/16"			
HEIGHT	14'-4"		14'-4 9/16"		14'-6"			14'-4¾"			
SWEPT TURNING CIRCLE	65'-0" DIA.		62'-0" DIA.		65'-0" DIA.			64'-6" DIA.			
PASSENGER CAPACITY	TWO CREW OPERATION	A.F.C. OPERATION	TWO CREW OPERATION		TWO CREW OPERATION		A.F.C. OPERATION	TWO CREW OPERATION		A.F.C. OPERATION	
UPPER SALOON SEATED	41	41	36 (36)		44 (41)		44 (41)	47 (44)		47 (44)	
LOWER SALOON SEATED	26	23	28 (26)		27 (25)		24 (22)	28 (25)		24 (22)	
TOTAL SEATING CAPACITY	67	64	64 (62)		71 (66)		68 (63)	75 (69)		71 (66)	
TOTAL STANDING CAPACITY	–	22	– –		– –		21 21	– –		23 21	
TOTAL CAPACITY	67	86	64 (62)		71 (66)		89 (84)	75 (69)		94 (87)	
ESTIMATED WEIGHTS											
UNLADEN KERBSIDE (FUEL, OIL & WATER)	7·28 tons	7·28 tons	7·4 tons	7·4 tons	9·95 tons	9·95 tons	9·9 tons 9·9 tons	9·5 tons	9·5 tons	9·5 tons 9·5 tons.	
PASSENGERS & DRIVER	4·63 tons	5·92 tons	4·1 tons	4·3 tons	4·55 tons	4·55 tons	5·65 tons 5·7 tons	4·8 tons	4·75 tons	5·94 tons 5·9 tons	
TOTAL LADEN WEIGHT	11·91 tons	13·20 tons	11·5 tons	11·7 tons	14·50 tons	14·50 tons	15·55 tons 15·6 tons	14·3 tons	14·25 tons	15·44 tons 15·4 tons	

COMPARISON OF XRM, RM, DM & B15 D/D VEHICLES

NOTES. 1a. PASSENGER CAPACITY SHOWN IN PARENTHESIS ARE AS XRM STANDARD I.E. PROPOSED G.R.S.A. EUROPEAN STANDARD.

1b. ALL WEIGHTS RELATIVE TO THE ABOVE ARE ON THE BASIS OF 150 LBS./PASSENGER (G.R.S.A. STANDARD) COMPARED WITH THE U.K. STANDARD OF 140 LBS./PASSENGER.

2. REGULATIONS PERMIT 8 STANDING PASSENGERS TO BE CARRIED ON CREW OPERATED VEHICLES.

The original proposal for the XRM was for an eight-wheeled design, with the objective of permitting a low floor line with minimal upward intrusion of the wheel arches.

Technology, rather confirming this and indicating that the only way was to use a computer-aided mechanism.

The steering and brake problems really ended the idea of having twin axles at the front. Since it is normal practice to fit new tyres on the front axles and then, after regrooving, run them out on the rear, any suggestion about having larger wheels at the front and retaining the small wheels on twin axles at the rear was not going to receive any support. Thus the four-axled XRM died.

Right from the start the engine position was to be on the offside, and with the four-axled vehicle the transmission line was somewhat difficult, compounded by the low floor level and accommodating differential units. There had been interest for some time in a hydrostatic drive, in which the engine drives a pump from which oil under pressure is fed to hydraulic motors mounted close to the wheels or at the wheels themselves. The Department of Trade and Industry funded an experiment carried out at the National Engineering Laboratory, East Kilbride, to fit a vehicle with hydrostatic transmission.

One of our Fleetlines, DM1787, a Leyland-engined vehicle that had entered service in February 1975, was sent to the NEL in the autumn of 1976 and converted. The pump took the place of the gearbox and in this case the hydraulic motors, of NEL design, were incorporated in the rear axle hubs themselves, there being four such motors in each of the two hubs. Flexible hoses fed the hydraulic fluid to the hubs, eliminating the need for both propeller shafts and a differential. It was envisaged that in the XRM design the wheel motors would be body-mounted and drive the rear wheels by short shafts, reducing the unsprung weight.

The design was based on the idea that with the engine running, pump pressure would be supplied to the wheel motors (each bank of four) causing the vehicle to accelerate. At a pre-determined speed (approx. 17mph) the supply of oil to two of each bank of motors was cut off and this caused further acceleration of the vehicle to its maximum speed of 45mph. When road trials began late in 1977 this caused some problems since the cut-off of the two motors each side left nowhere for the oil to go at this instant of what could be called

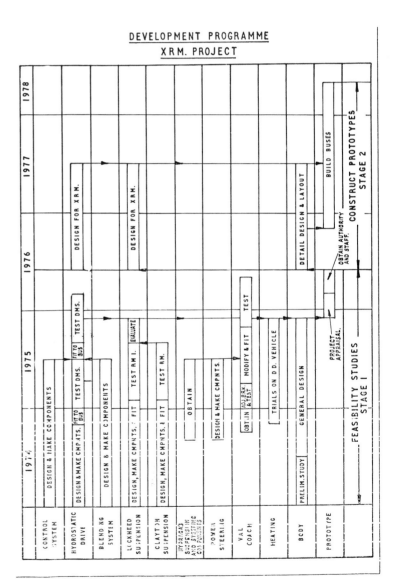

The planned development programme for the XRM would have led to the completion of prototypes by 1978.

123

This view shows Fleetline DM1787 as converted to hydrostatic transmission by National Engineering Laboratory. In place of the gearbox was a pump, feeding fluid to hydraulic motors in the rear wheel hubs.

consuming and costly, it would probably delay the XRM programme.

Another advantage claimed for hydrostatic transmission was that when slowing down the hydraulic system could be used to generate stored energy in accumulators which could be released when the vehicle accelerated again, thus saving fuel in the same manner as regenerative braking in use on some trolleybuses. However, the conversion of DM1787 never got beyond the non-regenerative stage. The bus was converted back to standard once the decision had been taken in 1980 that hydrostatic transmission would not be used for the next generation of buses. It was not until later that Volvo perfected a stored-energy system.

The coil-spring suspension had given good spring life (eight years for the front springs and fifteen years for those at the rear) with about two years for the shock absorbers, but it had limitations in the aim of achieving a low step height.

To further improve the suspension of the new vehicle earlier work in 1968 had indicated that, from a cost point of view, suspensions could be classed as follows, taking the most favourable as 1:-

'gear change', and the seals blew out. Provision of an expansion space overcame the trouble. However, when eventually completed, the drive noise was unacceptable and oil leaks under the somewhat high pressures were excessive. Because there was no provision of a lock-up in the drive, fuel consumption was also too high to be tolerable. To overcome these problems a good deal of work needed to be done on a control system to enable the vehicle to operate at optimum efficiency and it was considered that, apart from being time-

Type of Suspension	Initial Cost	Cost per annum in Maintenance
Leaf Springs	1	1.6
Coil Springs	1.35	1.02
Air Suspension	3.2	1

Unfortunately, with the idea of having a lower step height, both the leaf spring and coil spring present problems in not keeping a constant step height so the lowest step design that can be incorporated is governed by when the vehicle is laden. In the case of air suspension a constant height can be achieved

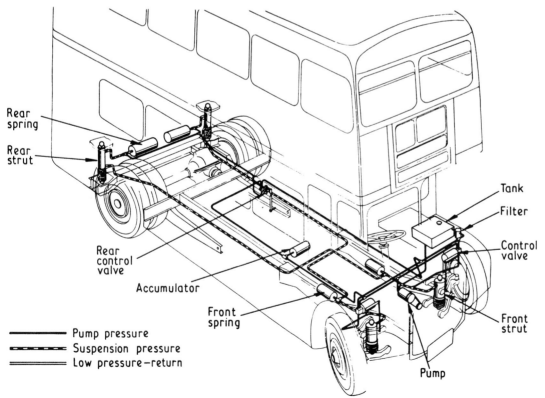

Rear spring
Rear strut
Rear control valve
Accumulator
Front spring
Pump

Tank
Filter
Control valve
Front strut

▬▬▬ Pump pressure
▬·▬·▬ Suspension pressure
══════ Low pressure—return

The idea of 'active ride', in which pressure could be applied within a hydraulic suspension system rapidly enough to counteract roll as well as giving a lowered step facility was developed to the stage of being tested on RM1 by Automotive Products and then transferred to RM116 in 1978 for trials in service. Such principles are still at the fringes of automotive design technique in 1990 and are another instance of how LT helped to pioneer new ideas of value far beyond its own activities.

throughout the load range, a feature desirable for elderly or disabled passengers. In spite of this, there were still some disadvantages with the air suspension system such as a delay in pumping up the system on run out in the morning. Sometimes the air bag became unseated when the air system deflated overnight and damage to the air bag could occur when roads were being tarred.

The advantages of coil suspension were further developed by trying a constant frequency coil spring by employing a spring with coils closer at each end than in the centre. Such a spring operates under the same frequency whether the vehicle is laden or unladen. RM7 was so fitted and gave a favourable ride. Unfortunately under lightly laden conditions coil slap occurred with the end coils emitting a noise like machine gun fire. Other than coating the spring in a plastic encasing it was impossible to get over this rattle and the proposal was dropped.

The Active Ride Suspension system developed by Automotive Products and mentioned in Chapter Six was taken up and it was planned to adopt it for the XRM. The principle, in brief, was to employ a hydraulic strut not dissimilar to a shock absorber to be fitted at each wheel station — there would have been independent suspension using wishbone linkage similar to that at the front of the RM. Sensing or levelling valves were fitted, and the struts were cross-connected diagonally across the vehicle. In addition to limiting roll, it was possible to lower or raise the vehicle so as to further reduce effective step height and its response was more rapid than the air system used on the 'kneeling' suspension developed by South Yorkshire PTE on a Leyland National.

The equipment was fitted to RM1 and a test programme carried out in conjunction with AP. It was then arranged to transfer the equipment to RM116 operating from Mortlake on route 9, though later transferred to Stamford Brook for route 27/9. A paper, *The Application of Hydraulic Suspension to the Public Service Vehicles* earned its three authors, Bob Pitcher of AP, Harry Hilled of the Dynamics Division of London Transport, and the writer, the Gresham Cooke Award in 1977.

Much thought was given to the power steering system. It was common practice to use a ram acting on the linkage but this had the disadvantage of imposing high loadings on the linkage. A system with power applied within the steering column, as on RML3, had also been tried but had the same disadvantage. The Leyland National system with the power applied at the Adwest rack-and-pinion unit mounted on the axle put the loadings nearer where they were wanted, almost at the road wheel. When the twin-steer layout was being considered, two such units were proposed, each controlled by lightly-stressed linkage from the steering column. When this was abandoned, it was intended to retain the same Adwest unit for a single axle layout, though there were problems of seal life related to the geometry which had not been overcome before the project was abandoned.

Another area of concern in relation to steering was the preservation of adequate self-centring effect. Applying more power than had been chosen for the RM made it easy to apply full lock at such a rate that it was difficult to straighten up, an effect which could arise with the Leyland National.

At this stage, only a little work was done on the structural design of the body, it being considered that the RM form of construction should be used.

So far as the choice of power unit was concerned, three options were considered initially, the first two being the Mercedes Benz OM421, an 11.0-litre V6, and the Leyland L11, which was the successor to the O.680, an in-line 11.1-litre six-cylinder unit. Although a Gardner six-cylinder unit of the LX series was considered, it was too long and too high to be fitted in the side position under the staircase and the revival of the five-cylinder then projected would not have been ready for the programme. Later the Perkins V8 was considered and one of the MS-class Metro-Scania single-deckers was retained to allow the idea to be investigated. However, beyond making a mock-up for a V8 installation in the XRM no further action was taken and the MS sold by Bus Sales.

The programmed date for design work to start in earnest was 1977 but because the Operating Department was unsure how bus operation was likely to take shape in the 1980s, the decision was made not to proceed further. A final review was made in 1980 on the future of the XRM and it was decided to terminate the project, as the questions of one-man operation and fare collection methods were still not settled. Meanwhile deliveries of the MCW Metrobus (M-class) and Leyland Titan (T-class) double-deckers had begun in 1978, though this in itself did not imply the end of the project which had been intended as the successor to these models as well as the replacement for the RM.

Enter the QRM

In any case, the basic idea was not entirely dropped and some work was done on a related project, the QRM. By that date the rear-engined Routemaster, FRM1, had been withdrawn from service and was allocated to my Experimental fleet, along with RM1 and RM2, and thought was given to converting the FRM to a QRM but the financial climate was not right for this development.

In essentials, the QRM would have revived the side-engined concept of the Q-type double-decker, of which two vehicles, Q2 and Q3, were built for the Central Area in 1934, but using RM design features, or those of the FRM in such features as the rear suspension with axle mounted over the side-members of the pivoted sub-frame rather than passing through them.

Around this time the Maxwell gearbox was in the pipeline and this had the capability of taking the drive line out of the box in several ways, rather than being restricted to either end. Indeed this gearbox had a lot going for it and its development was terminated not because of mechanical problems but due to market recession in the building of double-deck buses. With a side engine, and utilising the 'B' frame of the RM, the normal transmission line had a little difficulty avoiding the side-member but by taking a drive from the side of the box it would have been possible to avoid the side-member.

Although London Transport gave up the policy of developing its own vehicles, the basic idea did not die entirely. MCW had produced the Metrobus Mark I and then the Mark II with a good deal of standardisation and more extensive use of glass-fibre and thoughts were turning to the next stage. The policy of giving much thought to accommodating the elderly,

The QRM was to have revived the mechanical layout of the AEC Q-type bus of the mid-1930s. This picture shows Q3, one of a pair of double-deck examples supplied to London Transport for Central Area service in 1934, The side engine position is indicated by the louvred panel. These two vehicles had the entrance positioned ahead of the front wheels, in much the same manner as now considered usual, but at that time the whole concept was quite unlike any other double-decker in the fleet, and there were only a handful of other examples in service elsewhere.

infirm and disabled was pursued further and in conjunction with Ogle Design, an idea pioneered by Brighton Hove & District on Bristol Lodekka buses in 1961 was taken up and further developed. This was the split-step entrance, with the portion nearer the axle set at a lower level to take advantage of the reduced ground clearance needed at that point. There was also a desire to revert to independent front suspension to give better riding and stability, and these items were to be the basis for the Mark III. Indeed a place for such a vehicle was slotted in the Alternative Vehicle Evaluation. Working very closely with a good friend, John Brown, at that time with MCW, an underframe was produced and was such that although designed to have a rear engine could accommodate a side engine or even a front engine.

Allegedly because London did not order Metrobuses that particular year — there had been strong pressure from Leyland, which had threatened cessation of production of the Titan unless it received the whole of London's 1982 order — the idea was scrapped. Such an idea would have led to a good deal of standardisation in the body design, allowing the operator to have the engine where he wanted and also fit out the body to his style. There would have been a great bonus to the industry generally, much better than that which existed when Bus Grant was around. However, after an artificially induced cut back in bus orders, there are signs that after the great upheaval of privatisation and once the mini, midi bus saga has come and gone, that there may be a return to logical thinking again. The work has been done so there should be no need to re-invent the wheel again.

Although the project did not come to fruition at this stage I think perhaps it illustrated the thoroughness with which London Transport carried out such work and did not just fit new ideas to new generations of buses without full investigation. Critics may say that it should be left to the manufacturers to carry out such work but they must have some encouragement to do so. Money is not available to try every new idea and they need some evidence that the ideas do have some commercial substance. This is probably where the close co-operation with AEC was of great benefit not only to London Transport but to the bus industry generally, a fact which is not generally recognised.

Chosen for London service while the XRM project was in its early stages, the MCW Metropolitan double-decker was derived from the Metro-Scania single-decker. It offered good standards of performance but London traffic showed up problems with the two-speed automatic transmission, which rarely got into the equivalent of top gear. Seen here on the 36B at Marble Arch is MD92 which entered service in October 1976 from Peckham (PM), home of most of the class — it was withdrawn in March 1983, after six and a half years service. The first of the class, MD1, has been restored to original condition by the Birmingham & Midland Motor Omnibus Trust and was displayed at the Wythall Museum in July 1990 before going to the Scania Museum in Sweden.

10. A time of change

Foreign visits and some foreign products

The visits of London buses to various parts of the world are well-known and many have been documented elsewhere. The author was privileged to lead a tour to New Orleans and Memphis with a Routemaster in 1963, this being my first visit abroad and leading to many more.

Until the 1970s, because LT had almost always bought British, there had been little need to talk with foreign manufacturers, though there had long been friendly relations with several of the world's leading city transport undertakings. However, Leyland's decision to develop its own integral single-decker, which emerged as the Leyland National, led MCW, previously associated with Leyland in the manufacture of the Olympic integral single-decker (which had continued to sell well in various export markets up to the early 1960s) to look elsewhere. The result was the association with Scania of Sweden and the production of the Metro-Scania, of which the body shell was built by MCW to a design derived from Scania's home-market model but adapted for Britain with opposite-hand layout and other features.

One Metro-Scania demonstrator had been operated on loan as early as 1969-70 and six, forming the MS class, were acquired to operate alongside a similar number of Leyland Nationals in 1973, as described in Chapter Eight. However, MCW reacted to the renewal of demand for double-deckers in the early 1970s by developing a double-deck version of the same basic design called the Metropolitan, of which the first was completed late in 1973, visiting LT shortly afterwards. Both types used Scania's ingenious sub-frame construction in which the front and rear units—somewhat akin to the Routemaster 'A' and 'B' frames though the rear one incorporated the complete power train—were assembled together to form a chassis, capable of being driven, though at that stage having a much shorter wheelbase than when unbolted, spaced out and attached to the body structure. Both used the Scania 11-litre vertical six-cylinder engine mounted transversely at the rear, the transmission being a simple torque converter, with lock-up acting as the equivalent to top gear, giving a two-speed effect, overall.

The single-decker sold only in limited numbers but the double-decker became available just as output of the Fleetline dropped badly behind schedule due to the transfer of production from Coventry to Leyland and aggravated by the troubles that arose in consequence. Indeed, MCW was itself affected by the latter as Fleetline chassis for both London Transport and West Midlands PTE, due to be bodied there, became delayed.

A visit was made to Scania Vabis in 1975 to discuss London bus requirements, but in the main the mechanical units for the vehicles ordered were to be as made for Swedish operation. The main criticism was that the acceleration was, if anything, too good and in consequence the braking allowed the driver to abuse the vehicle. In addition, there was a tendency for following vehicles to fail to stop in time when drivers of the buses braked sharply, following use of the acceleration available. Whilst in Sweden we went to Malmo to visit SAB who were introducing an automatic brake adjuster to replace the Clayton Dewandre unit which was going out of production.

The resulting fleet of 164 Metropolitan double-deckers formed the MD class, delivery beginning in December 1975 and being completed early in 1977. They entered service at Peckham and New Cross garages. Operation on the 36 route soon showed the weakness of the transmission. In theory this was fine, but in London operation the gearbox rarely got into lock-up and thus remained in torque converter mode, giving very heavy fuel consumption and causing overheating of the transmission, sometimes causing failures. Attempts were made to lower the lock-up speed so that some advantage could be gained from direct drive. When slowing down with no throttle the disengaging speed was too low, such that the vehicle became very jerky.

It must be said that the vehicle was extremely quiet, so much so that tyre noise became noticeable. Attempts were made to reduce the maximum level of braking available in response to normal pressure by fitting a spring-loaded stop in the pedal, but before this got very far it was decided to withdraw the vehicles, creating another instance of short life by comparison with traditional London standards. All had gone by March 1983.

Another consideration was that MCW were bringing out their own bus—the Metrobus. In all fairness to Scania, it must be said that in the next version an additional speed was incorporated in the transmission which overcame the problems that London experienced.

With the advent of the MCW Metrobus, described more fully later in this chapter, it had been decided to accept a German gearbox, namely the Voith D851, which was a torque converter transmission backed up by three speeds. Within the torque converter was an integral retarder which was to become a statutory fitment under EEC law. An MBS had been fitted at Wood Green with the earlier Voith D501 box which gave a very good account of itself. When the Metrobus was in course of development it was felt worthwhile to fit one of the D851 boxes to a Red Arrow MB, namely MBA458, operating out of Walworth, from late 1976. Brake liner life was increased considerably due to the inbuilt retarder but it was not felt correct to drawn any strict comparisons, even though indications were as much as five-fold, as Red Arrow operation was a special type of service. Nevertheless, brake temperatures were halved, which in itself points to a potential life improvement. In all the gearbox lasted four and a half years until all the MBAs were withdrawn and replaced by Nationals.

As the performance of the Voith had been so impressive the loan of an ex-Leeds City Transport 1959 Daimler CVG6 bus

This 1959 Daimler CVG6 with Roe bodywork originally operated by Leeds City Transport, was fitted with Voith D851 automatic transmission to act as a mobile test bed for Dennis, which concern was proposing to use the D851 in its new double-decker. In 1977, it was accepted for trial on route 27 from Turnham Green and behaved well.

which had been fitted with the Voith D851 was accepted in 1977. The loan was arranged through the good offices of Bob Crouch, another good friend of many years standing, mainly with Daimler and now working for Hestair Dennis at Guildford, who had purchased this vehicle for development purposes. The arrangement was that for the price of a repaint London Transport would operate the vehicle for three months. Bob was a well-known figure of the Daimler organisation, having also been concerned with the Royal cars, and was around during the days of Pomeroy and the introduction of fluid transmission. Many hours have we spent listening to Bob's account of events of yesteryear over the dinner table after our meetings.

The bus was quite old-fashioned by current standards — no power steering — and really a provincial standard double-decker of the period as the photograph will show. With tongue in cheek I approached the union representative at Turnham Green, where it was thought it would be a good idea to operate it. Perhaps as Turnham Green had long suffered major experimental vehicles, what was one more? Rex readily agreed to accept the vehicle and also agreed that it could operate on route 27 along with RMs. Hardly a murmur was heard from the drivers — and the same could be said of the Voith gearbox. For the three months it operated at Turnham Green the gearbox did not require any oil, nor did it require any attention. Really this operation confirmed the reliability of the Voith gearbox and this was to be upheld by the Metrobuses, which were shortly to appear.

Frequent visits were made to Heidenheim, the headquarters of Voith, where they had located mainly the paper making machinery side of their business plus their Experimental shop. On one visit a long-life transmission had been deliberately

removed from a Metrobus so that it could be sent back to Voith for an examination. The system at Voith was such that the original test report was available and the removed box would still be acceptable to new standards. It was then decided to strip the box just to confirm these results, and nothing needed to be changed other than, of course, oil seals etc. The box was then rebuilt, tested and returned to be fitted to a London bus. This good life led to an upset in the number of spare boxes since it was customary to base spares on what was considered the norm. As this could only be judged against previous gearboxes, initially there was a large pile of spare boxes that did not move for several years! It would be true to say that the life of the Voith was at least twice that of the conventional Wilson box, quite apart from the increased brake liner life brought about by the retarder. In fairness to the Wilson box, it had shown almost double the life of the clash gearbox it replaced. This probably lulled us into a false sense of security, but automatic control highlighted the need for close control over the manufacture of brake bands. Voith had also begun with brake bands but by the time of the Metrobus had changed to plate clutches and sintered materials made them more responsive to full-throttle changes. Despite being brought up on the Wilson box, even I had to change my ideas.

Whilst in Heidenheim opportunity was taken to visit the Munich city operator who obviously used Voith and had several articulated buses. Such visits were always a great pleasure since stories can be exchanged of how each deals with what are often common problems. As a city, Munich has always impressed me with its fully-integrated transport system, a model for the rest of the World.

Other regular visits were to Northern and Southern Ireland. Northern Ireland was a good outlet for surplus London buses due to the vehicles they lost because of burn-outs. We also helped with the know-how in re-equipping second-hand Fleetlines that were not equipped with power steering. I was always amazed at the level of thought that went into the overhaul of units at their Falls Road works which really deals with the City Bus (ex-Belfast Corporation) side, and it was always a pleasure to meet up again with Tom Campbell, their Chief Engineer.

The other side of the organisation was Ulsterbus, where Ken Middleton, whom I came to know when I was looking at the Bristol LH as a replacement vehicle for the last RF buses because of its size, was Chief Engineer.

Werner Heubeck, who has recently retired, presided overall as Managing Director and managed both organisations in a manner to be admired. It was always a pleasure to meet him on my visits — in fact I nearly always found that on being met either at the airport or station, that I had to go via Milewater Road to have a chat. Indeed a character who will be missed.

Throughout my many visits to Belfast I saw very little of the unrest — except perhaps the obvious sign of guarded police stations, especially the one opposite the Falls Road depot which was the subject of an ambush.

My visits to CIE were just as interesting and enjoyable. There was particular interest in the wholesale re-organisation that CIE was undergoing somewhat in advance of London. Why some of the lessons learned in Dublin were not observed in London I do not know. I was always made exceedingly welcome by Joe Martin, who is the Chief Mechanical

Engineer, Bus Eireann, CIE now being the holding company much akin to London Regional Transport. Many of the problems associated with the early Atlanteans were common to both London and Dublin and John Kinnear of Leyland service was heard to remark that if either of us raised a problem there was some justification.

Later on CIE was to build its own buses based on a design by FFG in Hamburg. This concern was a development organisation with, I believe, some tie up with Hamburg Transport, and run by the Schultz family, father and son. I had the pleasure of meeting the son, Rainier, at one of the Hamburg Transport Fairs which are an excellent presentation by the Germans. The bus, a double-decker, was an integral construction vehicle built in Ireland by Bombardier. In design it was not unlike the Titan but did not have internal stress panels, relying instead on the structure to take the strain. Structural problems were experienced, probably to a greater extent than the Titan, and a re-work programme had to be initiated. I saw this being carried out at the Broadstone Works, and on my last visit to Dublin I was taken through all the modification details to put the vehicle to rights.

In the intervening period the Bombardier organisation was taken over by GAC Ireland and they produced the new single-deck Country bus for CIE. Unfortunately, lack of orders caused closure of GAC even though a lot of designs were in the pipeline, and the factory at Shannon is now back under Bus Eireann control, but mothballed.

It was customary to visit the Summerhill garage, where a computerised maintenance system had been installed in 1985, and in 1988 it was interesting to see how it was going. This had a lot going for it and I had hoped that the EMAG system being introduced into London Buses could have benefitted from a closer examination of this system.

One of my earlier recollections, soon after the announcement of the Ailsa B55 double-deck bus, concerns a prototype running with Dublin City Services. Little did I then realise that many years later I would organise the purchase of three such vehicles for evaluation since the engine was in the most desirable position—at the front of the vehicle—and despite this, the vehicle could be used of OMO. Whilst out with the bus we came across a student demonstration and the rapid way the Garda dealt with it was impressive. At the suggestion of the police we returned to the garage and watched the demonstration on closed circuit TV which happened to cover the area, though really for traffic purposes!

I have nothing but praise for the reception and hospitality that I was given during my many visits to Ireland generally, and felt that I was accepted as one of the family. It is a country of great contrast and a transport of delight. The Transport Museum at Howth is well worth a visit, not forgetting the dog.

Probably the most outstanding trip of my years with London Transport was in January 1986 when I was despatched to Beijing (Peking) in connection with a project to look into the prospect of selling surplus RMs to China.

Routemaster RM1863 had previously been sent to Hong Kong in 1984 for a Trade Fair. City Bus were down to act as agents for modifying the bus to suit Chinese operation, such as moving the staircase to the opposite side and putting in another entrance, but not modifying the driving position. The general idea was that the purchase of second-hand

Contact with operators in other countries was often valuable. Coras Iompair Eireann developed its own bus production, using a design by FFG of Hamburg. This is a single-deck example I saw on a Dublin visit.

RMs—suitably modified—would provide a stop-gap whilst the Chinese authorities planned an integral system which would take about five years.

The bus was despatched by road from Hong Kong to Peking, a journey of 1,000 miles. Since the journey would go through restricted areas I was unable to go with it, but spent the time trying to organise entry visas. The journey, apparently sometimes over rough roads, caused a great deal of excitement and apart from some minor roof damage and the loss of the exhaust system due to tight ground clearance, the RM arrived safe and sound. Arrival in Beijing was on 28th January, which coincided with my arrival from Hong Kong.

The next day a visit was made to the garage where the vehicle was to be operated. It immediately became apparent that there was no under-cover facility as the buildings were only high enough for single-deckers. The only place where any instruction on the vehicles could be given was on a ramp which was used for cleaning the underside of vehicles. Bearing in mind temperatures were below zero it was not the ideal situation! Some instruction was given in the classroom but some had to be done on the vehicle. On draining the air system of condensation the water froze as it came out of the drain plug hole, and could be broken off. Another shock in store was that anti-freeze is not used in Beijing and all vehicles were drained as they entered the garage and refilled when going out on service with hot water from a fleet of tankers continually on the boil! With the RM and its heater-radiator immediately above the driver's cab, it was essential to use anti-freeze which had to be obtained specially. Language was a difficulty which made all discussions somewhat lengthy, especially with the various dialects.

Later that day a presentation was made to the officials of the

Here I am seen with the Chief Engineer of the Peking undertaking.

The possibility of selling RM buses to China led to the conversion of RM1863 with opposite-hand entrance and stairs, an extra doorway and full-depth sliding windows throughout. This was done by City Bus, Hong Kong and then, in January 1986, we sent it to Beijing, where I joined it to supervise the demonstration. This picture was taken not far from the infamous Tiananmen Square.

Corporation and police and then a trip to the now infamous Tiananmen Square, which is like the Red Square in Moscow. From the police inspection there were a few omissions in meeting legal requirements but there were two points where I was unable to accept their assessment:

Firstly, there were no pressure gauges for hydraulic brakes, gearbox pressure, water temperature etc, and secondly, the brakes were not good enough when crawling along in traffic.

After a lengthy explanation they conceded that the warning flag was all that was needed with the red light for air pressure. The absence of a water thermometer was explained by the fact that with the engine where it was the driver would soon be aware of any boiling. As far as the brakes were concerned, it appeared that the performance of a brake was judged by whether the wheel locked and skidded. We had to try and explain through an interpreter that RM was designed so that whatever the loading it was only on the verge of skidding. After a practical demonstration the police gradually accepted my explanation, having difficulty in appreciating that hydraulic brakes are much smoother in operation than air brakes.

The working week in Beijing is a six day one of about twelve hours each, nearly everyone being free on Sunday. Opportunity was taken to look at bus operation and it was obvious that the buses were quite old. Each vehicle seemed to be provided with a broom, water and bucket. Once the drivers appreciated the power-assisted steering of the RM, and the automatic gear change, their method of driving changed. It is their practice to accelerate a vehicle up to 30mph and then drop into neutral to save fuel. This would be totally unacceptable on any bus in Britain and especially on the RM as the brake pump drive is taken from the input to the gearbox. To drive keeping one's foot on the throttle, with automatic change, pleased the officials greatly and it was a job to hold them back.

For a visitor to China a trip to the Great Wall and the Forbidden City is a must and this was done as a guest of the bus company. The full story of the visit has been told in a department report but the foregoing is included here to give the reader an idea of bus operation in China.

In order to return home after seeing the RM into service on the run from Tiananmen Square to the Summer Palace it was necessary to return via Hong Kong, where I had some business with China Motor Bus. After a meeting with an ex-London Transport colleague, Alan Leech, who was Chief Traffic Superintendent of Hong Kong Tramways, I was invited to visit their organisation and be taught to drive one of their trams. This turned out to be quite an experience especially as the mechanisms were so worn that it was somewhat hit and miss, though not literally I hasten to add!

Titan, Metrobus and Olympian

While the XRM project was still in its early stages, work was beginning on the contenders for the major part of London's bus requirements from the latter part of the 1970s and early 1980s. Although the FRM project had been dropped, apart from the building of a prototype, in 1966, we continued to make it clear that something of similar specification was what was wanted when the question of a successor to the Fleetline was being considered in the early 1970s.

Early outline designs, which were the subject of discussion between John Bloor of Park Royal and my colleague Stan Speed, were along the lines of an updated FRM but then the project went to Leyland and was turned into a completely new design, given the code B15, although having the same main features — integral construction, independent front suspension, hydraulic brakes, plus, of course, automatic transmission and power steering. It was claimed at this stage to require fewer man-hours to complete than the Routemaster. Five prototypes were put in hand at Park Royal in 1974, and one of these was used for the public announcement of the project in November 1975 before being sent to us, registered NHG 732P, for a period of experimental service in February 1976. Another of the prototypes, BCK 706R, also spent some time in London but was also used for the second 'launch', at which the model was given the name Titan, in June 1977.

Progress on the project was slow. There had been consultation with ourselves, the Passenger Transport Executives and the National Bus Company on the specification and inevitably there were differences of opinion. Leyland wanted to use its 500 series engine — the vertical version of the unit used in the Leyland National, but we made it clear that we wanted the Gardner 6LXB, with the Leyland O680 as a possible second choice. British Leyland, with its huge Austin and Morris car business in difficulties, was also looking for financial partners in the scheme, somewhat along the lines of the Leyland National exercise, and inevitably this exercise — ultimately fruitless — tended to delay matters.

There were many meetings between representatives of LT and the manufacturers. Basically the LT team was led by Mr J. W. Wicks and once the high-level decisions had been taken, subsidiary meetings were held on a regular basis with the interested parties — mechanical and electrical subjects were covered in meetings at Leyland, and body meetings at Park

Royal. Those involved included R. A. Fryers, J. McGowan, M. Dunn and, at Park Royal, J. Bloor.

Meanwhile, MCW had also been developing a new bus design, this time one for which it would be responsible for the vehicle as a whole. Leyland's decision to transfer production of the Fleetline chassis from the Daimler works in Coventry to its own plant in Leyland and the consequent closure of Daimler's bus design office released staff experienced in such work at a time when MCW, based on the outskirts of Birmingham nearest to Coventry, was in need of such people. Notable among senior staff in this category with whom I came in contact were John Rook, John Brown, Bernard Evans and, as a consultant, Peter Windsor-Smith.

The Metrobus had a complete underframe which was virtually a self-contained chassis (indeed some were sold as such for bodying by Alexander) and was also less advanced than the Routemaster or B15 in retaining a beam front axle, even though air suspension was standard. On the other hand, MCW recognised the potential for major orders from LT and incorporated a continuous-flow hydraulic brake system as one of the standard options from the beginning. The first prototype to be completed for demonstration duty, registered TOJ 592S, paid a first visit to LT for a brief period of loan on 20th December 1977, at the same time as one of the Titan prototypes. An initial order for five production vehicles had been placed, these having Gardner 6LXB engines and Voith transmission, this combination being chosen for most later London examples. At first the class letters were to be MT and the first vehicle, MT1, was delivered on 21st April 1978 — later it was described to identify the type simply as M, and the vehicles were numbered M1 upwards.

During 1977 it had been decided to order 450 double-deckers and an initial order for 50 Metrobuses and 50 Titans was confirmed — later these were increased to 200 and 250 respectively. All were to have Gardner 6LXB engines but the Titans had Leyland's Hydracyclic gearbox, which reverted to the original Routemaster concept in being hydraulically operated though retaining the familiar Wilson epicyclic gearing. The Titans were to be numbered in a TN series but this, too, was simplified, becoming T and thus arousing memories of AEC Regal single-deckers! The first of London's Titans, T1, was delivered on 16th August 1978.

Delivery of production Metrobuses was fairly slow at first, the first five having been followed by only ten more by the end of 1978, though the combined total of 205 had been delivered by a year later. Titan deliveries were even slower, with seven in stock at the end of 1978 and it was not until May 1980 that the delivery of the 250 buses of the first batch was completed.

Both local and national politics had their effect on these batches of vehicles and although most of this is beyond the scope of this volume, it can be mentioned that production plans for the Titans were affected by British Leyland's decision to close the AEC works (where at one stage it had been planned to build the Titans) announced in October 1978, and put into effect in May 1979. Then Park Royal's factory was also closed, the 250th Titan for London being the last vehicle built there. Thus was ended bus production in London and the last vestige of the link between the main operator of buses in the capital and their manufacture in the area—a sad day in more ways than one for London!

It had been planned to resume Titan production at Eastern Coach Works in Lowestoft, but this fell through and in the event it was transferred to Workington, where a production line was set up, alongside the facilities for Leyland National assembly. Output did not resume until 1981. By that date the Titan had virtually become a London-only model, partly because of the repeated delays, and partly because Leyland had developed another double-deck model, the Olympian, technically slightly less advanced than the Titan, with a self-contained chassis and beam front axle, but more readily produced in a variety of lengths and with other alternative features to suit different operators' needs — in particular, it met the NBC's requirement for a low-height model to replace the Bristol VRT, and attracted large-scale orders from operators in Britain and abroad.

Inevitably, this meant that Titan production was becoming more costly, and making continuation of production more uncertain. The delays in production had put the Metrobus well in front in terms of deliveries—during 1980, the fleet had grown by a further 300 examples to reach fleet number M505, while Titan deliveries from Workington beginning at T251 did not get under way until early in 1981, but by the end of 1982 had reached T675; Metrobuses had got to M805 earlier in the year.

The rear-engined Leyland Titan had begun life as the B15 project in the early 1970s. This example, T530, was placed into service in August 1982 and was built at the Workington factory where production had been transferred the previous year.

The MCW Metrobus has visual similarities to the Metropolitan, notably with the continued use of an asymmetrical windscreen, but is based on a quite different design below the skin, with a chassis-like underframe. The Gardner engine was chosen as standard for London examples. Seen here is M628, dating from September 1981. Omission of MCW from the 1982 order, which went entirely to Leyland, discouraged further involvement by MCW in the Metropolitan Mark III project in hand at the time.

For 1983 delivery, the order was split between 210 Titans and 150 Metrobuses but towards the end of that year it was decided that the programme for 1984-85 would include the completion of the Titan deliveries with a final 240 vehicles, ending production of the model. The Metrobus orders for 1984 and 1985 were 150 and 335, bringing the total of what was later called the Mark I type to 1440. As planned, Titans up to T1125 were completed towards the end of 1984. By that date the London Transport Executive had become London Regional Transport, the change of title marking the end of the Greater London Council era. In retrospect the Titan was disappointing in that the integral construction did not produce the weight saving expected with such construction as did the RM.

It was decided to carry out an Alternative Vehicle Evaluation Programme (AVE) on three examples each of Leyland Olympian (classified L), MCW Metrobus Mark II (added at the end of the M series), Dennis Dominator (H) and Volvo Ailsa B55 (V), in order to decide on the choice of further double-decker orders, the replacement of Routemasters being particularly in mind. Most were delivered during the earlier part of 1984. Specifications were deliberately varied, to gain experience of a variety of units as well as the models quoted.

Thus there were to be alternative engines within the batches of Olympians and Metrobuses and two different transmissions for the three Dominators. Gardner 6LXB engines were to be found in two of the Olympians, a Metrobus and both the Dominators, and all but one of these 6LXB-powered buses had Voith D851 transmission, which was also used with a Cummins engine in another Metrobus and with the Volvo TD70H engines in the three Volvo B55 buses. One Leyland Olympian had a Leyland TL11 engine and Hydracyclic transmission, whilst one Dominator had a Maxwell gearbox coupled to its 6LXB.

The original plan was that there were to have been two Metrobus Mark II buses, with the 'simplified' body design which had been adopted for Metroliner deliveries outside London, and a third, the Metrobus Mark III with independent front suspension which would have been the forerunner of the next generation of MCW double-deckers. The Metrobus Mark II buses (M1441 and 1442) were duly built, entering service in July 1984 (M1442) and September 1984 (M1441), when deliveries of production Metrobus Mark I buses had yet to reach M1100. However, the Mark III, which would have been M1443, did not come to fruition, unfortunately, this being an MCW decision.

Deliveries of the other AVE buses had begun with the three Olympians, which entered service in March-April 1984, and the first two Volvo B55 buses were put on the road in July of that year. The Dennis Dominators went into service in February 1985 and the last of the series was the final B55,

The Alternative Vehicle Evaluation Programme was drawn up on the basis of comparative trials of sets of vehicles from four manufacturers, the individual specifications also varying. The first of three Leyland Olympians with Eastern Coach Works bodies, L1 differed from the rest of the AVE fleet in having a Leyland TL11 engine and Hydracyclic transmission. It entered service in March 1984 and is seen here leaving Aldwych in August that year.

The two MCW Metrobus vehicles delivered in 1984 for the AVE exercise were of the Mark II type and M1442, seen here in Trafalgar Square in May 1985, was fitted with a Cummins L10 engine instead of the usual Gardner 6LXB. The Routemaster alongside was RML2608, already overdue for replacement by normal standards, being nearly eighteen years old at the time.

Also a member of the Alternative Vehicle Evaluation fleet, H3 was one of three Dennis Dominator models with Gardner 6LXB engines and Northern Counties bodywork. These were the first new Dennis buses to be added to the fleet since LGOC days, and the first buses with Northern Counties bodywork since the era of the wartime Guy Arab. The vehicle shown was one of two with Voith transmission.

(Below right) The three Volvo buses in the AVE programme were of the Ailsa-designed B55 type and hence briefly reintroduced front-engined layout to the intake of new double-deckers for the first time since Routemaster days. Noteworthy in this view of V2 in Trafalgar Square in April 1985 is the offside cab door of the Alexander bodywork — it had been in service since the previous July.

(Below) The third Volvo B55 did not arrive until March 1985 because of its special layout, with the exit doorway of the rear and a second staircase. Seating capacity was reduced to 65, compared to 76 on the other two B55 buses. It is seen at Chiswick soon after arrival.

which was later because it was of different layout. Instead of the combination of front entrance and centre exit which applied to the other AVE buses, and indeed London double-deckers in general since the Fleetline era, it was provided with a rear exit, taking advantage of the absence of the rear engine installation on this front-engined model. In addition, there was a second staircase. This vehicle, V3, went into service in

Only limited numbers of the rear-engined Leyland Titan were supplied to operators other than London Transport. Among them was West Midlands PTE, in whose fleet the five vehicles of this type, all dating from 1979, were regarded as non-standard and were sold to LT in 1984, taking fleet numbers which followed on from those of the buses supplied direct. They were equipped with coach seats but T1129, in Selkent Travel livery, is seen on bus duty, bound for Plumstead garage.

March 1985, completing the planned AVE fleet apart from the abandoned M1443. All the vehicles were allocated to Stockwell (SW) garage.

A fourth Volvo was added to the fleet on a leasing basis in September 1985, though not as part of the AVE programme. This was C1, a Volvo Citybus with the Cumulo energy storage system, described later in this chapter. Its horizontal engine was of the THD100EC type, of 9.6-litres rather than the 6.7-litres of the TD70H in the B55-type buses, the latter dictated by the space question mentioned in the previous paragraph. The drive was taken through a conventional automatic transmission, in this case a ZF HP500 four-speed unit, but the Cumulo device could either draw energy from the system, acting as a retarder, or feed it back, aiding acceleration. This work was intended as research for the future rather than a basis for placing orders for the next batch of new vehicles.

In the event, it was decided to order 260 further Leyland Olympian buses with bodywork by Eastern Coach Works, of which delivery began in January 1986, these being for London Buses Ltd, as we had become from 1st April 1985, as the 'bus' subsidiary of London Regional Transport. The announcement was made in June 1985 and indicated that features derived from an Ogle design study of factors making for easier loading described later in this chapter would be incorporated. Competition for business had become intense as the phasing out of New Bus Grant was completed in March 1984 and the position was further complicated by the move to privatise Leyland Bus Ltd, whose empire included the Leyland premises for bus production in Leyland and Workington and the ECW factory at Lowestoft. With far more capacity in the industry than could be kept busy, it was decided to close ECW and the completion of the L4-263 batch in January 1987 also marked the end of ECW.

Research and Development

The view is often held that Research and Development is an expensive luxury and allows a select body of people to carry out experiments behind closed doors with little or no relevance to the present day. Obviously one must be looking ahead — otherwise the horse bus would still be around! A true Research and Development section must have very close ties with the operation of the business as without it there would be no finance, and should contain staff who are familiar with such operation. What better test, having created a prototype, than to go out into the field and operate it with the normal equipment available? A Research and Development section — which I think is better named as Experimental — is a useful asset in solving problems away from the day-to-day hassle. After all, solutions are not always so obvious. At the end of the day all changes must be cost-effective, except perhaps safety problems where mandatory regulations apply, and it was for this reason that I undertook a review each year on the work done and how much, hopefully, was saved.

For instance, during 1984/5 a lot of work was carried out on oil leaks after pressure from the Department of Transport. It should be realised that the RM had been operating since 1959, but opportunity had not been taken to update gaskets with new and better materials. A review of the critical areas indicated that some change could be made in certain applications. Longer life could be obtained since oil leaks could be prevented which in the extreme prevented premature unit change.

Changes in oil formations led to extended oil change periods, and the fitment of oil filters once again proved an advantage. Again maintenance costs were reduced by less frequent changing, better performance and life from units and so on.

Another task undertaken on a continuing basis was the compilation of an *Approved Source of Supply Register* where details were listed of the best materials for items such as hoses (air, water and hydraulic) and from whom they could be purchased to be of the right quality.

One item which did not give a saving on the books was the purchase of fuel. It was the policy to take a sample of fuel deliveries and analyse for calorific value, gravity and so on to compare against the specification supplied (London Transport had its own high specification). Depending on the results from the Laboratory an adjustment was made in the next month's price. In spite of the cost of the analysis, a saving over seven times that cost was averaged over the year. Unfortunately the savings were absorbed by the garages without credit to the centre. This applied to nearly all the savings and only in the last year were Budget adjustments made to allow for these savings.

Typical figures for such savings for the years were as follows:-

1984/5	£297,000 saving over budgetted labour costs.
1986	£753,190 saving over budgetted labour costs.

By 1986 these savings equalled the budget costs of my section. So far as the Experimental Shop was concerned, outside work was taken on (quite apart from the altering relationship with London Buses which was being re-organised into self-accounting units in preparation for privatisation) and we were covering 50 per cent of the costs of the shop on that basis.

In earlier periods, when major projects such as the production of the Routemaster prototypes were in hand, costs would have been high. The RM was designed for a 17-year life, and, of course, it has far exceeded that. In layman's terms it thus more than paid for itself but accountancy doesn't quite work like that, so the RM carries a book value of the vehicle that would have to be purchased to replace it. However, the savings made as a result of the model's reliability and lack of need for expensive repair or early replacement by comparison with the off-the-shelf models that came later are virtually impossible to quantify but must run into the £multi-million range.

Much of the Research and Development work was able to be incorporated in new vehicle production so that the problems solved would not repeat. It was this liaison with manufacturers that was able to benefit London Transport, particularly with the RM programme. Once Bus Grants came into the picture, with the 'standard' bus, it became difficult to get one's own way and unsatisfactory performance resulted.

As has been stated before, London Transport maintained a very close relationship with many of the vehicle manufacturers, and such a case applied with Vauxhall Motors Limited, going back to the 1960s. In those days Vauxhall was the manufacturer of Bedford commercial vehicles, of which LT had a number, though it was more on a basis of mutual respect between research and development staff in quite different organisations that co-operation was built up.

With the aid of a brittle lacquer, Vauxhall had developed an extremely useful method of stress analysis, the work being done at their Chaul End Engineering Research Laboratory. The developed method is to spray the lacquer evenly over the area to be tested and the secret is to ensure that temperature changes are kept to a minimum. At the same time calibration bars are used to compare with the cracks that develop in the test area, and hence stress levels and the direction can be observed. To assist in observing the cracks the part is treated using the statiflux technique, and the result photographed. Having established the level of the stress, a more detailed test can be carried out using strain gauges fitted in the appropriate direction. This method successfully reduces the strain gauges to be used and hence the number of readings necessary to determine the absolute stress level.

Some problems had arisen with the rear suspension sub-frame of the RM (ie 'B' frame) and Vauxhall offered to assist in

Stress crack analysis trials were carried out on RM1278 at the Vauxhall Motors research premises at Chaul End in 1962.

carrying out tests using their stress lacquer method. A new Routemaster, RM1278, was taken from AEC and delivered to Chaul End where plastic sheeting was put around the skirt of the vehicle to prevent temperature variations as much as possible. A variety of tests including driving over planks, tight turns and severe braking were carried out. By examining the level of cracks in the lacquer approximate stress levels could be determined. From this work sufficient information was obtained to carry out more detailed strain gauge tests. As these tests were so successful it was decided to adopt this system of stress coat analysis in future work.

The co-operation with Vauxhall continued for many years including some similar work on the FRM when another leading vehicle builder showed possible interest in developing this vehicle in a larger capacity version. By this time Vauxhall had opened its new establishment at Millbrook in Bedfordshire, covering about 700 acres, where these later tests were carried out.

When the question arose of designing buses with lower floor levels to assist loading and alighting, considerable help was again given in this direction by Vauxhall, when a multi-axle bus was being considered, as described in Chapter Nine. I think the co-operation in the industry generally is something that can only be built up over the years with trust between all parties. Perhaps it might be worth concluding this comment by remarking that when Vauxhall were looking at possibly entering double-deck design, they borrowed a Routemaster commenting 'that for a 1959 design it represented a bus of very advanced ideas'. What better tribute to those concerned in its creation?

An entirely fresh approach to the braking problem was taken by Volvo. Initially they produced a flywheel which, on braking, would absorb the appropriate energy by being speeded up. This rotational energy could then be used to accelerate the vehicle when it needed to move off again. Thus not only was the life of brake linings improved, but it also gave a saving in fuel consumption which London felt it had a duty to pursue in the interests of prolonging the life of hydrocarbon fuels. Unfortunately this view did not appear to receive the support it should have held in Government circles.

As an example of longer-term research it might help to outline the work that was done in conjunction with Ogle Design of Letchworth. It was early in 1983 that Dr David Quarmby, the then Managing Director of London Buses, decided to commission a 'Human Factors and Design Research Study' in three specific areas relating to bus operation. These were:-

1.   Driving the Bus.
2.   The Cab as a Sales Counter.
3.   Passenger/Human Factors Interface.

The study was referred to as *The New Omnibus Concept and Systems Programme*, code named *NOCS*. The object was to make the bus a more attractive package, not only to those who used it but also to those who drove it.

In all such studies work starts with a review of the information already available, followed by visual observations in the field. This covered discussions with drivers at selected garages, and observations by video camera in service both of the driver actions and passenger boarding and alighting. From these observations it became clear that the two main objectives were:-

1.   To maximise the passenger boarding speed if One-Person-Operation was to be workable in Central London.
2.   To improve the attractiveness and accessibility of the London bus to achieve greater numbers and different types of travelling passenger.

Once this basic information had been achieved and digested a mock-up double-deck body was built in the Ogle workshops at Letchworth. On this mock-up it was easy to make changes to put the various ideas and theories to the test by carrying out user trials with a cross section of the community ranging from the old and infirm, young with children and pushchairs, shopping trolleys and so on. Once ideas had been firmed-up a parallel exercise was going on at Chiswick to convert a DMS in line with the proposals, DMS2456 being the vehicle in question. Perhaps it is worth recording that one of the salient points that arose from the analysis of the videos was the difference that the additional step at the exit made in the manner in which elderly people left the vehicle. With the two-

The Human Factors Buck. This mock-up of a bus, designed to allow easy modification of the entrance and exit layout and dimensions, was built in the premises of Ogle Design at Letchworth and a series of tests of loading and unloading carried out with a carefully balanced selection of passengers of all ages and types.

The result of the Human Factors study was incorporated in a conversion carried out on a Daimler Fleetline, DMS2456. These views show the entrance, with a split step layout rather similar to that used at the rear of some Brighton Hove & District Bristol Lodekka buses, and the exit, with additional step and handrails designed to facilitate descent by elderly passengers.

step arrangement it was noticed that the majority of elderly people turned as they stepped off the bus, leaving the vehicle in a backwards manner so that they could hold on to the grab rail. With the additional step it was apparent that after about the second trial passengers no longer turned round but left the bus in a forward direction. This was important because many accidents involving elderly people concerned hands trapped in doors — where they were carrying a bag they were reluctant to let go. This modification was put in hand for all new bus deliveries, starting with the Olympian.

Some of the Ogle work was incorporated in the delivery of

the 260 Leyland Olympians mentioned earlier in this chapter, the bulk being received during 1986. During the *Alternative Vehicle Evaluation Trials* Ogle were asked to carry out an assessment of the various vehicles on trial as they contained an assortment of current body manufacturers.

Looking ahead to the 1990s, a suggested exterior design of the body was produced, complete with interior decor. As well as giving a high standard of illumination an attempt was made to get away from the untidy effect of pasting adverts on the coving panels of the saloons. A scheme of detachable adverts was devised with the help of Transmatic (Europe) Limited, such that adverts could easily be replaced should a bus be transferred to another area. Ten Metrobuses were converted at Hounslow with this scheme and gave a very high level of illumination.

Finally, to finish off the project, a wind tunnel test was conducted at MIRA which showed that even at the relatively low speeds of a double-deck vehicle, the shape of the front of the bus played an important part in the 'mud line' along the side of the bus. Cleanliness of the door glasses, an important feature, was affected by the positioning of the doors in relation to the side of the bus.

Although this work was totally funded by London Buses it shows how important it is to have such fundamental information to hand rather than use trial and error. Much useful information was obtained from this investigation and it showed how co-operation between design consultants and those concerned with operating the buses can be put to good use.

One of the advantages of having a Central Workshop for any bus organisation is that where the Research and Development unit is part and parcel of the Technical set up, a close watch can be kept on the performance of components and units. In the main, garages are concerned with keeping buses on the road and are usually quite rightly concerned in meeting their service requirements. Of course there are garages that take a very close interest in the life of the units, and do keep in close contact with the Technical side at Headquarters.

On the other hand there is a second level of interrogation in the Works, where the staff draw attention to what they find in overhauling the defective units. When the Works cease to be part of the organisation they have little interest in improving unit life.

An example of these related to the RM differential. This was a spiral bevel unit as opposed to the worm drive of the RT and earlier models, giving greater efficiency due to less churning. Both units incorporated identical compensating gear (the mechanism allowing the near wheels to rotate at different speeds on each side during cornering) yet the Works reported a higher failure rate on the RM. Tests in the Experimental shop on units fitted with perspex panels and driven at different speeds showed that there was an intermediate range of speed with no oil flow to the compensating gear in both cases but that the flow did not resume as speed increased until a point 2 mph higher on the RM. Further tests established that a small change in design — machining flat areas on the spider in which the gears revolved — improved matters, and this modification was adopted from the end of 1972. Both London Country and AEC co-operated in this work.

In 1984 the *Alternative Vehicle Evaluation* programme already mentioned, was instituted to examine the most suitable chassis or underframe to take London Buses into the 1990s; it was to combine with the work instigated with Ogle on the body aspect. For the 'chassis' four manufacturers were selected, one of which was Volvo with the B55 double-deck chassis, this having a front-mounted engine. It has been a well-known fact of life that a front-mounted engine gives the best life possible and the choice of the B55 was to see whether it was practicable to use such a vehicle as One-Person-Operated in London conditions.

Although West Midlands PTE had operated such a vehicle, there was a foreseen problem in London with the 2½ stream boarding being evolved — providing cancellors or machines either side of the entrance but giving an area where an intending passenger could stand while he or she purchased a ticket if a pre-paid ticket or travel card had not been obtained.

At this stage design work was undertaken with Volvo to install a flywheel energy system at the rear of the vehicle under the transverse rear seat. Flywheel energy systems always bring forth comments on what might happen should the flywheel over-speed and, in the extreme, disintegrate. In an application such as this the flywheel was made in sections — like a series of clutch plates pressed on to a shaft — such that if excessive speed was reached the plates would slip on the shaft. As an additional precaution the flywheel was encased in a steel casing. A flywheel operating in a vacuum would hold the stored energy for a longer period, but this would involve maintenance problems.

There was a school of thought that with such a system it would be possible to utilise a smaller engine, but if for any reason the flywheel had given up all its energy the bus would not meet its normal operating specification. Thus any weight saving and cost in this direction was not considered acceptable.

A visit was made to Volvo in Sweden to test a single-deck vehicle so fitted, and the results were quite impressive. Before moving off the engine was started and the flywheel speeded up to run at about 10,000rpm. Leaving the engine running at idling speed the bus could then be moved off at normal acceleration by utilising the stored energy by means of a hydraulic pump supplying oil pressure energy to a motor mounted on the transmission line. As the energy was used up, the flywheel slowed down, and at a pre-determined speed the engine was speeded up to increase the flywheel speed without affecting the movement of the vehicle.

When the brakes were applied the motors on the transmission line became pumps and fed oil pressure to the 'pump' which was driven by the flywheel, changing its operation to a motor which then accelerated the flywheel thus creating more stored energy. For normal operation the energy from braking produced enough energy to accelerate the vehicle into top gear on moving off. Even on ascents the flywheel was able to cope with reasonable distances before it was coupled into the engine to restore the stored energy.

A review of the application of a typical London bus schedule rather suggested that the large amount of idling in gear that took place (as much as 30% of the journey time due to traffic, etc) would mean that the flywheel was not perhaps the best system. Therefore thoughts turned to hydraulic energy storage, a system with which both Volvo and London Buses were very familiar. A system was devised which utilised hydraulic accumulators, much on the lines as used on the RM

A further Volvo experimental vehicle added to the London Buses fleet in 1985 was C1, looking similar to the three B55 models included in the AVE programme with its Alexander bodywork. However, this was based on the underfloor-engined Citybus chassis and its main function was to allow investigation of the Cumulo energy storage system.

hydraulic brake system, but of course much larger in size.

It so happened that Volvo were about to launch the Citybus, which was a mid-underfloor-engined double-decker. Although the lower-deck floor was perhaps a little higher than the 'experts' were proposing, the engine was in the next best position to being fitted at the front. After a lot of discussion it was finally agreed that one such vehicle, fitted with the hydraulic energy storage system, would be leased from Volvo. By now the system had been marketed as the 'Cumulo' system.

Basically the Citybus had an underfloor-mid-engine with a gearbox and transmission line to a standard rear axle. Interspaced between the gearbox and the rear axle was fitted a take-off clutch to which was fitted a pump/motor. This latter unit served either to transfer the rotational energy of the propeller shaft to storage accumulators fitted across the rear of the vehicle, or transmit the stored energy to the motor turning the propeller shaft. A full description of the system was contained in a paper by the author presented by the Institution of Mechanical Engineers Conference in Bath in 1986.

The vehicle came to London Buses, classified as C1, in 1985, for initial tests based on Routes 11, 170 and 406 (LCBS) in both the laden and unladen condition. As was to be expected, the fuel savings were greater on the routes with frequent stopping and starting, being as high as 38%, with minimal savings on the high-speed less-frequent stop routes such as 406. Thus with an operational area with a spread of route types, the advantages of such a system would be reduced, unless, as an alternative it would be necessary to run two types of vehicles, Cumulo for City and West End and non-Cumulo for suburban routes.

In driving the vehicle the take-off in hydraulic mode could be classified as similar to a trolleybus, and the transition to mechanical drive was excellent, there being little sensation of any change whatsoever. Application of the brakes in the regenerative mode was noticeable in that there was a degree of hydraulic noise but it was not really objectionable. The Citybus was allocated to Palmers Green garage but facilities were limited which made control somewhat difficult and although the system behaved very well the diagnostic system fitted gave irritating problems, often with false indications. Changes in the London Bus organisation and the fact that Volvo had decided to proceed with this system based on all their researches caused the tests to be terminated before a real value could be put on the maintenance aspect of the energy storage equipment.

Although in the first place fuel economy was the driving force in this experiment, there had been a dramatic change in the general outlook. It appears to be a fact of life that we are assured that hydrocarbon fuels will be with us for 30 years or more (even though recent events act as a reminder that cost and supply can fluctuate) and the emphasis switched to the importance of reducing pollution from exhaust gases. A system such as Cumulo reduces pollution because the engine is run under strictly controlled conditions and using the stored braking energy in place of the engine must reduce the amount of exhaust gases dumped into the atmosphere.

In addition to Volvo, MAN in Munich had also been involved in developing an energy-storage system for buses. In 1986 I was invited to a presentation in Munich of the MAN ideas on energy storage. Manufacturers in West Germany are favoured with generous grants to pursue worthwhile development projects, and periodically reviews are undertaken where the hardware is demonstrated to their benefactors as well as to senior people in the bus industry in West Germany. Much like Volvo, MAN had dropped the idea of the gyro and flywheel in favour of the hydraulic method, but from there on they went their own way. Believing in an infinitely variable transmission for starting MAN had opted for a hydrostatic take-off, and then to use a mechanical split to the rear axle. With this arrangement it was possible to charge-up the storage accumulators. The relative merits of the Volvo and MAN ideas are outside the remit of this book but I was pleased to be able to try out the various attempts at energy storage systems. It was always a pleasure to visit MAN and to discuss the problems of bus operation and the various methods being looked at to solve them and I hope that I shall be able to keep in touch.

A somewhat routine and mundane task which the Experimental Shop was called upon to perform was that of a Quality Assurance function. With a move from the previous Inspection system to that of Quality Assurance, it was quite easy for output checks to be made on engines after overhaul in Chiswick as the Shop was fitted up with both an electrical and water brake dynamometer. Having tested the engine it was then customary to strip the unit and visually inspect all components and submit a report on what was found. Often advice was sought in overcoming problems discovered, with my staff working in close collaboration with both the Quality and Production staff. With the separation of Chiswick Works to Bus Engineering Limited an arm's length relationship was supposed to be the order of the day but after so many years of working as a team, this was somewhat difficult as we all had the same goal—running a successful bus operation. Once London buses started to employ outside organisations to repair units, based on commercial quotations, the task of carrying out quality checks increased including some endurance checks. One particular case involved the rejection of a batch of 50 engines following the failure by seizure of one unit on endurance test.

Although the Voith transmission had been introduced into the fleet there were no facilities for the overhaul of such a unit. In order to facilitate testing, one of the rigs in the Experimental Shop was modified with the aid of an old trolleybus motor to carry out a form of testing until facilities could be made available in the Works.

At an earlier stage, when the RM was introduced into service in 1959, provision had to be made to test the hydraulic units. Individual test rigs were designed to carry out such checks, utilising as much of the equipment used on the bus as possible. Most of the equipment designed to these specifications is still in existence, having been transferred by Frontsource (who purchased Bus Engineering Limited) to Alder Valley Engineering. The introduction of the Metrobus with the Clayton hydraulic system operating at higher pressures caused some problems with the existing rigs, and Bus Engineering Limited ordered an up-dated machine to do the work. This was made for them in the Shop and used by the Production staff.

Research and development work must go hand in hand with quality assurance and hence having evolved a design it is the prerogative of the design section to produce a technical data sheet as to its performance. This was used as a guide to the workshop staff as well as assisting with the design of the test rig. Any problems relating to the obtaining of the required output were soon referred back. With every new piece of equipment a technical data sheet was required so it was an on-going task. Once work started to go outside London Regional Transport the Technical Data Sheet was used as a document to call up the performance required. It was never the policy of London Buses to merely repair components by just putting the defect right but to ensure that it would give an almost identical performance to that when new. This principle was always difficult to put over to the Finance and Contract people who were inclined to think that repair and overhaul were one and the same thing except for the difference in price!

Another essential service provided by the Vehicle Engineering Centre, as it was to become in its latter years, was to provide a control of safety Critical Items. This consisted of drawing up a list of approved items relating to brakes, steering and suspension components. As already described, each type of vehicle has an approved brake lining fitment based on tests carried out on buses by the Division which ensures that the bus will meet all the legislation. This is issued in chart form to which the garages must comply.

In a similar manner hoses play an important part in the brake system and elsewhere, and there are many varieties of hose from water to armour-plated. Again, a chart lists those acceptable after laboratory tests have been carried out on strength and ozone cracking, deflection under load etc and before price is ever considered. Oil and air filters are another item which needs strict control since again price is not the governing factor. Oil leaks have been receiving a lot of attention from Ministry Examiners and with modern developments in jointing materials, required standards were laid down based on tests carried out on buses in service.

A new test rig to suit the higher operating pressure of the Metrobus hydraulic brake system was made in the Experimental Shop to the order of Bus Engineering Limited.

These examples tend to illustrate the non-glamorous side of Research and Development which is nevertheless absolutely essential. The Bus Industry is one which is labour-intensive and anything that can be done to reduce this must be of benefit — but to add to this philosophy a change is needed in the financial appreciation.

Accountants tend to work on an annual basis but total life costs are more realistic. Often a more efficient component will have a higher initial cost but give a better life. Provided this extra cost is outweighed by better life it is worthwhile to adopt, but this does present problems on long-living components.

I hope that the foregoing will illustrate some parts of the valuable role performed by a Vehicle Engineering Centre which is composed of dedicated people with many years of experience in the industry, acting as a back-up to those operating the buses. It should not be considered as a unit hidden away, dreaming up new ideas for the sake of it, but one on the look-out for new ideas which will be of benefit to the organisation and at the same time being in close contact with the operators. Neither can be effective without each other, a fact which is not always recognised. Each learns from the other.

In London, certainly, those who operated the buses had enough to do in maintaining their vehicles according to the Rota Charts (produced by the Vehicle Engineering Centre), ensuring that spare parts were always in stock, and that all service requirements were met, not to mention coping with their labour problems, so that they would never have had time left to delve into the world of research.

Perhaps I might be forgiven for some degree of understandable bias but I feel entitled to pose the question "who now will look after London's buses, and who will point the way to the future?"

Not, on past showing, those who build and sell their products as being ideal for the job, but who, when things go wrong, will turn and say 'no one else has had that problem', itself a statement which was sometimes shown to be untrue. Time alone will tell whether London's buses will ever be quite the same — and the reader must judge whether the case for the individuality of the vehicles operated in the Capital has been demonstrated, or proved.

The Experimental Shop interior when new. The engine on the test stand to the right of the picture and that on a stand alongside the workshop machines on the left were both AEC units of the 8.8-litre family, while the engine with cylinder head removed by the office wall was a Leyland of 8.6-litre type — both of these types were to influence the design of the RT 9.6-litre engine then being developed.

The Experimental Shop

'The Shop', as I came to know it, was erected in 1937 and had a recognised standard of achievement until I was forced to close it down in March 1986 as part of the economy measures then being implemented.

My first contact with the Shop as far as large scale work was concerned was with RTC1, the double-deck Green Line conversion of RT97 mentioned in Chapter Four.

It was in March 1951 that a large scale exercise was undertaken to find out the service behaviour of a London bus under all the various conditions of operation. To this end RT3995, then only about three months old, was withdrawn from service and extensively instrumented in all respects. Temperatures of all the various units were arranged to be displayed, measuring fuel meters fitted, and gauges for recording brake pressures were fitted as well as gear counters.

The test was then to follow a service bus in the peak and off-peak. As well as recording the aforementioned readings, records of bus stops, both request and compulsory, traffic stops and journey times were also taken by a team of observers on board. In those days much of the modern recording equipment was not available and it had to be done the hard way. The whole parameter of routes was observed from 6, 11, 65, 88, 321, 406 to 704. After covering the routes with the unladen RT3995 the vehicle was fully laden and the whole saga repeated. The report, written under the number S.6934 which became firmly imprinted on my mind, was a standard reference work and was used by many of our suppliers. The vehicle was retained by the department, never resuming normal duties — it was sold in 1966.

Following a service vehicle, especially when the test vehicle is laden and the followed vehicle lightly loaded, demands a very high standard of driving in order to do almost everything the first bus does. It can be argued that braking and acceleration is perhaps a little more severe, but it is a good safety factor. Throughout the tests the drivers being followed co-operated to the full and were very understanding although the same could not be said for some of the motorists.

Similar tests have continued until more recent times, but there were modifications to the routes selected, especially when One-Man-Operation became the norm on a larger percentage of routes operated; for this purpose route 220 was substituted, being one of the earlier routes to go from RM to DMS. Recording gear improved with the advent of data loggers and the work became much less labour intensive. It is surprising that many of the results remained the same except that buses spend longer idling and cover less mileage in proportion due mainly to traffic congestion and omo. Whether the latter affects the former is debatable. Sadly, so far as I am aware, no-one is doing such work nowadays.

Probably the greatest contribution of the Experimental Shop to the London bus scene was the development of Routemaster. It was always the policy of London Transport to look at all new developments in the bus world to see if there was any advantage to London. Hence, as already described, a lot of the RM development work had been carried out on RT vehicles, such as hydraulic braking and so on, and the real test was to fit all those features considered desirable in a new bus design. The general specification for the vehicle had been laid down by the Chief Mechanical Engineer, and the decision was taken to build four prototypes. As far as the Experimental Shop was concerned its part of the work was to build RM1 and 2 in conjunction with AEC and Park Royal Vehicles Ltd.

RM1 made its appearance at the Commercial Motor Show in 1954. A good deal of testing was carried out by Experimental Shop and technical staff however, before it

Among work carried out in the early days of the Shop in 1937-39 was the recording and analysis of bus noise. In this photograph, an ST-type bus had been taken to Epsom race course, no doubt to avoid noise from other sources, the vehicle trailing a bicycle wheel driving a precisely calibrated speedometer. Such work was rare at that date.

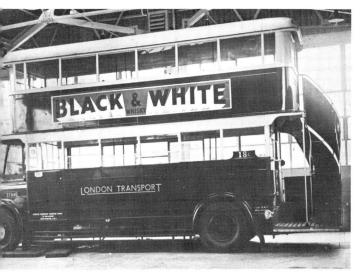

The first chassis to the new RT design was completed in June 1938 and to allow operational experience of the many new mechanical features it was fitted with this open-staircase body, built by Dodson, removed from a TD-class Leyland dating from 1931, taken over from the City Motor Omnibus Co. The resulting vehicle was given the temporary fleet number ST1140 — oddly enough, ST1139 was the LPTB's oldest AEC Regent, dating from July 1929. It is seen here with HW (Hanwell) garage plate and stencil for route 18c but is seen in the Experimental Shop at Chiswick, possibly after the vehicle was withdrawn at the end 1938 and the body about to be removed for scrap.

In April 1939, the former ST1140 emerged, renumbered RT1, with the body designed for it and built in the Chiswick body shops. It is seen outside the Experimental Shop in an early experimental livery — the polished aluminium bands were later painted over.

(Foot of page) The four 'pioneer' RM prototypes — RM1, RM2, RM3 (originally RML3) and RMC4 (originally CRL4) at North Weald Rally, 1985. By then, all had received variations of the production-style front panels and grille.

entered service in February 1956 from Cricklewood on Route 2.

Whilst RM1 was clocking up service miles, RM2 was being assembled at Chiswick and opportunity was being taken to carry out a strain gauge test at MIRA at Nuneaton to prove the design. Also a smaller engine was tried with a rating more in line with the requirement, but it proved the old well-known adage that a larger engine derated is a more economical proposition than a small engine uprated.

It then fell to the Experimental Shop to rebuild RM1 to incorporate the features that service operation had brought to light and those found on testing RM2 in its prototype form. RM1 then resumed service in March 1957 to be followed by RM2 from Reigate in May 1957. Because the Country area did not see a need for the RM, RM2 came back to the Experimental Shop and, painted red, began to operate from Turnham Green on route 91. Suggestions were then made

that air suspension would offer an even better ride than coil springs, so RM2 was withdrawn to fit this in December 1957. This rather sounded the death knell for the Self Changing Gears RV35 gearbox so an AEC railcar-type box had to be fitted which had a facility for driving an air compressor.

In all new design affecting vehicles nowadays it is customary to carry out crash testing to see how safe are the occupants. Whilst the tests carried out on RM2 showed that the design was adequate for all requirements, none of the four prototype vehicles had been involved in any serious accident. Whilst there was talk about creating a simulated crash, no one could really justify such action. However, it is always said that if one waits long enough it will happen. Sure enough on 29th January 1959 it happened — in the Edgware Road of all places. A sand and gravel lorry somewhat misread the traffic lights, thinking he had the right of way for a right hand turn, and RML3, the third prototype, with Weymann-built body

In their later years, the prototype buses appeared at various rallies — here I am with the Shield awarded for RM1 at the British Heart Foundation Rally, North Weald.

structure to our design, and Leyland mechanical units, hit the lorry broadside on. The force of the impact projected a passenger from the third seat back in the lower-deck into the bulkhead behind the driver, leaving a large dent in the panel work. This was another job for the Experimental Shop to repair, and they were able to report that the design had been well and truly proven!

Throughout its operating life the Experimental Shop staff undertook the maintenance and overhaul of these vehicles. Readers may care to note that a full history of the RM development is contained in the author's work — *The Routemaster Bus*.

Having mentioned earlier that simulated testing was the normal test procedure, there was one exception which rather proves the point for the need for such a test. When the prototype Leyland Titan, then code named B15, was being developed it was agreed that Leyland would do the testing and then hand over to London Transport for service trials. The bus duly arrived at Chiswick and after much representation I was allowed to do a limited test. This took place on a Sunday morning when route 11 was to be followed. We duly left Brook Green following an RM but by the time the B15 had reached Walham Green the gearbox oil was boiling. The need for a gearbox oil cooler was identified and the test aborted.

Once this was done a repeat test indicated that all was well. In all fairness to Leyland, their test work had been carried out on their test track — at that time at Spurrier Works — which enabled accurate repeatable tests to be carried out but without the problems associated with traffic. After the repeat test on route 11, the Leyland representative, who also took his turn at the wheel, admitted that this type of test found out nearly all the problems. Once the vehicle entered service at Chalk Farm on route 24 it was watched as to maintenance problems, but was continually dogged by going off on sales promotions. If anything, Leyland put in too much service help when it should have been left to the garage.

Probably the most rewarding job at the time was the 50 years celebration of London Transport when a Gala Day was organised at Chiswick in 1983 with a combined Bus Rally. The opportunity was taken to open up the Shop to let the public see what went on behind the scenes with vehicles of new

types, air cooled engines, development of new transmissions, engine testing, etc.

After such a successful event transport enthusiasts clamoured for yet another — so 1984 and 1985 saw repeats. Naturally each year became more complicated due to the improvements that could be introduced, and as Chairman of the co-ordinating Committee I was very fortunate in having James Roach, who was on a training scheme, to assist me, especially in the administration. The part played by John Bedford of the London Bus Preservation Group in respect of the Rally side must also be mentioned. Each time an attempt was made to change the exhibits in the Shop to let the public see what was done behind the scenes. Reference to the photographs will probably give a much better idea of what took place.

Unfortunately the changes that took place in the structure of London Transport in ensuing years prevented another Festival being held. The Chiswick works site became known as BEL, then a wholly-owned subsidiary of London Regional Transport, and it was an impossible task to co-ordinate such a repeat show. All who took part in these three Festivals, many giving their time voluntarily, felt that it was an extremely good public relations exercise and thoroughly enjoyed the effort.

The restructuring within London Transport brought about a total change in the way of working. Each business was charged with justifying its operation and this meant that the Experimental Shop had to make an effort to pay its way. It had always done work for other departments as a matter of course, and now the emphasis was to improve the situation. Work was undertaken for the British Transport Police in maintaining special surveillance vehicles which could not be sent outside for fairly obvious reasons, and tilt testing of foreign coaches for Cranfield Institute which yielded some very interesting results. For a time work was undertaken on behalf of BEL in providing a back-up technical service until they set up their own for a short period.

With the need to obtain competitive tenders for engineering work it had been decreed that a certain quantity of work had to be sent out to other than BEL to obtain a measure of the market. The Experimental Shop took on endurance testing of engines and, as already indicated, revealed an unacceptable standard of work from one such supplier.

When the decision was take above my head to close the Experimental Shop the work for outside parties had reached 50% of the total budget and, given more time, this could have been improved. As a temporary measure the essential equipment was stored in one of the lock-up garages at Chiswick where the St. John Ambulance was stored. Under BEL's management a revamp was made of the Works and a further move was necessary, this time to two of the lock-up garages adjacent to the main office block. With the general evacuation from Chiswick an out-station was established at Shepherds Bush garage, using one of the railway arches for storing equipment. This is how things were when I retired in 1988.

The responsibility for seeing that safety standards were met as far as vehicles were concerned, meant that testing of brake liners had to be continued, particularly as non-asbestos materials were coming to the fore. Selected garages were used to carry out tests with vehicles fitted with experimental liners

A ride in a bus over the skid pan was a source of excitement at the open days.

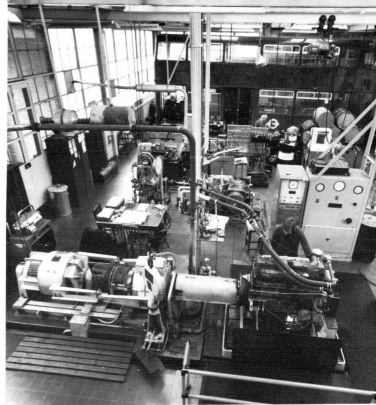

A general view inside the Experimental Shop in its latter days — rather more filled with equipment than at first but still at the forefront of technology.

The Chiswick open days held in 1983, 1984 and 1985 were both enjoyable in themselves and an opportunity to show the public some of the work we did. Below a parade of historic vehicles led by S742, representative of LGOC practice of the early 1920s, passes visiting vehicles including three from Southampton and more modern London buses at the 1985 event. The Experimental Shop is visible in the background.

Turning a double-decker on to its side, to demonstrate how it could be righted, was a spectacular event at the open days. Here a Fleetline performs a final function before being sold off.

(Below) An engine that might have had possibilities was Gardner's revival of the five-cylinder layout in the form of the 5LXCT, here seen displayed at the 1985 event.

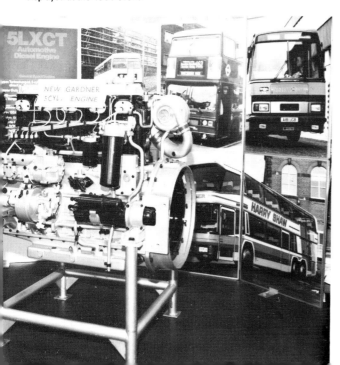

The first Experimental test vehicle is believed to have been this Yellow Y-type — Lord Ashfield had a 9-seat 'parlour coach' on similar chassis for his personal use delivered in 1927. Significantly, it had been designed by G. J. Rackham while he was Chief Engineer of Yellow in Chicago — Ashfield was to appoint Rackham as Chief Engineer of AEC in 1928.

The final Experimental test vehicle was RM1368, originally dating from 1962 but which was converted to a single-decker for use by the department following the burning-out of the top deck in 1973 — it allowed RM8, which had been used for similar duty since its appearance at the 1958 show, to enter public service for the first time in 1976.

and my thanks are due to the staff at Shepherds Bush, Stamford Brook, Norwood and New Cross for assisting in this essential work. BEL allowed the used of Chiswick Works site on weekends when up to three vehicles could be tested. In order to meet service requirements it often meant an early start at 6.00am in order to complete what I considered was a vital part of the work of the Department.

Looking back over the years, I believe the Experimental Shop was an essential part of London Transport that was never really appreciated and rather taken for granted. To illustrate this I can probably do no better than quote the serious incident involving a Leyland National bus, LS186, at Archway, mentioned in Chapter Eight. As a fatality had resulted and there were doubts as to what had caused the apparent uncontrolled acceleration which was being blamed for the accident, LS186 was taken to Chiswick Experimental once the initial examination had been cleared by the Police and Ministry.

A full examination was made of LS186 and only two minor faults were found. The vehicle was too badly damaged to be used as a test vehicle, so the engine, flywheel and gearbox were removed and fitted to LS331 enabling a full range of tests to be carried out.

At the end of this work it was decided to make eight modifications to these vehicles which in themselves could have a bearing on the phenomenon that drivers reported, but not in themselves cause it. This modification work was again entrusted to the Experimental Shop and it was arranged that as Turnham Green garage was not in use, this was to be used as the base. The Shop Foreman, Peter Parry, was sent there to supervise the work. Every National in the fleet was so treated and to my knowledge the allegations against the Nationals have been eliminated. There was no way that such a task could have been done at garages in a reasonable time.

Such work does not receive wide publicity and therefore few know what goes on. Obviously when working with vehicle and equipment manufacturers much of the work cannot be divulged on the grounds of industrial security, but I have no reason to believe that any thought other than that the work was not only important but essential.

With the closure of the department a highly-motivated skilled staff was broken up, many leaving the industry for good. The long-term ramifications will be interesting to see — perhaps even more so with the complete change in the structure of the manufacturing side of the industry, and the growing length of the lines of communication. Once it was just a five-mile trip to AEC, quite apart from the close historical ties that linked the two organisations. Then it became necessary to go to Coventry or Leyland, and now it may not suffice to go to Workington, for example, when key decisions are liable to be made in Sweden.

Professional associations

The extent to which London Transport has contributed to the various engineering bodies by its membership of the various professional and learned bodies is probably not realised. This support by London staff was always completely funded by London Transport, it being felt that whatever was of benefit to London would rub off to some extent on the rest of the industry, and bring economies of scale beneficial to all, including LT itself.

My contribution in this direction was firstly in my membership of various British Standards Committees. This included the main Automobile Standards Committee which was the parent of many other subsidiary Committees on which I served:- Mechanical and Pneumatic Couplings and Braking Systems; Commercial and Public Service Vehicles; Helical Springs; and Rubber Components and Fluids for Vehicle Braking Systems. The composition of the various Committees brought together not only the manufacturers, but also the Department of Transport, Ministry of Defence, SMMT and, of course, to a much more limited extent, the user, and formed a forum in producing standards.

In the days of the British Transport Commission, when transport was first nationalised, joint meetings were held with the principal organisations under the name of Research Co-ordination Committee (RCC), of which London was a fairly important constituent. Largely as a follow-on from this, when the Passenger Transport Executives were set up under the powers in the Transport Act of 1968, there were obvious common interests in the provision of public transport in major city areas. As a result, a series of meetings followed. From the top, Director Generals conferred and to advise them, the Chief Engineers' Committee met. To assist in carrying out the Technical aspect of this work a Technical Liaison Group was formed of which latterly I was the Chairman. In this Technical Liaison Group, much information was pooled and often shared and it was my task to present reports of the work to the Chief Engineers' Committee at their meetings.

One of the earliest jobs for the PTE Chief Engineers' Committee was in 1975 when an engineering specification for a bus in urban operation was produced. It was felt that with such a standard requirement for all the PTEs there could be a great financial benefit. Such a document is always a compromise and understandably there is always a reluctance to accept compromise when it actually comes to purchasing! The meetings of the Motor Bus Sub-Committee formed to handle this work always took place in Manchester at the Greater Manchester Transport (GMT) offices in Devonshire Street North and formed the start of a very close relationship with my counterparts. It was Harry Taylor who was the leading light in this idea of a PTE standard bus specification, which began when he was Group Development Engineer of SELNEC PTE, the predecessor of GMT.

The meetings of the Technical Liaison Group were held at each of the members' premises on a rotational basis and it was very interesting to see first hand how each PTE ran its organisation. Probably more important was the exchange of information in the later years of members' experience on mini-bus operation, particularly the reliability of the various makes of vehicles. Often it enabled a joint approach to be made as many of the vehicle manufacturers had only limited experience of such operation, the mini-buses being derived from vans. This latter point continued to be a problem, particularly in respect of brakes.

The Chief Engineers' meetings were usually hosted by a manufacturer in the industry, examples being Optare, Leyland, MCW, Ferodo, Mintex Don, and Duple and it was thus possible to include a tour of the Plant, always a useful and interesting exercise.

How these functions will fare as and when the PTCs (as they are now called) are broken up into smaller units, and probably privatised, remains to be seen but they have fulfilled an excellent purpose.

For many years London Transport ran a first-class Graduate Training Scheme whereby students in their final year were interviewed with a view to offering them, if they graduated, a two-year training period with London Transport. It was in this connection that I formed a close relationship with Loughborough University, whence we usually filled our two places. In former years we were occasionally able to take Vacation Students, again from Loughborough, thus giving both London Transport and the student time to gain some idea of what it was all about. The quality of the training was spoiled when the integration of the Buses and the Underground took place as it was designed to give a broader training to suit both disciplines, rather than to specialise in one. Once the 'shot gun' wedding was over, the training was segregated and the student gained a much deeper insight into the workings of one and not both. Several of those who completed the scheme were offered positions with London Transport.

The Graduate Training Scheme was recognised by the Institution of Mechanical Engineers in their Professional Training Requirements and with the advent of the Monitored Professional Development Scheme, I acted as Mentor to some of these people whom I am glad to say are now gaining their Corporation Membership.

Over the years there have been numerous trials with non-standard engines. Among experiments on display at the 1985 open day was the installation of a Deutz air-cooled diesel engine in Metrobus M205, which had entered service in 1980.

11. In retrospect

Having completed over 42 years involvement in the bus industry, one can be excused for looking back over that time and making a few comments. Having decided that working in the industry was my aim I had the idea that it was essential to put my theoretical background to the test by getting some practical experience, hence a Student Apprenticeship at AEC. This naturally brought me in close touch with London buses in the wider sense and perhaps strengthened my view that working for municipalities was not ideal as control was liable to be in the hands of a politically flavoured Transport Committee. So at the end of my time at AEC it was a choice of the Tilling companies, BET or London Transport. As the book details, the latter was my choice but little did I know how politics would enter into the organisation when the GLC took over on 1st January 1970.

The London Passenger Transport Act of 1933 provided for the establishment of a public authority, the London Passenger Transport Board (LPTB), which was charged with the general duty of providing an adequate and properly co-ordinated system of public passenger transport for a specified area. In addition there was the requirement to avoid the provision of unnecessary and wasteful competition and take such steps as to extend and improve the facilities for passenger transport in a most efficient and convenient way. Its area was somewhat similar to that covered by the London Traffic Area already in existence for the route licensing system set up under the Road Traffic Act of 1930, with the addition of some further territory situated roughly to the north and south. Certain runnings were allowed beyond this designated area such as Forest Row, Tunbridge Wells, Ascot, Maidenhead, Aylesbury and Royston, etc. Here was an area of operation which included all types of services as far as the buses were concerned — city, surburban, country and Green Line services and I felt that there was an opportunity to learn about the various facets in one organisation.

The LPTB had embarked on a degree of standardisation in its bus fleet after inheriting what could be described as a motley collection of vehicles from independent operators, though the bulk of the fleet, inherited from LGOC, was standardised and mostly of AEC make, and to this end worked very closely with AEC. Such an arrangement appealed to me and I felt that having a manufacturer in day-to-day contact with the organisation was a great help. In those days costs in a short-term sense were not quite so important and the opportunity was there to examine new ideas to improve the running of buses. I am sure that had it not been for the forward thinking of LPTB, the diesel engine and the planetary gearbox would not have been the success they were. Indeed, investment in design improvements must have saved vast sums in fuel economy and reliability over the years as well as making bus travel more attractive for passengers and improving working conditions for staff. The size of the LPTB fleet was such that it was possible for AEC to produce a special design for London, but at the same time much of it had a spin-off for provincial operators. There was perhaps an unusual arrangement in that London dealt with the design side of AEC, not the service side, and it was much easier to bring about changes in the interest of reliability etc through the joint meetings which in later years I was to attend. AEC was an ever-open door and there was a continual exchange of information. On occasion, in order to assist AEC, LPTB would operate certain experimental features in which AEC were interested but not necessarily LPTB, so that experience could be obtained under arduous conditions. This was an ideal arrangement and after the demise of AEC, was to continue with Daimler, MCW and to a large extent with Leyland. With the take-over of Leyland by Volvo and MCW's bus building activities taken over by Optare and now part of the DAF organisation, it is difficult to see this level of co-operation carrying on to the same degree.

London Transport always maintained a close contact with their component suppliers with the blessing of AEC and such an example is the application of the Lockheed Power Hydraulic Braking system to the RM. Fortunately the level of co-operation was unaffected by take-overs until fairly recently, and then we were usually on good terms with the affected partners.

Much of the work towards the RM was being carried out as separate experiments on RT-type vehicles and it all came to fruition with the building of the four prototypes, two of which were built at Chiswick, and their testing. This work produced great enthusiasm in the department as everyone was working to a time scale and could see the end product. Sight should not be lost of the fact that the service problems of the fleet were still being dealt with and I am not sure how we managed it all. Once the preliminary testing was over, experimental service operation followed which involved being on call all the time the vehicles were in service. There followed production and further monitoring as some production problems arose from one of the contractors who produced sub-frames. There is no doubt that these were the best years, finally ending with the 'off the peg' era and Merlins and Swifts.

It was partly the Bus Grant situation that started to bring about the changes in the industry whereby encouragement was given for operators to re-equip their fleets with vehicles suitable for one-person-operation. Unfortunately the requirement went a little too far in that it specified a rear engine configuration for double-deckers amongst other things. As events were later to prove with the Ailsa and the Citybus, it was possible to have an engine at the front, or underfloor amidships, and still have the possibility of one-person-operation. Unless the manufacturer declared his vehicle as a standard it was not possible to claim Bus Grant. At the start the 25% grant was not of a great long term benefit but when it was increased to 50% this was no longer the case. Thus it became impossible to have special designs and the emphasis changed to try and get improved reliability into the buses once again.

Added to this was the short-term belief that single-deck was the way to go, which meant a lot of changes in garages such as lengthening pits for the new longer single-deckers and changes in servicing since engines, flywheels and gearboxes were now contained in a power pack needing fork lift trucks. This occupied a good deal of time and labour and it was not until double-deckers returned to popularity in 1971 — with the Fleetline — that there was a return to more forward thinking. Credit must be given to Daimler who co-operated fully in this regard and gradually improvements were made in the Fleetline chassis bearing in mind that, technically, it was not on a par with the RM, but more a rear-engined equivalent to the RT with its combination of a beam front axle, leaf springs and air brakes and needed a labour allocation appropriate to that vehicle rather than an RM, with the addition of further staff to deal with the door gear, fare collection equipment, etc.

The loss of the Country area in 1970 saw the start of the break up of London Transport and I think this was partly brought about by the short sightedness of the GLC in that they didn't fully appreciate that the green buses penetrated the GLC area. As part of its execution of the 1933 Act, LPTB operated services according to traffic needs and not area boundaries, and hence nearly all the Green Line services ran into Central London and often right through it. Later, London Transport were to pay subsidies to London Country to run such services. Although the Country Buses became part of the NBC, they were to some extent a special unit as they carried certain agreements pertinent to their days with LPTB and so on. However, from a technical point of view, full co-operation was kept up for quite a long period as there was an agreement to give support to vehicles that were inherited from London Transport — but not any that they were to purchase themselves. As a result LCBS representatives attended my Divisional Meetings until route tendering started in 1985 when they became competitors in the full sense of the word. LCBS has now been sold off privately in four units and London Buses is being restructured to follow suit, with eleven units which were designed to be offered for sale ultimately. It seems as if it has gone full circle, returning to the pre-1933 era, but with the major difference that the LGOC was then already part of a largely integrated organisation with the tube and Metropolitan railways.

Although the Country area was an integral part of the organisation, it was different in many ways. The control was centralised at Reigate, there was a good deal of autonomy traffic-wise, and the Chief Inspectors at the garages were locally identified people. The garages, being more distant, operated with a good deal more flexibility in order to keep the service going. In vehicle types they often felt that they were the poor relations but nevertheless it was always a pleasure to work with the garages, the staff being so co-operative beyond their normal duties. In spite of criticisms of London Transport being a faceless image it did prove that it could operate a more

This chart shows how unladen vehicle weight per seated passenger carried has fluctuated in successive double-deck bus types since 1910. Note that the low points, implying the greatest efficiency in this respect, were the K and S-types of 1919-20, which combined relatively high seating capacity with a very 'basic' specification (no top cover for the upper deck, brakes on the rear wheels only), and the RML (72 seats, aluminium alloy integral construction and such advanced features as independent suspension). The off-the-peg era brought unwanted extra weight and hence increased running costs.

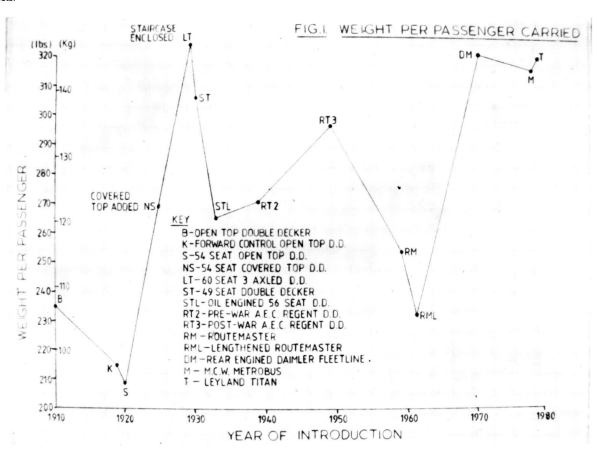

FIG.1 WEIGHT PER PASSENGER CARRIED

KEY
B - OPEN TOP DOUBLE DECKER
K - FORWARD CONTROL OPEN TOP D.D.
S - 54 SEAT OPEN TOP D.D.
NS - 54 SEAT COVERED TOP D.D.
LT - 60 SEAT 3 AXLED D.D.
ST - 49 SEAT DOUBLE DECKER
STL - OIL ENGINED 56 SEAT D.D.
RT2 - PRE-WAR A.E.C. REGENT D.D.
RT3 - POST-WAR A.E.C. REGENT D.D.
RM - ROUTEMASTER
RML - LENGTHENED ROUTEMASTER
DM - REAR ENGINED DAIMLER FLEETLINE.
M - M.C.W. METROBUS
T - LEYLAND TITAN

WEIGHT PER PASSENGER

YEAR OF INTRODUCTION

accountable structure within that large organisation. Country operation was different with higher scheduled speeds for the buses, with yet another variation in the Green Line operation, and provided a variety to the again different operation in the 'Red Bus' area.

When the Leyland B15, later to become the Titan, was being developed, there was a return to some involvement in this. There was a great deal of exchange of information between Leyland and London and it was a pleasure to note that the vehicle incorporated independent suspension. Although it was recommended that it would be worthwhile to adopt the RM Lockheed hydraulic braking system, spring brakes unfortunately were added instead of the customary hand brake and this led to service problems. With the RM the vehicle weight was such that a manual non-assisted hand brake would meet the parking brake requirement, but with the Titan with a two-ton increase, assistance would have been required.

For an integrally-constructed vehicle the weight of the Titan was a great disappointment. Had it not been for strong pressure from London, supported by West Midlands PTE, the B15 would probably have had the 500 series engine instead of the Gardner 6LXB although Leyland were given the option of using the O680.

At the same time work was being done with MCW who were producing their Metrobus. When working on two projects for rival companies there cannot be a lot of commonality, unlike the RTL which was developed after the RT had been produced. From the operators point of view, where there is a degree of commonality a useful reduction in stores holdings follows. Again the Metrobus came out in the heavier range, which was not entirely unexpected as it had an underframe construction with a beam front axle and a rear axle sub-frame with air suspension.

Although a good rapport existed with Leyland there were quite a lot of internal reorganisations which didn't help. In the case of the MCW personnel, several had come from Daimler, in some cases via Leyland as a result of the take-over, and it was possible to do some future development work on what might have been the Metrobus Mark III. Work was done on fitting independent suspension which was developed for the Metroliner. The Ogle front entrance was also incorporated but for other reasons the prototype was never completed. Again another disappointment as I felt that the Mark III offered a lot in meeting the various operators' demands.

London always wished to have dual sourcing and it was worried regarding the future of the Gardner engine in the Titan and Metrobus. As already described, attention fell on the Cummins L10 and some interesting work was carried out with the organisation with the fitment of 22 Metrobuses at Brixton. Cummins realised that the L10 was performing well in goods vehicles but that bus operation was liable to prove sufficiently different to need careful monitoring and development. Several visits to the States left me impressed with their organisation and I believed that they were offering a soundly-built product, which was subsequently proven. I had made many good friends in the States and I am sorry that I shall not have the first-hand experience of some of their new developments which will be taking off shortly. Through Cummins and another organisation, Transmatic, I was able to make contact with Seattle, who were another go-ahead transport authority in the States.

When the switch to mini buses came, I don't think we were given a fair crack of the whip. It is not difficult to grasp that a more frequent service usually results in increased ridership — this was proved in reverse when RMCs were put on Green Line 715 service in places of RFs, increasing the interval from 20 minutes to 30 minutes. I believe this caused a 50% drop in ridership. More to the point, the mini bus vehicles were often 'stretched vans' and the foundation brakes would not stand up to bus operation. Once overloading occurred it was realised that a bigger vehicle was required and often the 'stretched van' had reached the limit so it was back to the drawing board again. Both Leyland and MCW had quite wisely refrained from getting involved in the mini bus market but had quietly been working on the midi range. Unfortunately it was difficult to fully record all the problems of these vehicles as they were operated by satellite companies who tended to work directly with the manufacturers, except perhaps Westlink with whom a close relationship existed. The manufacturers have now accepted that the foundation brake design leaves something to be desired and have started fitting retarders which is rather an expensive cure. Nevertheless it proves once again that heavy duty service operation needs a rugged brake. Accepting that mini buses have a limited use in housing estates, where full size buses would have difficulty, I wonder what might have happened if more frequent services had been operated with normal buses. In this connection it is of interest to note that double-deck bus purchases and hence

The last of the rear-engined Leyland Titan buses were delivered in 1984. I visited the Leyland Bus factory at Workington and am seen here, second from the right, in a group of Leyland and LRT staff on that occasion with three of the last examples to be completed — T1121 is nearest to the camera.

output has grown again in the last year or two, though more recently held back by financial pressures and uncertainties.

Much could be said of recent events in London Buses, with the present break-up into eleven units, but I will leave this to others. In a more general way the feed-back of information from operators throughout the whole country to the manufacturers is going to be more difficult as the small units of 250-450 buses will not support a full-time technical service. Also there will be a reduced possibility of getting what the operator wants as it is not worth building 'specials' in the small numbers such operators would need. We have now gone full circle and it will be an interesting guess as to when the industry will start inventing the wheel again.

Nevertheless, and in spite of all this, I would not have changed things in my career as I have made many good friends in all walks of the industry which I hope I will retain during my slight change of direction into the consultancy field.

Considering that as far back as 1968 thought was being given to closing down the engineering function of design and development by 1970, the Division succeeded in living a further eighteen years and gave an exceedingly useful account of itself.

The drawing office at Chiswick, where many important advances in bus design were first committed to paper. This view dates from the early '80s.

The end of an era. Chiswick Works in course of demolition in 1989. The concept of central engineering works and research facilities for city transport systems is out of favour in Britain nowadays, but will this remain so?

Ending on a lighter note, I was invited to drive ST922, the preserved ex-Tilling AEC Regent dating from 1930, on one of its appearances in the Historic Commercial Vehicle Club's London-Brighton rallies and am at the wheel in this view. The bus, which had been converted to a canteen for use by LT in 1947-54, was rescued for preservation by the late P. J. Marshall in 1966 and re-entered service in London several times on special duties since restoration. My first recollections of buses are of very similar vehicles in Brighton — see page 8.

INDEX

150

Photocredits